中國學術思想研究輯刊

三八編

林慶彰 主編

第10冊

美國漢學與中國思想研究論集

李哲賢 著

花木蘭文化事業有限公司

國家圖書館出版品預行編目資料

美國漢學與中國思想研究論集／李哲賢 著 -- 初版 -- 新北市：
花木蘭文化事業有限公司，2023〔民 112〕
序 4+ 目 4+212 面；19×26 公分
（中國學術思想研究輯刊 三八編；第 10 冊）
ISBN 978-626-344-398-3（精裝）

1.CST：漢學 2.CST：漢學研究 3.CST：比較研究 4.CST：文集
030.8　　　　　　　　　　　　　　　　　　　112010421

ISBN-978-626-344-398-3

9 786263 443983

中國學術思想研究輯刊
三八編　第十冊　　　　　　　　　ISBN：978-626-344-398-3

美國漢學與中國思想研究論集

作　　　者　李哲賢
主　　　編　林慶彰
總 編 輯　杜潔祥
副總編輯　楊嘉樂
編輯主任　許郁翎
編　　　輯　張雅淋、潘玟靜　美術編輯　陳逸婷
出　　　版　花木蘭文化事業有限公司
發 行 人　高小娟
聯絡地址　235 新北市中和區中安街七二號十三樓
　　　　　　電話：02-2923-1455／傳真：02-2923-1452
網　　　址　http://www.huamulan.tw 信箱 service@huamulans.com
印　　　刷　普羅文化出版廣告事業
封面設計　劉開工作室
初　　　版　2023 年 9 月
定　　　價　三八編 16 冊（精裝）新台幣 42,000 元　　版權所有 · 請勿翻印

美國漢學與中國思想研究論集

李哲賢　著

作者簡介

李哲賢，台北人，美國亞歷桑納大學漢學博士，曾任國立雲林科技大學漢學研究所教授、所長。著有：《漢學視野下之荀子思想研究論集》、《荀子之名學析論》、《荀子之核心思想——「禮義之統」及其現代意義》、Chang Ping-lin（1869～1936）：A Political Radical and Cultural Conservative 等書及〈弱者道之用——老子弱道哲學析論〉（中、英文）、〈美國漢學視野下之中國古典文學研究及反思〉等中、英文論文多篇。

提　要

　　在中國思想之研究領域，中文學界之研究成果極為豐碩，然而，或許受限於自身之學術文化傳統，研究成果不易積累消化，或突破傳統藩籬，而只能在自身之文化傳統中迂迴摸索。

　　依此，作者以其二十多年來在美國漢學領域之教學與研究為基點，透過美國漢學界之中國思想研究成果之分析、詮釋，由此提出新的問題和觀點，擴大學術研究視野，並超越自身文化傳統之框架，可提升中文學界之中國思想研究之水準。本書極具國際視野，相信此種視野之研究進路（approach）當是中文學界未來學術研究之必然趨勢。

自　序

　　《美國漢學與中國思想研究論集》一書係本人歷來所撰寫的單篇論文之選集。本論集收入與美國漢學研究相關之中國思想研究之中、英文論文 10 篇，並收入兩篇美國漢學名著之中文書摘，共計 12 篇。其中，兩篇係以美國漢學為研究主題之論文，四篇中國思想研究之英文論文及由之分別改寫為中文之論文四篇。本論集所收諸文多曾先後刊登於國內、外之學報〔註1〕，且多稍作修訂與潤飾。

　　本書之所以名為《美國漢學與中國思想研究論集》，實因其所收諸文皆不出「中國思想」此一研究主題，且是從「美國漢學」之視角予以探究。此外，本人歷來之研究重心和關切所在亦是環繞此一主題和視角而展開。底下試就「美國漢學」與「中國思想」之間的關係作一說明，希冀本論集之主旨可由之而更為明確。

　　長久以來，世界上有關中國思想研究的中心，是在兩岸，而不是在海外。在中國思想之研究領域，中文學界之研究成果最為豐碩，然而，或許長期以來，受限於自身的學術文化傳統、儒家的道統觀念或政治因素的影響，研究成果不易積累消化，或突破傳統的藩籬，而只能在自身的文化傳統中迂迴摸索。

　　然而，國外漢學界尤其美國學界長期以來即非常關注中國思想的研究，近年來，他們的研究成果頗為豐碩，相形之下，美國漢學界可不受中國傳統文化的影響與限制，因此，能從不同的視角或切入點來研究中國思想，從而，可獲

〔註1〕　〈戴震之考證哲學析論〉一文係邀稿之作，並刊登於 *Asian and African Studies*。

得令人耳目一新且具有啟發性的見解。由於其所提出之觀點極為新穎且具啟
發性，非常值得中文學界的借鏡。

然則，何謂「漢學」？「漢學」一詞源自西方，相當於英文之 Sinology，
不過，現在則多用 Chinese Studies（漢學或中國學）一名。它大致和我國過去
習用之「國學」一詞在實質上相近，而涉及之範圍則更廣泛。簡單地說，「漢
學」就是外國人研究中國學術文化的學問，且是以中國為探究對象之人文和社
會科學為主。具體而言，它包括語言、文字、文學、歷史、考古、人類學、哲
學與藝術等。就時間範圍而言，「漢學」是兼包古今，亦即涵蓋現代歷史（思
想、文學）之研究，不似「國學」以研究古代為主。至於所謂「美國漢學」則
是指曾在美國從事教學或研究之學者的漢學研究成果。

既然在中國思想之研究領域，中文學界之研究成果最為豐碩，那麼，為何
需要借鏡美國漢學之相關研究？底下試以「章太炎之研究」為例，予以說明，
當可明其一、二。

雖然，章太炎在革命運動中極為有名，然而，其聲望及盛名實多得自其國
學方面之成就。實者，章氏在政治方面之貢獻不可謂之不大，然而，其在學術
方面之貢獻則更大，此所以章氏被稱為國學大師。況且，章氏在政治方面之觀
點及靈感實大多來自其學術方面之見解。究實而言，章氏之思想實包含學術和
政治兩個側面。因此，欲全面而深入地把握章氏之思想，對於這兩個側面的研
究，實缺一不可。

依此，中文學界普遍認為章氏在歷史上之重要性主要在其學術方面，因
之，學者對章氏之研究多側重其學術方面之探究，而較疏於對其政治方面之探
討。至於在美國漢學界，學者則較偏重對章氏之政治思想和活動方面之全面而
深入之探究。其所探討之議題頗為多元且甚或中文學界所未能觸及或予以發
掘者。如，民族主義、文化立場、政治立場或思想之一致性，保守與激進、革
命與國粹、生涯之抉擇及文化之承續性等，且其所提出之觀點亦頗為新穎、獨
到且具啟發性，非常值得中文學界之借鏡。

綜言之，在中國思想研究方面，透過美國漢學界研究成果之再研究（分析，
詮釋），可提供或發掘新的問題或觀點，由此擴大學術研究視野，並提供新的
學術研究方向或論題。此外，藉由彼此的對話或學術交流，可提供中文學界一
種國際視野，超越自身文化傳統的框架，並提升中文學界中國思想研究的水

準。此即是美國漢學研究對於中文學界之中國思想研究所可能賦予之意義，並可作為中文學界在從事中國思想研究時之參照、借鏡及反思。

　　本人多年來以中國思想，尤其是荀子哲學作為研究之重點，2001 年國立雲林科技大學漢學研究所成立時〔註 2〕，本人負責籌設漢學研究之學程〔註 3〕，並開設美國漢學等相關課程，除了引進並推動漢學研究外，並培養諸多研究生從事美國漢學之研究且已有具體成果。〔註 4〕同時，在多方省思本所未來發展方向之際，更深深體會到，學術研究國際化乃中文學界未來研究發展之必然趨勢。因之，本人不揣鄙陋，試從漢學之視角去扶發荀子名學之義蘊，於 2005 年完成《荀子之名學析論》一書〔註 5〕，本書將中、外學界，包括兩岸、美國及日本等學者之研究成果予以分析、詮釋，並由此提出新的問題和新的觀點，可說極具國際視野，相信此種研究視野必是中文研究未來之趨勢。

　　實者，中文學界引進並推動漢學研究雖已有二十年多年之歷史，然而，漢學之引介對中文學界之教學與研究，其作用與意義為何，學界迄今尚未有進一步或深入之反思或探究。因之，本書《美國漢學與中國思想研究論集》旨在以個人多年來在美國漢學領域之教學與研究為基點，試圖尋繹出美國漢學研究對於中文學界之教學與研究所賦予之意義、價值及貢獻，並希冀對中文學界之中國思想研究能有正面而實質之助益。

　　本書得以出版，首先要感謝花木蘭文化事業有限公司杜潔祥總編輯之協

〔註 2〕　由於本人曾負笈美國，接受西方漢學之學術薰陶，因之，籌設研究所之初，乃以「漢學」名之，旨在強調學術研究國際化之特色，以與傳統中文系所有所區隔。本所係全台第一且唯一之一所以「漢學」命名之研究所，成立迄今已有 20 年之歷史。

〔註 3〕　有三種學程，分別是美國、歐洲和日本之「漢學研究專題」和「漢學家及其名著專題」。

〔註 4〕　漢學研究可分成兩類；一是「漢學家之研究」，如，賴亭融：《他山之石——宇文所安及其唐詩研究》（2004 年）；謝丹邵：《梅維恆（Victor Mair）之變文研究析論》（2013 年）；張乃云：《韓南及其白話小說研究析論》（2017 年）。另一則是「漢學主題之研究」，如，蘇郁銘：《近十年（1994～2003）來美國的荀子研究》（2004 年）；郭興昌：《三國演義研究在美國》（2006 年）；彭振利：《老子研究在美國》（2007 年）。以上皆是本人指導之研究生所完成的美國漢學領域之碩士論文。

〔註 5〕　《荀子之名學析論》（台北：文津出版社，2005 年），又本書於 2018 年 7 月出版第二刷。

助，並慨允出版。此外，最要感謝的是協助繕打、整理和編輯書稿的張乃云助理的百般辛勞。最後，藉此向內子吳玉妹老師之默默支持、付出與奉獻致以最深摯之謝忱。

兌山　李哲賢

謹識於逸哲齋

2023 年 3 月 6 日

目

次

壹、美國漢學篇

荀子名學研究在美國 〔註1〕

一、前言

　　西方漢學界對於《荀子》的研究，最早可追溯到十九世紀後半葉，英國學者 A.Wylie 在其論著 *Notes on Chinese Literature*（1867 年）中對荀子的介紹。〔註2〕其後，同樣是英國學者，James Legge（理雅各）在 1893 年出版的 *Chinese Classics* 中，將荀子之〈性惡〉篇收於《孟子》譯文後之附錄中。〔註3〕然而，《荀子》一書之翻譯，則要等到二十世紀之後，才開始出現。荷蘭漢學家 Jan J.L. Duyvendak 在 1924 年首先英譯荀子之〈正名〉篇〔註4〕，其後，美國學者 Homer H.Dubs（德效騫）在 1927 年出版荀子一書之專著〔註5〕，次年，又出了一本《荀子》之選譯。〔註6〕Dubs 可說是西方漢學界最早全面譯介《荀子》之學者，由此而開啟美國漢學界的荀子研究。

　　然而，直到 1950 年代，《荀子》始有新的譯作出現。梅貽寶有《荀子》

〔註1〕 本文係兩岸學界以荀子名學為主題之美國漢學研究之開山之作。

〔註2〕 Homer Dubs, *Hsüntze : the Moulder of Ancient Confucianism* (London : Arthur Probsthain , 1927),p.xx.

〔註3〕 James Legge,"That the Nature is Evil", in *Chinese Classics:with a Translation ,Critical and Exegetical Notes, Prolegomena ,and Copious Indexes* ,v.2,ch.2,Appendix 1(Oxford :Clarendon Press,1893),pp.79~88.

〔註4〕 Jan J.L. Duyvendak ,"Hsün-tze on the Rectification of Names", *Toung Pao* 23(1924), pp.221~254.

〔註5〕 Homer Dubs ,*Hsüntze :the Moulder of Ancient Confucianism.*

〔註6〕 Homer Dubs ,tr.,*The Works of Hsün Tze (London :Probsthain,1928).*

之三篇譯作：〈正名〉、〈勸學〉、〈王制〉。〔註7〕Burton Watson 在 1963 年出了
《荀子》之選譯本〔註8〕，而陳榮捷則有〈天論〉、〈正名〉、〈性惡〉三篇譯
文。〔註9〕將上述 Dubs、梅貽寶、Watson 及陳榮捷等四人之譯作加以比較，
可發現，在四種《荀子》之選譯作品中，〈正名〉篇是唯一四家皆有選譯之篇
章，由此可見，〈正名〉篇頗受學者之重視。然而，從目前美國漢學界已出版
之《荀子》相關論著看來〔註10〕，有關荀子名學之研究，在量方面實明顯不
足。

　　荀子乃先秦儒學之殿軍，其學無所不窺，舉凡政治、社會、經濟、名理、
心性及人生等皆有其個人之弘識。有關荀子之研究，在美國漢學界已作出極為
可喜之成績。唯美國學界歷來有關荀子之研究多著重其心、性、天、禮或政治、
倫理學說之闡述，而較疏於其名學之探究。然而，就目前已發表之論著而言，
無論是在釐清荀子之哲學立場，抑或對於名學之分析等亦頗有獨到之處，值得
吾人借鏡。

　　本文題為〈荀子名學研究在美國〉，所討論之對象以曾在美國從事教學或
研究之學者所已發表之英文論著為準，分別就一些較為重要之著作作一論述，
且就已有之研究成果，作一析論，並說明其未來可能之研究發展方向。

二、荀子名學研究述要

（一）德效騫：〈邏輯理論〉〔註11〕

　　本文乃德氏所撰《荀子——古代儒學之塑造者》中之第十三章。本書乃西
方學界第一本荀子研究之專著，在該書中，德氏除了對荀子之學說作全面性之
探討外，亦對荀子之生平和著作等相關問題作了介紹。

　　德氏在〈邏輯理論〉中，首先指出，在中文中，邏輯一詞在字面上乃意指

〔註7〕 Y.P.Mei, "Hsün Tzu on Terminology", *Philosophy East & West* 1(1952), pp.
　　　　51~66;"Hsün Tzu's Theory of Education ,with an English Translation of the Hsün
　　　　Tzu ,Chapter 1",*Ts'ing Hua Journal of Chinese Studies* 2/2 (June,1961),
　　　　pp.361~377;"Hsün Tzu's Theory of Government ,with an English Translation of the
　　　　Hsün Tzu ,Chapter 9",*Ts'ing Hua Journal of Chinese Studies* 8/1~2 (Aug. ,1970).
〔註8〕 Burton Watson ,*Hsün Tzu :Basic Writings* (N.Y.:Columbia University Press,1963).
〔註9〕 Wing-tsit Chan ,"Naturalistic Confucianism :Hsün Tzu",in *A Source Book in
　　　　Chinese Philosophy* (Princeton :Princeton University Press ,1963),pp.115～135.
〔註10〕 請參見本文末之附錄。
〔註11〕 Dubs, "Logical Theory", in *Hsüntze :the Moulder of Ancient Confucianism*, pp.
　　　　198~241.

名學（the study of terms）而言，且邏輯問題之出現，首先是關於名之問題而非關於辭或判斷（judgment）之問題。德氏以為，荀子係中國古代哲學思潮中儒家之殿軍，因此，他受到所有不同學派思想的影響。雖然，荀子對於先秦諸子之學說有所評騭，但是，他也深深地受到他們的影響。因此，德氏認為，他必須提供中國古代邏輯理論發展之歷程，如此，始能理解荀子之邏輯學說。底下德氏即略述各家之邏輯思想：

1. 孔子之邏輯思想

孔子邏輯之基本概念是「正名」。任一行動或思想皆起於觀念，名代表觀念，名賦予行動以方向，且是生活和社會組織的焦點。因此，正名乃改革社會和道德所不可或缺的。而下列這段話則是了解孔子哲學的最重要陳述：

> 子路曰：衛君待子而為政，子將奚先？子曰：必也，正名乎。子路曰：有是哉！子之迂也。奚其正？子曰：野哉，由也。君子於其所不知，蓋闕如也。名不正則言不順，言不正則事不成，事不成則禮樂不興，禮樂不興，則刑罰不中，刑罰不中，則民無所措手足。

孔子以為，所有的改革，以及以正道去教導人民，皆必須透過正名的媒介。因此，孔子提出：正名之所以正政之主張。此外，正名之目的在於建立一種是非的客觀標準，因此，孔子提出「君君、臣臣、父父、子子」之主張，由此，正名乃成為儒家倫理學和是非之判準的來源之一。而孔子在正名方面努力的結果是促成中國古代邏輯的發展。荀子之邏輯即是孔子學說的直接產物。同樣地，我們發現墨子和楊子也發展了邏輯。孔子的正名學說成為中國邏輯之來源。

2. 老子之邏輯思想

德氏以為，在中國古代邏輯之發展中，另一具有重大影響的是老子。老子乃是第一位處理名實關係此一中國邏輯之重大問題的哲學家。

老子和孔子的邏輯思想頗為不同。老子以為，名並非存在，而是在於表達實之本質。名和實或事物是不同的。更重要的是名與名之間彼此是相對的。由此，吾人發現相對主義（relativism）之萌芽，而此亦日後非正統思想之特色。

3. 楊子之邏輯思想

楊子是一位快樂主義哲學的個人主義者（The Cyrenaic individualist）。他對名實所作之區分與老子不同。老子主張，雖然事物改變，但是本質卻是真實而可靠。楊子則是反對此種實在論（realism），而走向另一極端：名並非實在，名是人為之產物，他並不承認任何共相（universal）之存在，而只承認殊相（particular）之存在。實並無名，而名亦無實。名只是人為之產物，名只是人類所創造，且不是真實的存在，而實當然亦非名所賦予的。這是極端的唯名論（nominalism）。

由此，楊子推論出兩個重要的結論：(1) 所有的名、禮和規則都只是人類的創造，本身並無相當的實在性；(2) 只有個人是重要的，因此，人倫關係是不重要的，並且每一個個人都可以做他所喜歡做的事。楊子以極端之個人主義和利己主義貫徹其學說。

4. 墨子之邏輯思想

墨子原是孔子的學生，但是，他脫離儒家之保守主義，想要斬斷過去，並且，以功利主義來加以改革。這種凡事皆根據一種單一原則的企圖，表現出墨子的邏輯心靈。為了使他的新學說具有說服力，墨子乃提出三表法。所謂三表法是：(1) 本之於古者聖王之事，(2) 原察眾人耳目之實；(3) 發以為刑政，觀其中國家人民百姓之利。在三者當中，墨子特別強調第三表，因為墨子是依據邏輯來表現出他的功利主義。但是遺憾的是，墨子的詮釋太過狹隘，且使用它來批判音樂是浪費且無用。墨子這種功利主義之所以失敗的主要理由之一就在於它太狹隘。

墨子之後，其後學則發展出墨辯之邏輯學。在墨辯中，名可分為三類，即達名、類名、和私名。此外，根據墨子之三表法，墨辯亦發展出一套知識論。而墨辯對於古代中國哲學的貢獻如下：(1) 墨辯發展出一種介於孔子之實在論和楊子之唯名論之間的概念論（conceptualism），此種概念論是使實只作為主詞，即被論謂之主體，是指一個具體的對象；而名只作為謂詞，即論謂之內容，是從具體對象中抽象出來的本質。(2) 他們的科學方法 (3) 強調研究和推論，因此，開啟通向科學貢獻之門戶。

荀子對於先秦諸子思想之批評仍然持續且非常嚴厲。他不僅寫了一篇〈非十子書〉來批判諸子，並且他的學說亦持續地針對他們而加以批判。

作為孔子的真正傳人，荀子將「正名」視為他基本的邏輯原則。正如孔子一樣，荀子相信，公私生活中之所有罪惡和困境都是來自於名之不正，因而，沒有是非之真正標準。故荀子曰：

> 今聖王沒，名守慢，奇辭起；名實亂，是非之形不明，則雖守法之
> 吏，誦數之儒，亦皆亂也。

故唯有王者起而制名，名定而實辨，始能建立是非之正確標準。可見，對於荀子而言，邏輯是以倫理政治之要求為正名之目的。

德氏在本章中，主要是根據荀子〈正名〉篇之內容來加以疏解。其中包括，「所為有名」，論制名之目的；「所緣以同異」，論同名異名之所由起；「制名之樞要」，論制名之原則，及名之類別和名之用法等。在制名的原則方面，荀子特別強調名的社會性格。荀子認為，名具有固定而確定的意義，但只是由約定俗成而來。但是約定俗成並無法賦予一種絕對而固定之標準，如荀子所想的，因為個人可以決定不去贊同約定俗成之原則。因此，荀子決定藉由王者或政府之力量來賦予名之絕對之性格。

又德氏亦提到荀子對於名之分類。德氏認為，墨辯將名分為達名、類名和私名三類；而荀子只分為達名和類名兩類（即大共名和大別名）。德氏以為，荀子可能並不認為私名是值得加以分類；或可能荀子認為所有的名都是類名，雖然，荀子並未明說。此外，德氏指出，對應於制名之三項原則，荀子亦提出各家用名之謬誤，即所謂三惑。所謂三惑是指「用名以亂名」、「用實以亂名」和「用名以亂實」等。

（二）顧立雅：〈荀子之權威主義〉〔註12〕

本文係顧氏所著《中國思想：從孔子到毛澤東》一書中之第七章。顧氏在本文中將荀子之生平、著作和學說作一般性之論述，其中亦有涉及荀子之名學，試略述如下：

顧氏指出，作為一位哲學家，荀子令人感到興趣的是，當他討論語言理論時。荀子所處理之問題，甚至仍困擾著今日之哲學家。荀子提出之問題有：何謂名或語詞？何謂概念？概念如何產生？何以人們在使用概念時是如此的不同？

在中國古代有所謂的辯者（dialectician）提出詭辯，如「白馬非馬」等來贏得人心。作為當時儒家之主要代表，荀子必須與這些論辯對抗。荀子並不滿足於只是處理這些問題，而是，試圖研究語言的本質，並且建立語言之正確使用的規則。

荀子首先提出的問題是「所為有名」，荀子的回答：名是為了滿足談論事

〔註12〕H.G.Creel, "The Authoritarianism of Hsün Tzu", in *Chinese Thought: From Confucius to Mao Tse-tung* (Chicago: University of Chicago Press, 1953), pp. 115~134.

物和事件之方便的需求而來，同時，名亦是人們所發明來提供這種需求。荀子指出，制名之目的在於辨同異和明貴賤。

其次，荀子提出「名之同異的基礎」此一問題。顧氏指出，荀子認為名之同異的基礎在於感官。根據感官，感官認為事物屬於同一類的，就是同類。顧氏指出，荀子並不相信名與實之關係是固定不變的。荀子說：

> 名無固宜，約之以命，約定俗成謂之宜。……名有固善，徑易而不拂，謂之善名。

荀子使用各種不同的關於語言的原則來分析先秦諸子之令人困惑之命題。此外，他更確立語言之正確使用來表達觀念。可惜，後人並未重視荀子之學說。

（三）柯雄文：《倫理論辯：荀子道德知識論之研究》〔註13〕

柯氏指出，荀子之〈正名〉篇被視為具有極大邏輯興味（logical interest）之作品，然而，柯氏並不認為荀子之名學與西方之邏輯是實質之同義語，蓋荀子具有明顯的倫理取向，因之，荀子並未以系統之邏輯理論的形式來詳述其基本觀念。荀子之正名學說主要在於關心道德地秩序井然之社會此一問題。依此，當荀子在解說與辯護其價值主張時，其所提出之論辯可被視為是倫理的。甚而，當荀子在論述其主張時，會有若干之推理作用，然而，此等推理與嚴謹之邏輯推論是有所不同。易言之，荀子在其名學中所提出之論辯，本質上是倫理的，而非思辯的，故柯氏對於荀子名學研究之重心即在於釐清其倫理論辯（ethical argumentation）觀，並進而研究其道德知識論（moral epistemology）。

本書旨在藉由儒家論辯概念之說明來對荀子倫理理論之某一面向作一哲學之重建。本書共分四章，首先提出倫理論辯的一些基本要素，其次，轉向倫理推理之問題和使用準定義公式來解釋評斷倫理判斷之標準的意義和表述。最後，則以荀子對於錯誤的倫理信念的診斷之討論作結。

本書共分四章，茲分別略述如下：

第一章〈表現之風格和勝任之標準〉：柯氏指出，論辯本質上是一種賦予理據之活動，用來解說和辯護其價值主張。此種論辯活動，廣義而言，可視之為倫理的。此一倫理論辯之看法，對荀子而言，尤為貼切，蓋荀子在其思想中，並未嚴格區分道德價值和非道德價值。

〔註13〕Antonio S. Cua ,*Ethical Argumentation :A Study in Hsün Tzu's Moral Epistemology* (Honolulu :University of Hawaii ,1985).

　　柯氏在本章中描述倫理論辯之某些面相。首先對表現之風格和勝任之標準作大略之區分。柯氏指出，要使論辯成為一種合作之活動，參與者應具備的理想素質有：不爭辯、自尊與尊重他人、謙和之禮節和以仁心說、以學心聽、以公心辨。至於勝任之標準，柯氏說明此乃作為一種理性活動的論辯之精華所在。所謂勝任之標準如下：1. 辨與合，2. 符驗，3. 說明論辯之目標（坐而言之，起而可設），4. 其主張可以施行（張而可施行）。

　　第二章〈論辯之階段〉：柯氏在本章中主要討論〈正名〉篇：「實不喻然後命，命不喻然後期，期不喻然後說，說不喻然後辨。」中之「命」、「期」、「說」、「辨」四種論辯活動。

　　荀子認為，語言之正確使用是實現良好秩序與和諧社會所必需。制名之階段有二：1. 認可，即對舊名賦予正當之地位；2. 設立新名。而在制名之前，必先了解「所為有名」和「所緣以同異」。制名之目的在於「指實」，亦即在於「明貴賤」與「辨同異」。

　　就論辯之四個階段而言，柯氏將「命」解釋成「限定名之所指」，此一解釋頗為符合荀子之基本假設，即制名之目的在於「指實」，尤其是指出實物之異同。而事物之異同完全依據感官，更根本而言，是依賴心之徵知。而「期」，柯氏則解為「語言理解之一致」。「期」與「命」二者之作用不同。「命」之作用在於指出事物；而「期」之作用則在於促進人們在語言溝通方面之相互了解。至於「說」和「辯」，柯氏以為，「說」是解說，而「辯」是證成。

　　第三章〈倫理推理和定義之使用〉：柯氏首先將荀子之推理作用解釋成類比推衍，亦即一種倫理知識之擴伸活動，或是一種將既有標準應用於非常情況之知識的擴伸活動。由於「理」與類之作用，此種活動或可被視為一種推理（reasoning），或具有推理作用之活動。此種推理與邏輯學者所研究之推論不同。

　　其次，柯氏指出荀子之「正名」在於正確使用「名」。荀子在論述時，極為注意定義之作用，此可由荀子屢次使用「謂」字得到明證，大部分之「謂」字皆是用來界定以解說荀子對於某些名之用法。在《荀子》一書中，「謂」字大約出現四百次。柯氏藉由荀子書中「謂」字之不同使用，而提出一些準定義公式（quasi-definitional formulas），此等公式在倫理解說與證成中可扮演各種不同之角色。柯氏指出對於區別四個「謂」之句式，大體而言，在斷定力之程度上有重大之差異。從「所謂」之不確定到「可謂」的確定但不強烈，再到「之謂」與「謂之」的較強烈斷定。

第四章〈錯誤信念之診斷〉：柯氏指出錯誤之信念由蔽而生。人若有所蔽，則可說陷於「惑」之狀況。荀子並未說明認識之迷惑的心理根源，而主要是注意這些症狀的語言性質，蓋錯誤之信念用語言之表述最容易處理，此乃正名說實用面向最主要之關懷所在。不過，荀子所關心的是各種思想家所提倡之信念和判斷。這些錯誤的信念主要包含於荀子有名之三惑說。所謂「三惑」是指「用名以亂名」、「用實以亂名」、「用名以亂實」。而荀子用來診斷三惑之圖式，則是一種概念之架構，此一架構則是依據荀子之制名原則即所謂三標而來。

（四）陳漢生：〈荀子：實用主義之儒學〉〔註14〕

本文係陳氏所著之《中國思想之道家理論：一種哲學之詮釋》一書中之第九章。在本章中，陳氏首先說明荀子之思想影響及其思想概述。其後，則主要探討荀子之名學思想，兼及性惡之問題。底下試略述陳氏對於荀子名學之看法。

1. 陳氏指出，荀子採用一種規範的、社會的正名學說，依此，名並非不變的。而名之改變之標準是歷史傳統，且唯有此一傳統是正確之標準。此即遵守已然存在之約定俗成之標準。而此一標準即是此一傳統之當前的擁護者——儒家之君子。荀子藉由成為一位關於道和詮釋的約定主義者來解決正名之問題。

2. 荀子之哲學目的集中於處理人性——心之哲學的名之問題。這些名或語詞主要在於說明心如何使用語言來作社會之統合。荀子專注於自然——約定之區分。荀子確定所謂性是來自自然。荀子並為性、情、慮、偽等術語下定義。

3. 荀子完成上述與人和人之行為相關之散名的界定後，指出此等名或語詞係來自後王。荀子之目的與孔子相同。社會菁英使用語言的任務就是教育。統治者如同父親，他們影響人民如何說和行動。當我們使用名，則我們可以區別事物或對象。而後，我們可以成功地彼此溝通心意。因此，君王可控制人民，且使其行為完美和諧。而政府的關鍵就在於塑造語言。荀子以為，正名之任務是屬於社會菁英，而非碰巧獲得哲學技巧之一般民眾。因此，

〔註14〕 Chad Hansen, "Xunzi :Pragmatic Confucianism", in *A Daoist Theory of Chinese Thought: A Philosophical Interpretation* (Oxford: Oxford University Press, 1992), pp. 307~334.

政府之目的宜持續以政治力控制名之使用。

4. 荀子指出，由於當今聖王沒，名守慢，奇辭起，以致名實之關係相亂，是非之形不明，甚至守法之吏和誦數之儒亦皆混亂。因此，聖王之使命必將有循於舊名，有作於新名。在荀子政治的制名理論中的這種進步的主意仍是權威主義的。荀子僅允許聖王制名。社會上若有新的術語出現，則它們一定是來自於中央的威權，而不是來自有爭議的哲學學派。

5. 荀子提出制名之理論，其原則有三：（1）所為有名，（2）所緣以同異，（3）制名之樞要。荀子指出，制名之目的首先在於明貴賤，而後才是辨同異。至於同名異名之所由起，荀子以為，同異之語言學基礎並不在於其外在之性質，而在於它結合我們作為一個類的性質，即荀子所謂同類同情之意。蓋凡為同類，如人類，感官情形相同的，其感官接受外在事物的刺激，所攝取的物象是相同的。易言之，感官賦予吾人對於事物同異之基礎。

6. 在制名之原則方面，荀子特別強調約定俗成之原則。所謂「名無固宜，約定俗成謂之宜，異於約則謂之不宜。名無固實，約之以命實，約定俗成，謂之實名。」荀子認為，制名之基本要求是約定的一致性。因此，簡易，實用和約定之使用即制名之基本要求。

7. 荀子雖受惠於名家，然而，對於名家之理論則是輕蔑的。他採取一種主要是政治的立場來批評名家的詭論。荀子討論名家，卻不是以哲學家的立場來談論哲學問題，而是採取一位關切維持秩序之統治者的觀點來探討名家之問題，而名家當然會危及國家社會之正理平治。荀子指出，當時之詭論有三種，即三惑：「用名以亂名」、「用實以亂名」和「用名以亂實」。陳氏以為，詭辯論者並不代表思想的挑戰。荀子之所以提出這些詭辯，只不過是在說明詭辯足以威脅制名之約定系統。統治者並不需要去研究或解決這些詭辯，而只要壓制他們即可。

（五）Makeham：〈墨辯和荀子中唯名論者之命名理論〉〔註15〕

本文乃 Makeham 所著之《早期中國思想中之名與實》一書中之第三章。在本章中，作者主要在考察中國古代思想中兩個最發達的命名理論，其目的在於確認這些唯名論的命名理論的主要特色，尤其是荀子的命名理論，蓋其命名

〔註15〕John Makeham, "Nominalist Theories of Naming in the Neo-Mohist Summa and Xun Zi", in *Name and Actuality in Early Chinese Thought* (Albany: SUNY Press, 1994), pp.51~64.

理論乃孔子正名思想之進一步發展。以下試略述 Makeham 對於荀子名學之看
法：

荀子所謂「實」是意指特殊之事物。這種對於「實」的了解，可由荀子對
於「實」和「物」之區分中明顯看出：

> 物有同狀而異所者，有異狀而同所者，可別也。狀同而為異所者，
> 雖可合，謂之二實。狀變而實無別而為異者，謂之化。有化而無別，
> 謂之一實。此事之所以稽實定數也。

依荀子而言，「物」是以概括之方式來指稱事物之對象，而「實」則是用
來指稱特殊之個別對象。事實上，「物」在〈正名〉篇中有其特別作用：

> 故萬物雖眾，有時而欲徧舉之，故謂之物；物也者，大共名也。

荀子將名分為三類：大共名、共名和大別名。其中，大共名是唯一的，它
是無所不包涵之最普遍的概念，而「共名」和「大別名」則是相對的。

對於荀子而言，命名之目的乃在於區別不同之對象：

> 名無固宜，約之以命，約定俗成謂之宜，異於約則謂之不宜。名無
> 固實，約之以命實，約定俗成，謂之實名。

這是荀子唯名論之命名理論的核心。藉由制定特別的名稱，統治者建立了
區分對象的界域。唯有此時，命名始是約定俗成之事。

在近代語言學家中，語言是一種社會約定的觀念乃一平常之事。而陳漢生
也有類似的主張。荀子也確實承認對事物命名主要是一種隨意而約定的性質。
然而，對荀子而言，將實在劃分成被命名之對象的方式是統治者的特權。荀子
對於名的主要關切是實用主義的，而非語意學的。

至於制名之目的，則荀子述之如下：

> 故知者為之分別制名以指實，上以明貴賤，下以辨同異。貴賤明，
> 同異別，如是則志無不喻之患，事無困廢之禍，此所為有名也。

名代表事物同異之標準。然而，最終的認可則是政治的而非哲學的：

> 故王者之制名，名定而實辨，道行而志通。……今聖王沒，名守慢，
> 奇辭起，名實亂，是非之形不明，則雖守法之吏，誦數之儒，亦皆
> 亂也。若有王者起，必將有循於舊名，有作於新名。

對荀子而言，王者命名的主權乃是絕對必要的。荀子所呈現的命名理論的
圖像是聖王已創造出一個足以確保社會和諧和政治秩序的名之系統。

（六）Hagen：〈荀子之使用正名：作為一種建設性設計之命名〉
〔註16〕

本文旨在挑戰數位關於荀子名之地位的詮釋者之觀點。Hagen 主張荀子之觀點是與孔子相一致，即在於努力去影響語言的活動。根據他對翻譯之重新考察和一些主要章節的詮釋，Hagen 主張，名既不是稱謂也不是一種特別的現象分類法。實者，荀子將名理解為促進社會目的的構成概念。最後，Hagen 提出他對於名如何形成及誰將負責其形成之看法。底下試略述本文之主要觀點：

1. Hagen 指出，正名就像多數中國古代學說一樣，本質上是倫理的。正名並不是在知識論的意義上使名歸於正的工作，而是為了社會和倫理的目的使名具有效力。當我們探究荀子之正名觀念時，必須記住：正名是在整部論語中，當孔子回答各種倫理概念之問題時，孔子所持續從事之過程。正名並非一種解釋在語言中已有什麼之過程，也不是一種獨立於我們心靈活動之外有何存在的過程。

2. Hagen 指出，Makeham 主張荀子之名是約定俗成，並且制名只是統治者之特權。Hagen 認為，若依 Makeham 所言，則區分一個對象來符合任一標準，似乎是沒有必要。區分一名所指涉之對象並無內在之適當性，然而，區分一對象之範圍卻是由命名而來。易言之，聖人有權界定名之範圍。Goldin 亦認為名本身是任意的，因之，無需討論名之由來。而陳漢生則指出，荀子思想中之約定論之性格。

3. 關於制名之權責問題，Makeham 主張制名乃君主之特權。而 Hagen 則指出，此並非意謂著君主之制名乃是任意的。君主有其社會目的，而名之區分應要達成其社會目的。此誠如 Rosemont 所言，對荀子而言，統治者有一主要政治功能，即任命足以治理國家政治事務之官吏。當統治者要決定制名之約定原則時，他會尋求最有能力之官吏，亦即知者之建議。雖然，制名之職責在於統治者，然而，實際上積極影響正名的卻是其身邊之知者。

依此，對於制名乃聖王之特權以及制名之過程是居於統治階級之利益此一看法，Hagen 以為，這是不正確的。實者，Hagen 的主張是正名的過程係統治者、有才德之菁英和人民之間的一種複雜的磋商。

〔註16〕Kurtis Hagen , "Xunzi's Use of Zhengming : Naming as a Constructive Project", *Asian Philosophy* 12/1(2002), pp.35~51.

三、荀子名學研究析論

根據上述美國漢學界有關荀子名學之研究，可以發現，學者在某些議題上之觀點，頗為分歧，其中尤以荀子名學之本質，荀子正名之約定原則及荀子之哲學立場等三議題最具爭議性且最為重要，茲分別析論如下：

（一）荀子名學之本質

關於荀子名學之本質的探討，主要的問題是，荀子之名學是否即等同於西方亞里斯多德（Aristotle,384～322B.C.）所創之傳統邏輯（traditional logic）或形式邏輯（formal logic）。環繞此一問題，主要有兩種不同的主張，一是認為荀子之名學即等同於西方之邏輯；另一種主張則是認為荀子之名學並不即是西方之邏輯。對於荀子之名學採取「等同於邏輯說」之代表人物是德效騫。至於認為荀子之名學乃「非邏輯說」，主要是柯雄文和陳漢生。

德效騫在〈邏輯理論〉一文中指出，在中文中，邏輯即指名學而言。柯雄文則指出，荀子之〈正名〉篇被視為具有極大之邏輯興味之作品，然而，柯雄文並不認為，荀子之名學與西方之邏輯為實質之同義語。至於陳漢生雖然在其〈荀子：實用主義之儒學〉中，並未對名學之意義提出說明，然而，陳漢生曾在他文中對中國古代之名學和邏輯之關係加以說明。陳漢生認為，中國古代有語意學理論，但並無邏輯。西方史學家混淆了邏輯和語言理論，而使用邏輯學家（logician）一詞來描述那些中國人稱之為名家（name school）之哲學家，其中最著名的是惠施和公孫龍，而目前亦包括墨辯學者和辯者。可知，陳漢生認為中國古代並無邏輯。〔註17〕

根據上述學者有關荀子名學本質之看法，吾人實看不出其所言之「中國邏輯」或「邏輯」究是何義？易言之，荀子之名學究竟是否即等同於西方之邏輯，學者皆未予以明確之說明或證明。此即表示學者對於荀子之名學在定性方面之研究，仍有未明之處，且亟需予以釐清，否則，將有礙吾人對於荀子名學之確切理解與把握。

荀子之名學是否即等同於邏輯？欲解答此一問題，首先必須了解何謂邏輯學。根據 Copi 對邏輯學所下之定義，邏輯乃是一門研究推論法則和方法之學問。〔註18〕邏輯既旨在探討抽象之推論法則，此即明言邏輯僅研究推論形式

〔註17〕 Chad Hansen,"Logic in China", in *Concise Routledge Encyclopedia of Philosophy* (New York : Routledge , Taylor & Francis Group,2000),pp.495～496.

〔註18〕 Irving M. Copi , *Introduction to Logic* (N.Y.:The Macmillan Company,1972), p.3.

而不求推論之內容。此所以目前之邏輯學又稱之為形式邏輯。所謂推論是由前提推衍出結論之過程。任一推論之前提和結論皆是命題或判斷。易言之，推論是由命題所組成。因之，欲研究有效之推論形式，則必先研究命題之一般結構，或命題之邏輯形式，蓋僅研究命題之內容是無法獲得有效之推論形式。〔註19〕

　　試就荀子名學之內容加以考察，可以發現，荀子名學之核心乃是名或概念之理論。荀子對於辭或命題之探討較為簡略，雖然，荀子對於命題作過分析，且亦有合於有效推論形式之論述之實例，然而，荀子並未能抽象地提出有效之推論形式。因之，根據邏輯學之定義，可知，荀子之名學並不等同於邏輯。

　　在先秦時期，最富於邏輯思辯的，除了荀子之外，尚有名家之公孫龍和墨辯。然而，墨辯和公孫龍之名學皆非邏輯學，蓋二者雖有合於有效推論形式之許多論述或論辯之實例，唯二者皆未能有系統的研究命題之一般結構和有效之推論形式。〔註20〕

　　實者，在邏輯學產生之前，人們已然做過許多合乎邏輯之論述和思辯。此種自然之邏輯概念和能力所表現出之論述和思維形態，僅是邏輯之運用，而非即是邏輯學本身〔註21〕，蓋研究有效之推論形式和運用正確之推論，雖皆與推理活動有關，然而，二者卻是完全不同之兩回事。運用邏輯推論是第一序（first-order）之推理活動；而邏輯之本務是以推論形式作為研究對象，乃第二序（second-order）之活動。任一思想皆可表現出運用了正確之推論，然而，此並非意味著此種思想已對正確或有效之推論進行研究。研究有效之推論形式乃是邏輯之本務，此亦邏輯學之所以有別於其他學問之本質所在。〔註22〕依此，先秦名學，包括荀子、公孫龍及墨辯之名學，其內涵雖有種種合於有效推論形式之實例，然而，其名學僅能稱之為「運用邏輯」，而並非邏輯學本身。

　　此外，就名學與邏輯學之性格而論，二者亦不相同。徐復觀曾就二者之性格，作出極為精闢之分判：

　　　　自從嚴復以「名學」一詞作為西方邏輯的譯名以後，便容易引起許多的附會。實則兩者的性格，並不相同。邏輯是要抽掉經驗的具體事實，以發現純思維的推理形式。而我國名學則是要扣緊經驗的具

〔註19〕劉福增：《語言哲學》（台北：東大圖書公司，1981年），頁270。
〔註20〕劉福增：《語言哲學》，頁270～271。
〔註21〕劉福增：《語言哲學》，頁271。
〔註22〕葉錦明：〈中國邏輯研究的範圍和方法〉，收入葉錦明編：《邏輯思想與語言哲學》（台北：學生書局，1997年），頁113。

體事實，或扣緊意指的價值要求，以求人的言行一致。邏輯所追求
的是思維的世界；而名學所追求的是行為的世界。兩者在起步的地
方有其關連，例如語言表達的正確，及在經驗事實的認定中，必須
有若干推理的作用。但發展下去，便各人走各人的路了。〔註23〕

徐氏以為，中國古代之名學與西方之邏輯，二者之性格不同，蓋邏輯是要
抽掉經驗事實，以發現純思維之推論形式。而中國之名學則是根據經驗事實或
基於價值之要求，以追求行為之實踐或解決現實之倫理政治問題。徐氏所論，
甚為有見，此由中國古代最富於邏輯思辯之名家代表公孫龍、墨辯及荀子之名
學思想中可加以印證。茲略述如下：

公孫龍雖善於析理，長於論辯，然而，公孫龍之正名實，旨在冀求時君能
將之用於治理國事上，故公孫龍曰：

至矣哉！古之明王，審其名實，慎其所謂。至矣哉！古之明王。〔註24〕

所謂「審其名實，慎其所謂」即正名之意，乃〈名實〉篇通篇主旨之所在，
亦公孫龍造作此論之主要理由。而公孫龍亦以能正名實為古之明王。

此外，在〈跡府〉篇中亦敘述，公孫龍之所以提倡〈白馬論〉之原因在於
「疾名實之散亂」，而目的則在於「欲推是辯，以正名實，而化育天下焉。」
易言之，公孫龍學說之目的在於正名實，並欲以名辯之道理來化育天下。此亦
〈跡府〉篇之主旨所在。可知，公孫龍雖以名辯著稱，然而，其名學之目的，
並非全然在於純粹之思辯，而是欲將名辯思想運用於施政上，並以之化導天下
之人，亦即公孫龍之名學思想所追求的亦是行為之世界，而非思維之世界。

而墨辯中雖極富於講求邏輯之思想形態，其論辯之範圍除了知識及邏輯
方面，亦涉及倫理政治方面。墨辯論述辯說之目的如下：

夫辯者，將以明是非之分、審治亂之紀，明同異之處，察名實之理，
處利害，決嫌疑。〔註25〕

「明是非」、「明同異」乃知識、邏輯方面之功能，而其餘四項則是論辯倫理政
治方面之問題。可知，在先秦名學中，墨辯雖然最富於邏輯思辯，然而，其目
的並不在於講求純粹之邏輯思辯，而在於解決經世倫理之問題。

至於荀子之名學實極為明確地繼承並發展孔子正名之所以正政之正名主

〔註23〕徐復觀：《公孫龍子講疏》（台北：學生書局，1979年）頁7。
〔註24〕《公孫龍子・名實論》。
〔註25〕《墨辯・小取》。

義，亦即以倫理政治之要求為其正名之主要目的。其名實之辯雖具有邏輯意義，然而，荀子之主要目的並不在於建構一邏輯學之體系，而是為了倫理政治目的之正名。

綜言之，根據吾人對於中國古代名學之定性分析及對西方邏輯學之理解，中國之名學與西方之邏輯，二者之性格並不相同，易言之，名學在本質上並不等同於邏輯學。

（二）荀子名學之約定原則

荀子以為，制定事物之名必須遵守約定俗成之原則。至於將荀子約定俗成之語言約定論推至極致的，則是陳漢生。陳漢生以為，荀子之正名學說乃是一種約定主義（conventionalism），而荀子則是一位約定主義者（conventionalist）。其後，Makeham 亦認同陳漢生之看法。陳漢生首先區分兩種不同的約定主義，並予以說明如下：

> 約定主義有兩種說法：較弱的約定主義是將吾人所使用的聲音或符號視為社會之約定，只要他們被正確使用時，能夠被一語言社群所相互承認。簡言之，所謂馬，吾人亦可稱之為牛。較強的約定論則主張不僅聲音和符號是約定的，而且相關的區分之實踐亦是約定的。將實在劃分為被命名之對象之方式（完全不論社群所使用之符號或聲音）也是一種共同和約定的分類或區分的實踐，而為大眾所接受的功能。〔註26〕

依據上述約定主義之界定，陳漢生斷定荀子之正名學說乃是一種較強之約定主義，且荀子亦是唯一公開承認名乃是出於約定之儒者。〔註27〕根據陳漢生之論點，荀子之正名乃是一種約定主義之正名觀，依此，對荀子而言，命名乃是完全出於約定俗成，易言之，命名在本質上只不過是一種隨意之約定而成

〔註26〕此段文字之原文如下：

Conventionalism has two versions. The weaker version of conventionalism treats the sounds or symbols we use as social conventions, properly used as long as they are mutually recognized by a language community. Simply put, what we call horse, we could as well have called ox. The stronger version holds that not only the sounds and symbols are conventional, but so is the associated practice of division. The way of dividing reality into objects to be named (totally apart from what symbols or sounds the community uses) is also a function of common acceptance of a shared and conventional practice of classification or division. 參見 Hansen, *Language and Logic in Ancient China* (Ann Arbor :The University of Michigan Press,1992),p. 62.

〔註27〕Hansen, *Language and Logic in Ancient China*, p.81.

之習慣而已。

對於陳漢生之觀點，Makeham 持贊同之態度，Makeham 以為，荀子承認命名乃是一種隨意而約定之性質。〔註28〕而 Van Norden 則對陳漢生之說提出強烈之質疑。Van Norden 認為，陳漢生使用約定主義一詞是有歧義，且陳漢生並未提供充分之文獻證據來支持其論點。〔註29〕

由於 Van Norden 之論點極多，底下僅擇述其主要論點予以說明。Van Norden 指出，荀子似乎已明白地否認較強的約定主義之說法。Van Norden 認為，荀子在正名篇中已提出：命名時乃是經由感官分別事物之同異而後予以制名以指實，因此，對荀子而言，在判斷名之同異時，除了約定之標準外，尚有其他之標準，如，名之同異之制名原則。可知，荀子之命名並非完全出自約定俗成。〔註30〕

此外，Van Norden 指出，陳漢生之論點乃是依據下列一段引文中之「約」字所作之過度解釋而來：

> 如是，則其迹長矣。迹長功成，治之極也。是謹於守名約之功也。
> 〔註31〕

Van Norden 指出，陳漢生乃是將文中之「約」字譯為「約定」〔註32〕，且過度依賴此一「約」字而作出太多之論證。雖然，此一「約」字在想像中或許意指強烈約定之意，然而，實際上，它有其他之譯法，如，Watson 及 Dubs 皆將之譯為「同意」，且二人皆不認為荀子之說法乃是較強之約定主義。〔註33〕

〔註28〕 John Makeham, *Name and Actuality in Early Chinese Thought*, p.59.
〔註29〕 Bryan W.Van Norden, "Hansen on Hsun-Tzu", *Journal of Chinese Philosophy* 20/4(Sep.,1993),p.365.
〔註30〕 Van Norden, p.372.
〔註31〕 《荀子·正名》。
〔註32〕 Van Norden 指出陳漢生係採用 Wing-tsit Chan 之譯文而稍作修正。見 Van Norden, p.375. 又 Wing-tsit Chan 確是將「約」字譯為 conventional,而陳漢生則將之改為 conventionality,參見 Chan ed., *A Source Book in Chinese Philosophy*, p.124.此外，Chan 在同頁註30中指出楊倞註「約」字為「要約」(essential,本質),而劉師培在《荀子補釋》中，亦釋之為"to agree"即"同意"之意。實者，劉氏註「約」字為「要約」，並謂即今之「界說」。
〔註33〕 Van Norden, "Hansen on Hsun-Tzu", p.375.又上述引文中最後一句, Watson 譯之為：All of this is the result of being careful to see that men stick to the names which have been agreed upon. 參見 Burton Watson, *Hsun Tzu:Basic Writings*,p.141.而 Dubs 則譯作：This was the benefit of being careful in preserving the terms which had been agreed upon. 見 Homer Dubs, *The Works of Hsuntze*, p.486.

對於陳漢生之約定論，方萬全亦認為陳漢生不宜將「約定」一詞看得太當真，以為人們確是透過約定之程序而建立一種語言，否則，當初從事約定程序之人又是依據何種語言來進行討論。〔註34〕

綜合上述學者對荀子約定俗成之制名原則之看法，可知，其爭論之問題主要是荀子之正名學說是否即是一種「約定主義」。而此問題實與荀子名之涵義有關，因此，若能釐清荀子名之涵義，則上述問題當可獲得圓滿之解決。

荀子名之涵義實兼指概念（concept）和語詞或名言（term）。所謂概念是表達外在世界客觀事物之抽象義理或本質之語言文字符號，而語詞則是指示一具體事物之名稱的符號。如，「這一朵花」即是語詞，它代表在時空中佔有特殊地位的這一朵具體的花。而「花」則是概念，乃是概括所有的花而代表「花」之義理，而非指一具體的花。可知，語詞與概念僅有些微之分別，由概念轉成語詞只是將之「外在化」或「形式化」而已。〔註35〕概念必須使用語言文字來表達，概念是語詞之思想內容；而語詞則是概念之表達形式。

由上可知，概念乃是代表客觀事物。荀子以為，名是實之反映，是由實所決定，因此，制名須以實為依據，使名實相符。在認識客觀事物之同異後，即要分別制名以指實。指實即是代表客觀事物之意，可知，名具有概念之涵義。作為概念之名與其所代表之客觀事物或實即有一一對應之關係，可知，名與實之關係乃是確定的。荀子之名除具有概念之涵義外，尚有語詞之意義。語詞乃是人們思想交流，彼此溝通之工具，因此，荀子提出名之社會意義，強調「約定俗成」對於名之形成所產生之作用。

就作為語詞之名而言，制名之初，由於名與實之間並無一定之關係，故名之宜否，須由約定俗成之原則所決定。然而，誠如龍宇純所言，語言之約定原則有其適用範圍之限制，並非所有語詞皆由此原則所決定，而是僅有其中之原始語適用之。〔註36〕至於作為概念之名則與約定原則無關。因此，陳漢生主張荀子之正名乃是一種約定主義，以為荀子之命名乃是出於語言之約定，亦即，命名在本質上只不過是一種隨意之約定而成之習慣。其論點實是推求太過且有以偏概全之嫌，蓋荀子之制名原則除了約定俗成之原則外，尚有名之同異原

〔註34〕 方萬全：〈論陳漢生的物質名詞假設〉，收入葉錦明編：《邏輯思想與語言哲學》，
　　　　 頁 208。
〔註35〕 陳祖耀：《理則學》（台北：三民書局，1978 年），頁 27。
〔註36〕 龍宇純：《荀子論集》（台北：學生書局，1987 年），頁 111～112。

則等。無怪乎，陳漢生之論點會引發 Van Norden 之強烈質疑，而方氏亦批評陳漢生不宜將語言約定論無限上綱，以為人們確是透過約定程序而建立一種語言。蓋如此，將會產生無窮後退之難題。可知，陳漢生主張荀子之正名學說乃是約定主義，此一論點實值得商榷，之所以如此，主要在於陳漢生未能把握荀子名之涵義實兼指概念與語詞，且太過強調語言約定論之功能。而 Van Norden 及方萬全之批評則頗為的當。

（三）荀子之哲學立場

美國學者對於荀子名學之研究，主要並不在於對荀子名學所作之定性分析，而在於其哲學立場之釐清，亦即荀子之哲學立場究竟是唯名論或是實在論。主張荀子是唯名論立場的代表是 Makeham。所謂唯名論是指只承認有共名，而否認有所謂共相之真實存在之說。

Makeham 以為，對荀子而言，命名之目的是在於區分不同之對象：

> 名無固宜，約之以命，約定俗成謂之宜，異於約則謂之不宜。名無
> 固實，約之以命實，約定俗成，謂之實名。

Makeham 引述荀子〈正名〉篇中之此段文字，以為此乃荀子唯名論之命名理論的核心。〔註 37〕依此，Makeham 之所以主張荀子之哲學立場是一種唯名論，主要是根據荀子正名說乃是一種約定主義而來。而 Makeham 此一看法實是對於陳漢生之觀點的認同。蓋陳漢生首先斷定荀子之正名學說乃是一種較強之約定主義，且認為荀子是唯一公開承認名乃是出於約定之儒者。〔註 38〕根據約定主義之正名觀，正名乃是出於約定俗成，亦即命名在本質上只不過是一種隨意之約定而成之習慣而已。

由此可知，Makeham 以為荀子之正名說乃是一種約定主義，並由此而主張荀子之哲學立場是一種唯名論。而一般之唯名論者僅承認「名目性定義」（nominal definition）之存在，亦即名或概念只是用來區別某一物和他物之標記而已。〔註 39〕並且反對有所謂「真實之定義」（real definition）或「本質定義」（definition by essence）之存在。所謂「本質定義」是指名或概念在於反映

〔註 37〕 Makeham, *Name and Actuality in Early Chinese Thought*, p.58.

〔註 38〕 Hansen, *Language and Logic in Ancient China*, p.81.

〔註 39〕 "Nominal definitions ……contain only marks for distinguishing a thing from others." 參見 M.D.Wilson, *Leibniz' Doctrine of Necessary Truth* (N.Y. & London: Garland Publishing, 1990), p.117.

事物之本質。

　　然而，荀子名之涵義實兼指概念和語詞而言。即就作為語詞之名而言，制名之初，雖須由約定俗成之原則所決定。然而，語詞之約定原則亦有其適用範圍之限制，並非所有語詞皆由此原則所決定，而是僅有其中之原始語適用之，至於作為概念之名則與約定原則無關。更何況荀子名學之名主要是指概念而言，此由荀子對名所下之定義為「名也者，所以期累實也。」〔註40〕可知。因之，陳漢生及 Makeham 主張荀子之正名學說乃是約定主義，此一論點實有以偏蓋全之嫌。可知，荀子之名學並非是一種約定主義。

　　此外，在先秦名學中，荀子正名學說最重要之成就與貢獻是有關名之理論或概念論（theory of concept）。依西方邏輯而言，尤其是在概念論中是極為強調一概念或名之「內涵」和「外延」之區別。所謂「內涵」是指概念所指涉之本質；所謂「外延」是指概念所指涉之事物之範圍。一般而言，邏輯中之概念論得以成立之關鍵在於能區別一概念之「內涵」和「外延」。荀子已能清楚意識到一概念之「內涵」和「外延」之區別。此由荀子對於人之「內涵」與「外延」之明確說明可知。荀子曾明白指出人之「內涵」如下：

> 人之所以為人者，何已也？曰：以其有辨也。飢而欲食，寒而欲煖，勞而欲息，好利而惡害，是人之所生而有也，是無待而然者也，是禹、桀之所同也。然則，人之所以為人者，非特以二足而無毛也，以其有辨也。今夫狌狌形相亦二足而無毛也，然而，君子啜其羹，食其胾。故人之所以為人者，非特以其二足而無毛也，以其有辨也。夫禽獸有父子，而無父子之親，有牝牡而無男女之別。故人道莫不有辨。辨莫大於分，分莫大於禮，禮莫大於聖王。〔註41〕

　　依此，「人之所以為人者」即人之本質。所謂「人之本質」是指僅有人始具有而非人者則不會具有之特性。荀子指出，人之本質並非「二足而無毛」，而是「有辨」。「辨」即「辨別」，是理性之知。可知，荀子以為人與禽獸之區別是人具有理性之知。依此，人之概念或內涵即是理性之動物。至於人之「外延」則是指具有人之本質之概念，如，孔子、荀子，或聖人、君子、小人、君、臣、庶人等。

　　由上可知，荀子已能明白區分概念之內涵和外延，由此而有概念論之建立。

〔註40〕《荀子・正名》。
〔註41〕《荀子・非相》。

在概念論中，定義論乃是其中之一最基本之構成要素。先秦學者多是透過名與實之關係來論定義問題。荀子在定義論方面承認「本質定義」或「真實之定義」之存在。如，荀子對人所作之定義即是採取「本質定義」。荀子指出，「有辨」即有辨別能力或理性是人之種差或本質，且荀子是由無生物、植物、動物之層層區別中，來顯示出人之所以為人之本質。故荀子曰：

> 水火有氣而無生，草木有生而無知，禽獸有知而無義，人有氣、有
>
> 生、有知，亦且有義，故最為天下貴也。〔註42〕

荀子指出，「有義」即「有辨」之種差即是人之本質。荀子以為，人與動物之差別在於「有義」或「有辨」，而以此種差對人所下之定義即是人之本質定義。綜言之，Makeham 以為，荀子之名學乃是一種約定主義，並由此主張荀子之哲學立場是一種唯名論，其論點實值得商榷。蓋經由上述之分析，可知，荀子之名學並非是一種約定主義，因之，Makeham 以荀子之哲學立場是一種唯名論之主張，當然亦不能成立。此外，一般唯名論者會反對有所謂「本質定義」之存在，然而，透過上述分析，可明，荀子在定義論方面卻承認「本質定義」之存在，由此可知，荀子並非是一唯名論者。

四、結論與未來研究之展望

以上論述乃荀子名學研究在美國之概況。由於篇幅所限，本文僅選擇一些較具代表性之論著作一介紹。不過，從論述中，亦不難看出荀子名學研究在美國此一研究領域之概略情形。根據以上論述，可以發現，此一研究領域在質的方面，已呈現可喜之成績。雖然，在某些議題上，學者之觀點頗為分歧，然而，多元觀點之呈現，對於荀子名學之把握，應有正面而實質之助益。至於量的方面，則明顯不足。然而，由於美國漢學界人才輩出，再加上與華語地區之學術交流日趨頻仍，在此一領域之研究，應會交出更為亮麗之成績單，此當是可以預期的。

從上述已發表之論著看來，在美國學界，學者對荀子名學之研究比較偏重其哲學立場之探討和順著〈正名〉篇作一般性之論述。至於對於荀子名學之定性方面之研究則稍嫌不足。此外，荀子名學之旨趣既然是以倫理政治之要求為依歸，甚而，荀子在論述其主張時，會作若干之推論，然而，此種推論僅是邏輯法則之應用，而與嚴謹之邏輯推論並不相同。易言之，荀子名學中所提出之

〔註42〕《荀子·王制》。

論辯，本質上是倫理的，而非思辯的。因之，未來有關荀子名學之研究，或誠如柯雄文所指出的，宜著重於荀子之倫理學或道德知識論之探究，唯柯雄文對於荀子名學之內涵之分析，則稍嫌不足，因之，此後對於荀子名學之研究，宜全面而深入地分析其內涵。其次，根據荀子之名學理論來重建荀子書中之論證形式和結構，亦不失為研究荀子哲學之另一方向。

附錄

1. Allinson, Robert E., "The Debate Between Mencius and Hsün-tzu: Contemporary Application", *Journal of Chinese Philosophy* 25/1 (1998), pp. 31~50.

2. Bayerleova, Ema, "A New Introduction to the Thinking of Hsün-tzu", *Archiv Orientalni* 46 (1978) pp.174~179.

3. Berkson, Mark, "Death in Xunzi", in "Death and the Self in Ancient China Thought: A Comparative Perspective", Ph. D. dissertation(Stanford University, 1999), pp. 103~195.

4. Bodde, Derk, "Hsün-tzu", in *Encyclopaedia Britannica* 11 (1960), pp. 854~855.

5. Campany, Robert F., "Xunzi and Durkheim as Theorists of Ritual Practice", in Frank E. Reynolds and David Tracy eds., *Discourse and Practice*(Albany: SUNY Press, 1992), pp. 197~231.

6. Chan, Wing-tsit, "Naturalistic Confucianism: Hsün Tzu", in *A Source Book in Chinese Philosophy* (Princeton: Princeton University Press, 1963), pp. 115~135.

7. Chan, Keung-lap, "Confucian Politics and Christian Politics: A Comparison between Xun Zi and Augustine", in Beatrice Leung and John D. Young eds., *Christianity in China: Foundations for Dialogue*(Hong Kong: Center of Asian Studies, University of Hong Kong, 1993), pp. 155~178.

8. Cheng, Andrew Chih-yi, "Hsün Tzu's Theory of Human Nature and Its Influence on Chinese Thought", Ph.D. dissertation(Columbia University, 1928).

9. Cheung, Leo K. C,"The Way of the Xunzi", *Journal of Chinese Philosophy*

28/3 (2001), pp. 301~320.

10. Chung, Bungkil, "Feature Review: A. S. Cua, Ethical Argumentation: A Study in Hsün Tzu's Moral Epistemology", *Journal of Chinese Philosophy* 13/4 (1986), pp. 459~470.

11. Cook, Scott B, "Xunzi",in "Unity and Diversity in the Musical Thought of Warring States China", Ph.D. dissertation(the University of Michigan, 1995), pp. 372~456.

12. Cook, Scott B, "Xun Zi on Ritual and Music", *Monumenta Serica* 45 (1997), pp.1~38.

13. Creel, Herrlee G., "Confucius and Hsüntzu", *Journal of the American Oriental Society* 51 (1931), pp. 23~32.

14. Creel, Herrlee G., " The Authoritarianism of Hsün Tzu",in *Chinese Thought: From Confucius to Mao Tse-tung*(Chicago: University of Chicago Press, 1953), pp. 115~134.

15. Cua, Antonio S., "The Conceptual Aspect of Hsün Tzu's Philosophy of Human Nature", *Philosophy East & West* 27/4 (1977), pp. 373~389.

16. Cua, Antonio S., "The Quasi-Empirical Aspect of Hsün Tzu's Philosophy of Human Nature", *Philosophy East & West* 28/1 (1978), pp. 3~19.

17. Cua, Antonio S.,, "Dimensions of Li (Propriety): Reflections on an Aspect of Hsün Tzu's Ethics", *Philosophy East & West* 29/4 (1979), pp. 373~394.

18. Cua, Antonio S.,, "Hsun Tzu's Theory of Argumentation: A Reconstruction", *Review of Metaphysics* 36 (1983), pp. 867~894.

19. Cua, Antonio S.,, *Ethical Argumentation: A Study in Hsün Tzu's Moral Epistemology*(Honolulu: University of Hawaii Press, 1985).

20. Cua, Antonio S.,, "Ethical Uses of the Past in Early Confucianism: The Case of Hsün Tzu", *Philosophy East & West* 35/2 (1985), pp. 133~156. Rp in: Thornton C. Kline III and Philip J. Ivanhoe eds., *Virtue,Nature, and Moral Agency in the Xunzi*, pp. 39~68.

21. Cua, Antonio S.,, "Hsün Tzu and the Unity of Virtues", *Journal of Chinese Philosophy* 14/4 (1987), pp. 381~400.

22. Cua, Antonio S.,, "The Problem of Conceptual Unity in Hsün Tzu and Li Kou's

Solution", *Philosophy East & West* 39 (1989), pp. 115~134.

23. Cua, Antonio S.,, "Review of Xunzi: A Translation and Study of the Complete Works, v. 1, books 1~6, John Knoblock", *Philosophy East & West* 41/2 (1991), pp. 215~227.

24. Cua, Antonio S.,, "Hsün Tzu", in Lawrence C. Becker and Charlotte B. Becker eds., *Encyclopedia of Ethics* ,v. 3(New York: Garland Publishing Company, 1992), pp. 556~558.

25. Cua, Antonio S.,, "The Possibility of Ethical Knowledge: Reflections on a Theme in the Hsün Tzu", in Hans Lenk and Gregor S. Paul eds., *Epistemological Issues in Classical Chinese Philosophy* (Albany: SUNY Press, 1993), pp. 159~180.

26. Cua, Antonio S.,, "The Ethical Significance of Shame: Insight of Aristotle and Xunzi", *Philosophy East & West* 53/2 (2003), pp. 147~202.

27. Cua, Antonio S.,, "The Ethical and the Religious Dimensions of Li", in Tu, Weiming and Tucker, Mary Evelyn eds, *Confucian Spirituality* v. 1(New York: The Crossroad Publishing Company, 2003), pp. 252~286.

28. Dubs, Homer H., *Hsüntze, the Moulder of Ancient Confucianism*(London: Arthur Probsthain, 1927).

29. Dubs, Homer H., *The Works of Hsün Tze*(London: Arthur Probsthain, 1928)(Translation of Chapters 1, 2, 4~11 and 15~23).

30. Dubs, Homer H., "'Nature' in the Teaching of Confucius", *Journal of the American Oriental Society* 50 (1930), pp. 233~237.

31. Dubs, Homer H., "Mencius and Sun-dz on Human Nature", *Philosophy East & West* 6 (1956), pp. 213~222.

32. Edkins, Joseph, "Siün King, the Philosopher, and His Relations with Contemporary Schools of Thought", *Journal of the China Branch of the Royal Asiantic Society* 33 (1899~1900), pp. 46~55.

33. Eno, Robert, "Ritual as a Natural Art: The Role of T'ien in the Hsün Tzu",in *The Confucian Creation of Heaven: Philosophy and the Defense of Ritual Mastery* (Albany: SUNY Press, 1990), pp. 131~170.

34. Fehl, Noah E., *Li: Rites and Propriety in Literature and Life-A Perspective for*

a Cultural History of Ancient China(Hong Kong: Chinese University of Hong Kong Press, 1971).

35. Fung, Yu-lan, "Hsün Tzu and His School of Confucianism",in *A History of Chinese Philosophy*, v.1, Derk Bodde, trans. (N. J.: Princeton University Press, 1952), pp. 279~311.

36. Geaney, Jane, "Xunzi: Eye/Action and Ear/Speech", in "Language and Sense Discrimination in Ancient China", Ph.D. dissertation(University of Chicago, 1996), pp. 103~143.

37. Gier, Nicholas F., "Xunzi and the Confucian Answer to Titanism", *Journal of Chinese Philosophy* 22/2 (1995), pp. 129~151.

38. Goldin, Paul R., "The Philosophy of Xunzi", Ph.D. dissertation(Harvard University, 1996), Rev. version as *Rituals of the Way: The Philosophy of Xunzi*(Chicago: Carus Publishing Company, 1999).

39. Goldin, Paul R., "Xunzi in the Light of the Guodian Manuscripts", *Early China* 25 (2000), pp. 113~146.

40. Goldin, Paul R., "Xunzi's Piety", in Tu, Weiming and Tucker, Mary Evelyn eds, *Confucian Spirituality* v. 1, pp. 287~303.

41. Hagen, Kurtis, "A Critical Review of Ivanhoe on Xunzi", *Journal of Chinese Philosophy* 27/3 (2000), pp. 361~373.

42. Hagen, Kurtis, "Xunzi's Use of Zhengming :Naming as a Constructive Project",*Asian Philosophy* 12/1 (2002),PP.35~51.

43. Hansen, Chad, *Language and Logic in Ancient China*(Ann Arbor: University of Michigan Press, 1983).

44. Hansen, Chad, "Xunzi: Pragmatic Confucianism", in *A Daoist Theory of Chinese Thought: A Philosophical Interpretation*(New York: Oxford University Press, 1992), pp. 307~334.

45. Hsieh, Shan-yüan , "Hsün Tzu's Political Philosophy", *Journal of Chinese Philosophy* 6 (1979), pp. 69~90.

46. Hutton, Eric, "On the Meaning of Yi for Xunzi", Unpublished manuscript. ca. 1976.

47. Hutton, Eric, "Does Xunzi Have a Consistent Theory of Human Nature?" in

Thoenton C. Kline III and Philip J. Ivanhoe eds., *Virtue, Nature, and Moral Agency in Xunzi*, pp. 220~236.

48. Hutton, Eric, "Virtue and Reason in Xunzi", Ph.D. dissertation(Stanford University, 2001).

49. Hutton, Eric, "Xunzi",in Philip J. Ivanhoe and Bryan W. Van Norden eds., *Readings in Classical Chinese Philosophy*(New York: Seven Bridges Press, 2001),pp. 247~294.

50. Hutton, Eric, "Moral Reasoning in Aristotle and Xunzi", *Journal of Chinese Philosophy* 29/3 (2002), pp. 355~384.

51. Ivanhoe, Philip J. "Thinking and Learning in Early Confucianism", *Journal of Chinese Philosophy* 17/4 (1990), pp. 473~493.

52. Ivanhoe, Philip J. "A Happy Symmetry: Xunzi's Ethical Thought", *Journal of the American Academy of Religion* 59/2 (1991), pp. 309~322.

53. Ivanhoe, Philip J. "Human Nature and Moral Understanding in Xunzi", *International Philosophical Quarterly* 34/2 (1994), pp. 167~175. Rp in Thoenton C. Kline III and Philip J. Ivanhoe eds., *Virtue, Nature, and Moral Agency in Xunzi*, pp.237~249.

54. Ivanhoe, Philip J. "Xunzi",in *Confucian Moral Self Cultivation*(Indianapolis: Hackett Publishing Company, 2000), pp. 29~42.

55. Kaminsky, Jack, "Hsüntze's Philosophy of Man", *Philosophy and Phenomenological Research* 12 (1951), pp. 116~122.

56. Kenzig, Stephen R., "Ritual versus Law in Hsün Tzu: a Discussion", *Journal of Chinese Philosophy* 3 (1975), pp. 57~66.

57. Kline III, Thoenton C., "Ethics and Tradition in the Xunzi", Ph.D. dissertation (Stanford University, 1998).

58. Kline III, Thoenton C. and Philip J. Ivanhoe eds., *Virtue, Nature, and Moral Agency in Xunzi*(Indianapolis: Hackett Publishing Company, 2000).

59. Kline III, Thoenton C. and Philip J. Ivanhoe eds., "Moral Agency and Motivation in the Xunzi", in *Virtue, Nature, and Moral Agency in Xunzi*, pp. 155~175.

60. Knechtges, David R., "Riddles as Poetry: The 'Fu'", *Wen-lin* 2 (1989), pp.

116~122.

61. Knoblock, John, "The Chronology of Xunzi's Works", *Early China* 8 (1982~1983), pp. 28~52.

62. Knoblock, John, *Xunzi: A Translation and Study of the Complete Works*(Stanford: Stanford University Press, 1988~1994).

63. Kuller, Janet A. H., "Early Chinese Resistance to Taoist Thought: A Study of Anti-Taoism in the Hsün Tzu", Ph.D. dissertation(University of Chicago, 1974).

64. Kuller, Janet A. H., "The 'Fu' of the Hsün Tzu as an Anti-Taoist Polemic", *Monumenta Serica* 31 (1974~1975), pp. 205~218.

65. Kuller, Janet A. H., "Anti-Taoist Elements in Hsün Tzu's Thought and Their Social Relevance", *Asian Thought and Society* 3/7 (1978), pp. 53~67.

66. Kuppermann, Joel J., "Xunzi: Morality as Psychological Constraint", in Thoenton C. Kline III and Philip J. Ivanhoe eds., *Virtue, Nature, and Moral Agency in Xunzi*, pp. 89~102.

67. Lau, D. C., "Theories of Human Nature in Mencius and Shyuntzyy", *Bulletin of the School of Oriental and African Studies* 15 (1953), pp. 541~565. Rp in Thornton C. Kline III and Philip J. Ivanhoe eds., *Virtue, Nature, and Moral Agency in the Xunzi*, pp. 188~219.

68. Lee, Janghee, "The Autonomy of Xin and Ethical Theory in Xunzi", Ph.D. dissertation (University of Hawaii, 2001).

69. Machle, Edward J., "Hsün~tzu: a Revisionist View", *Iliff Review* 32/3 (1975), pp. 19~31.

70. Machle, Edward J., "Hsün Tzu as Religious Philosopher", *Philosophy East & West* 26/4 (1976), pp. 443~461.

71. Machle, Edward J., "The Mind and the 'Shen-ming' in the Xunzi", *Journal of Chinese Philosophy* 19/4 (1992), pp. 361~386.

72. Machle, Edward J., *Nature and Heaven in the Xunzi: A Study of the "Tian Lun"*(Albany: SUNY Press, 1993).

73. Makeham, John, "Nominalist Theories of Naming in the Neo-Mohist Summa and Xun Zi", in *Name and Actuality in Early Chinese Thought*(Albany: SUNY

Press, 1994), pp. 51~64.

74. Malmqvist, Göran, "The Cherng Shianq Ballad of the Shyun Tzyy", *Bulletin of the Museum of Far Eastern Antiquities* 45 (1973), pp. 63~89.

75. Malmqvist, Göran, "A Note on the Cherng Shiang Ballad of the Shyun Tzyy", *Bulletin of the School for Oriental and African Studies* 36/2 (1973), pp. 352~358.

76. Marshall, John, "Hsün Tzu's Moral Epistemology", *Journal of Chinese Philosophy* 14/4 (1987), pp. 487~500.

77. Mei, Yi-pao, "Hsün Tzu on Terminology", *Philosophy East & West* 1 (1951), pp. 51~66.

78. Mei, Yi-pao, "Hsün Tzu's Theory of Education, with an English Translation of the Hsün Tzu, Chapter 1", *Ts'ing Hua Journal of Chinese Studies* 2/2 (1961), pp. 361~377.

79. Mei, Yi-pao, "Hsün Tzu's Theory of Government, with an English Translation of the Hsün Tzu, Chapter 9", *Ts'ing Hua Journal of Chinese Studies* 8/1-2 (1970), pp. 36~83.

80. Mote, Frederick, "Early Confucianism: Hsün Tzu",in *Intellectual Foundations of China*, second edition(New York: McGraw-Hill Publishing Company, 1989), pp. 54~58.

81. Munro, Donald J., *The Concept of Man in Early China*(Stanford: Stanford University Press, 1969).

82. Munro, Donald J., "A Villain in the Xunzi", in Philip J Ivanhoe ed., *Chinese Language, Thought, and Culture*(Chicago and La Salle, Ill.: Open Court, 1996), pp. 193~201.

83. Nevile, Robert, "Ritual and Normative Culture", in *Normative Cultures*(Albany: SUNY Press, 1995), pp. 163~195.

84. Nivison, David S., "Hsün Tzu and Chuang Tzu", in Henry Rosemont Jr. ed., *Chinese Texts and Philosophical Contexts*(La Salle, Ill.: Open Court, 1991), pp. 129~142. Rp in Thornton C. Kline III and Philip J. Ivanhoe eds., *Virtue, Nature, and Moral Agency in the Xunzi*, pp. 176~187.

85. Nivison, David S., "Xunzi on 'Human Nature'" ,in Bryan W. Van Norden ed.,

The Ways of Confucianism: Investigations in Chinese Philosophy(Chicago: Open Court, 1996), pp. 203~213.

86. Nivison, David S., "Critique of David B. Wong, 'Xunzi on Moral Motivation'" ,in Philip J. Ivanhoe ed, *Chinese Language, Thought, and Culture*, pp. 323~331.

87. Parker, Edward H., "The Philosopher Süntsz", *New China Review* 4 (1922), pp. 1~19; pp. 360~372.

88. Robins, Dan, "The Development of Xunzi's Theory of Xing, Reconstructed on the Basis of a Textual Analysis of Xunzi 23, 'Xing e' 性惡 (Xing is Bad)", *Early China* 26 (2001~2002), pp. 99~158.

89. Roetz, Heiner, "Xunzi's Rationalism",in *Confucian Ethics of the Axial Age: A Reconstruction under the Aspect of the Breakthrough Toward Postconventional Thinking*(Albany: SUNY Press, 1993), pp. 213~226.

90. Rosemont, Henry Jr., "State and Society in the Hsün Tzu: A Philosophical Commentary", *Monumenta Serica* 29 (1970~1971), pp. 38~78, Rp in Thornton C. Kline III and Philip J. Ivanhoe eds., *Virtue, Nature, and Moral Agency in the Xunzi*, pp. 1~38.

91. Schofer, Jonathan W., "Virtues in Xunzi's Thought", *Journal of Religious Ethics* 21 (1993), pp. 117~136. Rp in Thornton C. Kline III and Philip J. Ivanhoe eds., *Virtue, Nature, and Moral Agency in the Xunzi*, pp. 69~88.

92. Schwartz, Benjamin I., "Hsün-tzu: The Defense of the Faith",in *The World of Thought in Ancient China*(Mass.: Harvard University Press, 1985), pp. 290~320.

93. Shih, Vincent Y. C., "Hsün Tzu's Positivism", *Ts'ing Hua Journal of Chinese Studies* 4/2 (1964), pp. 162~174.

94. Shih, Joseph, "Secularization in Early Chinese Thought-A Note on Hsün tzu", *Gregorianum* 50 (1969), pp. 391~404.

95. Shun, Kwong-loi, "Review of Ethical Argumentation: A Study in Hsün Tzu's Moral Epistemology, by A. S. Cua", *Philosophy East & West* 41/1 (1991), pp. 111~117.

96. Slingerland, Edward G., "Wu-wei in the Xunzi", in "Effortless Action: Wu-wei

as a Spiritual Ideal in Early China", Ph.D. dissertation(Stanford University, 1998), pp. 345~411.

97. Soles, David E., "The Nature and Grounds of Xunzi's Disagreement with Mencius", *Asian Philosophy* 9/2 (1999), pp. 123~133.

98. Stalnaker, Aaron D., "Overcoming Our Evil: Spiritual Exercises and Personhood in Xunzi and Augustine", Ph.D. dissertation(Brown University, 2001).

99. Stalnaker, Aaron D., "Aspect of Xunzi's Engagement with Early Daoism", *Philosophy East & West* 53/1 (2003), pp. 87~129.

100. Twohey, Michael, "Xunzi and Ancient Chinese Authority", in *Authority and Welfare in China: Modern Debates in Historical Perspective*(New York: St. Martin's Press, 1999), pp. 13~28.

101. Van Norden, Bryan W., "Mengzi and Xunzi: Two Views of Human Agency", *International Philosophical Quarterly* 32 (1992), pp. 161~84. Rp in Thornton C. Kline III and Philip J. Ivanhoe eds., *Virtue, Nature, and Moral Agency in the Xunzi*, pp. 103~134.

102. Van Norden, "Hansen on Hsün-tzu", *Journal of Chinese Philosophy* 20/3 (1993), pp. 365~382.

103. Van Norden, " Hansen on Hsun-Tzu", *Journal of Chinese Philosophy* 20/4(Sep.,1993),p.365.

104. Van Norden, "Liu Hsiang and Ts'ien Ta-hien on Sundz", *New China Review* 4 (1922), pp. 443~449.

105. Watson, Burton, *Hsün Tzu: Basic Writings*(New York: Columbia University Press, 1963)(Translation of Chapters1, 2, 9, 15, 17, and 19~23).

106. Wong, David B., "Hsün Tzu on Moral Motivation", in Philip J Ivanhoe ed., *Chinese Language, Thought, and Culture*, pp. 202~233, Rp in Thoenton C. Kline III and Philip J. Ivanhoe eds., *Virtue, Nature, and Moral Agency in Xunzi*, pp. 135~154.

107. Yearley, Lee H., "Hsün Tzu on the Mind: His Attempted Synthesis of Confucianism and Taoism", *Journal of Asian Studies* 39/3 (1980), pp. 465~480.

章太炎研究在美國 [註1]

一、前言

　　美國原無漢學傳統。其漢學研究，基本上是由歐洲漢學移植發展而來的。由於幾位漢學大師逐漸地凋零，象徵歐洲傳統漢學的式微。加上二次世界大戰後，歐洲不再是世界中心，國力衰弱，經濟萎縮，在在影響了歐洲漢學之發展，而人才外流亦是嚴重的問題。而美國則是國勢強，財力雄厚，此正是美國在二次世界大戰後，漢學研究所以「後來居上」的關鍵。

　　美國早年的漢學，基本上和其他各個學科一樣，都是歐洲學術的支脈，因此，留學歐洲以及客居美國之歐洲學者，便是美國漢學研究的另一個推動力量。尤其到了十九世紀末葉，二十世紀初期，美國已逐漸脫離「草創」時期，前來美國講學及研究之歐洲學者絡繹不絕，大大提升了美國的學術水準。

　　但直到 1930 年代，儘管漢學已經進入美國各大學的「學術殿堂」，但它並未受到真正的重視。在此期間，西方人研究中國，不外乎是為了傳教、通商，擴展殖民地，或乾脆視中國為一神祕而「遺世獨立」的國度，帶著「賞玩古董」，以個人興趣為主的心情來探究中國。也因為如此，西方人研究中國傳統的藝術、宗教、哲學、文學及科學，雖不乏學術價值及創見，但「中國的歸中國；西方的歸西方」，西方的傳統歷史觀裡沒有中國，而中國的興衰存亡也似乎不足以令西方學者掛心。

　　此種「心理瓶頸」一直到二次世界大戰後，才開始轉變。由於中國大陸淪

〔註1〕本文係兩岸學界之美國漢學研究之開山之作。

入共黨陣營，乃至於長達三十年的美蘇冷戰等，使中國在「世界體系」中之地位，愈來愈重要，而「漢學」也就從無關痛癢的冷門科目，逐漸「質變」成以近代中國（從鴉片戰爭算起）的政治、經濟及社會發展為研究主體的美國式「中國研究」了。

　　美國的中國研究起因於政治上需要一群中國問題專家，以深入了解「中國」。在 1950 年代，美國政府開始將大量資金投入高等學術研究機構，來推動研究工作。起初，研究是環繞近、現代史，且得出用「西力衝擊與中國回應」的模式，即可道盡中國近代種種轉折及變遷之結論。隨著不斷廣泛地探討，美國史家往上溯及思想問題，而著眼於中國近代思想史的研究，並以一些思想家之思想作為基點來探究中國近代之思想變遷。〔註2〕

　　在近代中國思想史中，章太炎實扮演一極其重要之角色。章氏不僅在政治上及學術上極其有名，且影響深遠。此外章氏之生平與思想呈示出他那一代之知識分子中政治及文化理想間所產生之張力，並預示了近代中國思想史上的一些重要思潮。有關章太炎的研究，在美國漢學界已做出可喜之成績。本文題為〈章太炎研究在美國〉，所討論之對象以曾在美國從事教學與研究之學者所已發表之英文論著為準，涵蓋之時間是 1969 年至 1993 年之間，分別就一些比較重要之著作作一論述，並就已有之研究成果，作一析論，並說明其未來可能之研究發展方向。

二、章太炎研究述要

　　（一）高慕軻：〈章炳麟〉〔註3〕本文乃高氏所撰《中國知識份子與辛亥革命》中之一章。本書主要討論一個短暫時期中少數中國革命份子之觀念。這個時期主要是 1905～1907 年，但也包括 1903～1905 年及 1907～1908 年。1898～1903 年和 1908～1911 年較少，而 1898 年之前和 1911 年之後則幾乎沒有。本書討論的人物是參與反清革命和建立民國之知識份子。高氏選擇這些人物是因為他們代表當時之支配性思潮，並且此一思潮是重要的，因為它代表一個新的知識階層的出現。「章炳麟」在本書中乃唯一列為專章討論之人物，由

〔註2〕 李哲賢：〈美國漢學研究的概況〉，《文理通識學術論壇》第 1 期（1999 年），頁 2～4。

〔註3〕 Michael Gasster, *Chinese Intellectuals and the 1911 Revolution: The Birth of Modern Chinese Radicalism* (Seattle and London: University of Washington Press, 1969), pp. 190~227.

此可見其重要性及高氏對章氏之重視。

　　高氏首先指出章氏在辛亥革命中，在某些方面是最保守的，但在其他方面卻是最激進的。他的觀念來源複雜，可追溯至古代中國及現代西方。整體觀之，章氏之思想似乎與他自己及其世界相衝突，章氏之所以如此，高氏引述蕭公權之說法：章氏之政治思想乃一深切沈痛而微妙之抗議。高氏同時指出章氏無疑的是革命份子中最著名之學者，其影響是不容置疑的，且其生平及思想亦有其重要性。以下試依本文之內容分項予以敘述：

1. 章氏轉向革命之路（頁191～198）

　　高氏指出，章氏於1895年加入康有為之強學會，因為他所閱讀之西書使他相信，欲救中國必須採取改革之手段。據說，在當時，章氏除了反對康氏之建立孔教論之外，已是一位堅定之改革者。但是，章氏自言，他已反對康氏所詮釋之儒學，並質疑只要滿清仍掌權，改革是否可能救中國。只是此等觀點並未影響章氏之支持改革。

　　1898年，維新運動失敗後，據說章氏曾自述，雖然孫逸仙只受過一點西式教育，卻能清楚地分辨種族之不同；而康、梁等著名學者卻是是非不明且仍持續支持滿清異族。值得注意的是，章氏早期對孫氏之看法是輕蔑孫氏之教育，但卻欣賞他的革命目標。

　　高氏指出，章氏和康氏二人之儒學觀點差異性極大，且章氏又是極端反滿，何以二人仍能合作？高氏提出的解釋是：二人之共同信念，如，為了避免外國勢力之征服，必須向日本學習及改革中國之制度等形成二人合作之基礎。至於，章氏何時由改革轉向革命？高氏認為章氏是在1900年或1901年才公開而明白地成為革命份子，因為，在義和團事件中，滿清無力抵抗外國勢力之侵犯，才使章氏投向革命。但高氏指出，更可能的解釋是，當時革命和改革之間的界線並未明白劃分，直到1902年至1905年間，他們的政治立場才逐漸穩定而劃歸其所屬之陣營。此由章氏曾將1897年至1901年間之康氏歸類為革命份子可知一般。

　　1903年章氏發表〈駁康有為論革命書〉，它被認為是一篇極具影響力之革命文獻，在文中，章氏主要是根據民族主義之觀點來駁斥康氏之改革主義和支持滿清政權，此文發表後不久，章氏即因蘇報案繫獄三年，值得一提的是，在獄中章氏開始接觸大乘佛學，尤其是唯識學。

2. 宗教和民族主義（頁 198～210）

1906 年，章氏出獄後，隨即赴東京演說，他強調：用宗教發起信心，增進國民的道德和用國粹激動種性，增進愛國的熱腸。章氏之所以重視宗教是因為他認為若沒有宗教，則道德不會增進，生存競爭專為一己。而他所說之宗教是指佛教而言。至於國粹，章氏並不是要人尊信孔教，而只是要愛惜漢人的歷史，廣義而言，中國歷史可分三方面，即語言文字、典章制度和人物事跡。高氏指出章氏之強調宗教與國粹，使他明顯地有別於參與革命運動之其他知識份子。高氏認為章氏之所以強調二者，乃是因為它們是章氏思想中最基本而持續的特色。

高氏指出，當初章氏之所以加入康、梁之陣營，可能是因為他認同康氏對防止中國傳統在西化潮流中被淹沒之關切所致。然而，康、章二氏對種族和傳統的認知不同，使他們之間保持距離，再加上政治思想之歧異，才使得二人最後決裂。因此，高氏認為在康、章之間的敵對因素總是存在著，而政治則是促使二人分手的觸媒。至於章氏與其他革命份子亦有所不同。誠如李文遜所言，章氏與革命份子中之保守學者不同的是章氏之革命觀點是來自於他保存國粹之關切，且章氏之國粹概念亦不同於其他傳統主義者。章氏不僅要保存國粹，且更強調道德之重要性。

章氏之所以要增進道德乃是因為他相信道德衰亡是亡國滅種之根源，因此，振興道德對救國救種而言，是必要的。在章氏眼中，道德僅是一種手段，而非目的，因為，他認為缺乏道德之人，則革命不成。因此，章氏之所以特別推崇宗教或佛教，乃是因為它對促進道德是有用的。誠如章氏所言，佛教之價值在於它可以培養革命之精神與道德，如勇氣、無私、平等、服務和責任等。章氏之提倡佛教，「但欲姬漢遺民，趨於自覺，非高樹宗教為旌旗，以相陵奪。」依此，佛教對章氏民族主義之主張有所貢獻。章氏之宗教和民族主義之概念也強化了同盟會之綱領。

3. 個人、社會和國家（頁 210～213）

章氏提出他對中國未來之看法而主張「五無論」。他認為國家必有政府，而共和政體於禍害為差輕，乃不得已而取之。但是，即使是最好的共和政體也只不過是解決世界問題的基本或暫時的方法。因此，若要求盡善，則必當高蹈「太虛」。而欲達於此，非有共和偽政以為基礎不可，且唯有百年之後，始可見五無之制。

章氏所謂五無論，依次是指無政府、無聚落、無人類、無眾生及無世界。章氏之所以會主張五無論這種政治的悲觀主義，是因為 1907 年夏天時的一些事件使他深感絕望所致，如，革命運動不順利、章氏批評孫逸仙，並與之決裂等。其後，章氏擔任陶成章所組織的光復會會長。

4. 章氏論政府（頁 213～219）

章氏曾自言，共和政體乃最進步的政治組織之形式。其後，則解釋說，共和政體可為無政府鋪路，因此，它是無可替代的。但是，一個共和政體需略加改革始可被接受：

> 一曰，均配土田，使耕者不為佃奴。二曰，官立工場，使傭人得分贏利。三曰，限制相續，使富厚不傳子孫。四曰，公散議員，使政黨不敢納賄。

章氏雖可接受共和政體，卻反對代議制，蓋共和非代議也。章氏之反對代議，其理由有三：（1）代議制乃封建之遺跡，不適於平等之社會。對章氏而言，西方代議政權之共通性是上置貴族院，民主之國則代之以元老。而中國已脫離封建甚久，且無階級區分，何需採用此一制度？（2）議員不能代表民意。（3）中國地廣人多不宜行代議。

章氏亦要求司法權之獨立行使，其首長之地位宜與總統平齊。而行政和司法之外，則另立一教育權，其首長則三者平齊。

高氏指出，章氏將代議制與封建制度及階級區分相提並論，實令人難以理解。高氏認為或許章氏所了解的是十三世紀剛發展時的代議制，當時此制度是代表貴族而非人民之利益，而對二十世紀議會制度之運作不甚了解吧！

5. 章氏之個人主義（頁 219～222）

章氏不信任權威和對國家之敵意乃來自於他對個人之深切信念。個人乃章氏政治思想之中心。章氏相信不僅國家之事業最鄙賤，而且，國家之作用亦是不得已而設之，非理所當然而設之。他主張個人是真實的；而群體是虛幻的。但是，章氏認為有時國家之存在是必要的，因為，中國是衰弱且身處危機中，且因為他國一日不解散，則中國也需要國家以求自存。

由此，章氏提出他對人際關係之看法：人非為世界、社會、國家及他人而生。因之，對世界、社會、國家及他人皆無責任。故人倫相處以無害為其界限。除了五無論外，在章氏人倫概念中，抗議之語氣在他的思想中是最明顯的。由於，不安和不妥協的精神，章氏持續地與同志甚至自己不和。他是一位儒家學者，卻反對儒家道德；作為一個革命份子，卻提倡國粹；身為民族主義者，卻鼓吹消除民族間之不同，並否認個人對他人有任何責任；雖提倡共和政體，卻譴責代議政治。或許對於這些矛盾的唯一解釋是章氏的生命是一種受挫的追尋思想之表現、方向和認同。

6. 章氏對吳稚暉（頁222～227）

章氏與吳氏之爭論首先表現在語言改革之議題。吳氏主張採用萬國新語（Esperanto）來取代中文，而章氏則強烈反對，以為此舉會對傳統有不良後果。章氏主要從語言及文字之發展及承傳來說明吳氏作法之不可行。而章氏與吳氏之衝突，亦顯示在二人對無政府主義看法之分歧。章氏是主張無政府主義不適用於中國，且不配稱為一種哲學；而吳氏則認為無政府主義是一種哲學，且植基於現代科學，尤其是進化論。因此，當然適用於中國。章氏和吳氏二人觀點之分歧主要在於章氏並不否認科學之價值，而是否認它的普遍適用性，並且他反對以未經批判之精神企圖將科學延伸至所有知識和行為之範圍。

最後，高氏指出，章氏在中國革命史上之地位難以評估。在某些議題方面，章氏與同盟會成員之觀點一致，如，反滿主義及反帝國主義等，但是章氏在革命運動中提倡宗教與國粹，使他與同志有所區隔。雖然，章氏與其他革命陣營中之知識份子有許多共通性，但是，他所堅持之傳統主義和保守主義，使他成為一位孤立者。他對社會改變所提出之計劃有時極其激進，如，五無論，但整體而言，他本身與其他革命份子相較，並沒有多少改變。章氏之思想遠離科學及民主之學說，而它們卻是在中國思想革命中的主要趨勢。

（二）傅樂詩：〈特立獨行之哲人——章炳麟之內在世界〉〔註4〕傅氏首先概述章氏之重要政治生涯，並指出在革命運動中，章氏難以歸類。有人主張他是一位特立獨行之人（a maverick），一種天生之怪人，其主要精神在於個人主義式地反對所有已建構之社會規範，他在任何時代都是一位孤立者，而在這個時代，他是一位革命份子。此外，傅氏指出，章氏對革命運動的重要理論貢獻是他的民族主義學說，這是民族主義意識形態在中國首次正式的表現。對章氏而言，民族主義意指反對清廷，並在政治和文化上，擴及到對外國勢力之反抗。章氏相信，中國人應在漢人之歷史和文化中尋求革命之靈感，並且革命最

〔註4〕 Charlotte Furth, "The Sage as Rebel: the Inner World of Chang Ping-lin", in Charlotte Furth ed., *The Limits of Change: The Conservative Alternatives of Republican China* (Cambridge, Mass: Harvard University Press, 1976), pp.113~150.

重要之使命是保存中國獨特之國粹。

傅氏指出，對 1898 年那個世代的人而言，西方勢力之入侵威脅中國之存亡。再加上社會達爾文主義引進中國，人們相信，世界上之民族與文化，皆必須為生存而競爭，由此，章氏亦試圖對中國之歷史和思想重新加以評估，希望能拯救中國於危亡。傅氏認為，章氏是本土論者（nativist），認為民族認同乃最高之價值所在，此一認同是植基於中國獨特的歷史所界定的文化及種族所界定之民族之上。以下試依本文內容分三方面來敘述：

1. 語言與學術（頁 118～128）

傅氏指出，漢學是形成章氏最早期學術訓練之基礎，且成為其終生奉獻之學科。在章氏之時代，今文學已成為一好爭論之學派，幾乎完全受康有為所支配。康氏把孔子看作五經之私家作者，及一個未來之烏托邦時代之先知，使孔子看起來既像政治之改革者又像未來世界之拯救者。章氏反對康氏之看法，而主張一較具批判性之現代歷史研究法，對章氏而言，史家之主要工作是分析歷代制度之變革，且其責任是將此分析建立在古代文獻之可靠事實之基礎上，其理想乃是超越利害之歷史（disinterested history），此亦今文學派政治動機之致用主義的對比。

在章氏之生涯裡，革命和政治只是插曲，而學術才是他終生之職志。章氏不斷地建議人們研究歷史，乃是因為它具有在中華民族之中激發愛國主義和一種共同的種族和政治團體的意義之價值。因此，章氏並不是工具性的利用歷史來為民族服務，他之所以重視民族，乃是因為國粹是依恃它而存在。章氏認為如果沒有歷史地植基於本土文化之激勵，民族主義運動是不會發生效用的。並且章氏也表達了他更根本的信念是：保存中國文化是民族的使命和意義之所在。

此外，章氏認為，最微妙而完美的本質中國之呈現，是要在民族的歷史本身及其獨特的語言中去發掘。章氏並指出中國語言更甚於其他文化產物的是：它包含了整個中國文化之歷史，並顯示其歷代有機之統一。

傅氏最後指出，章氏善用文言，行文古雅，其同時代之人皆視其作品晦澀而難懂。章氏之考據學（philological）理論，雖具啟發性及原創性，但他在語源學方面卻固守《說文解字》之精神，而拒絕接受甲骨文之真實性。如此，使他生前在這個領域之研究無法再向前推進。此外，章氏經學的成就使他在仍重視文人價值之社會中深具魅力與聲望。

2. 種族與進化（頁 128～139）

傅氏指出，章氏之種族革命（民族光復）或中華民族復興的理論是在 1898 年維新運動後發展而成的。在這方面，最重要的靈感是來自於王夫之及斯賓塞（Herbert Spencer）之作品。而章氏之民族觀則較符合伯倫知理（J·K·Bluntschli）之民族（nation）之用法：民族是指一種由比單純的政治關聯更為根本而有機的關係所結合而成的人群——一種基於血緣、歷史和習俗的認同感。

在章氏之心中，種族復興是與文化遺產的復興和強化不可分割的。民族乃一動態之有機體，不斷地受到國粹之滋潤與轉換，並且，其存在自始即由國粹所塑造。章氏對種族之解釋，是王夫之較為傳統的文化主義之反響，且提供了文化極端理想化之通路，這是後來民國時期保守思想之主旨。

此外，章氏以佛教思想來詮釋斯賓塞之理論。由於相信斯賓塞以分化為進步之理論（theory of progress as differentiation），非常接近佛教「變」的概念，章氏提出一個佛教式的結論。當世界在進化時，善與惡必同時進化，因為，所有的善與惡皆來自於自我意識。因此，苦與樂亦同時俱進。於此，章氏反映了佛教存在的悲觀主義——意識之積累及造作之後果，使人類深陷虛幻之現象世界中，而善本身即是最後之虛幻。

如果進步或善是一種虛幻，則人們為求生存而奮鬥之想法，顯然不切實際。從此，一位種族中心之民族主義者（an ethnocentric nationalist）因對自己國家及其過去歷史之熱愛，而陷入兩難。的確，追求國家生存和保存承自傳統之道德之間的衝突是整個改革世代關注之焦點。章氏對此問題的解決是：政治上的善必須由生存本身來界定。

3. 政治與道德（頁 139～150）

章氏認為立憲派所鼓吹的是以利益為出發點的私人政治，而西方之代議制亦是基於私心利益。因此，章氏完全統一與公平的政治理想在獨裁君主身上最能具現。對章氏而言，此一問題與國家生存相關。因此，他提出革命之道德——從所有私人之束縛中解脫出來，並將之內化為唯一的道德規範，是對公眾利益，即國家生存非關個人之奉獻的理想。

在政治上，章氏喚起一較部族化之中國，其國粹是植基於中國獨特的歷史、民族與語言上。章氏提出國粹與民族以取代聖人和王位，二者在王朝滅亡之後，已成為文化保守主義之重要主題。而章氏在 1905 年之後支持的國粹運動，乃是中國在文化上反抗西方模式之具體化。

傅氏認為章氏對民族之解釋，不僅是民族主義的，且是種族的本土主義的（ethnically nativist）。章氏從歷史、語言、土地和人民中尋求民族之根源，為民國時期之保守份子開拓新境。由中國之歷史文化與種族之特殊環境所界定之「中國性」（Chineseness）上，探求價值之所在。此外，章氏之觀念反映出中國民族主義的本土論之某些重要特徵。章氏之本土論並非狹隘地建立在生物學之種族群體之概念上，而是在於歷史文化本身及文化產物。依此，中國之民族及國粹之概念，在 1912 年之前被章氏用來反抗滿清，且繼續被其後之民族主義者所採用。

（三）孫華倫：〈章炳麟及其政治思想〉[註5]本文主要論述章炳麟之政治思想。孫氏藉著章氏一生所參與之政治活動來剖析其政治思想及其可能之貢獻。

孫氏首先簡述他對章氏及其政治思想之看法，以此為前提，來論述章氏之政治思想。

孫氏（頁 57～59）認為，一位重要的政治思想家常是一位受挫之行動家，並且他政治思想之重要性大多在於他對政治之否定。上述說法即孫氏對章氏之基本看法。

孫氏認為章氏很明顯地並不是一位成功的政治家，部分是因為他是一位仕紳，政治並非他的專業；部分是因為章氏從未擁有真正的權力。對章氏而言，政治並非他全力擁抱的活動；且甚而主張應使政治之重要性降至最低限度。因此，章氏想超越政治，藉著提出一種終極的哲學解答來斷然地排除對政府和政治的任何需求。因此，對章氏而言，政治在世俗世界中似乎僅具有限之價值。在此世界中，人們註定要受苦，並且沒有任何政治方法和努力足以帶來最終之救贖。姑不論章氏對超越政治之渴望，他的政治生活是活躍而多變的，並發展出一種獨特的政治思想。超過三十年的時間，他抗議的聲音和替代的建議時有所聞。在民國時期，幾乎所有身握大權的人都多少認識他，也幾乎無人能免於他的批評。也許就是這種勇於批判的精神，使他被賦予桀傲不馴之形象。

民國成立後，章氏之政治生涯是多采多姿的，這似乎證明章氏在政治上之重要性和影響力。然而，辛亥革命後，尤其在 1920 年代後期，章氏之聲望急

[註5] Warren Sun, "Chang Ping-lin and His Political Thought", *Paper on Far Eastern History* (September, 1985), pp.57~69.

遽下降。一般而言，章氏在民國時期仍備受尊重，但已遠離權力核心了。

以下試依孫氏文中之觀點，分幾方面來敘述：

1. 章氏對民族及國家的看法（頁 59～61）

孫氏認為章氏的「民族」觀點是前後一致的。章氏認為民族較國家具有優先性。若民族不存在，則國家亦無存在之價值。這種民族主義的前提，認為國家總是次要的，可以說明何以章氏在 1920 年代會主張聯省自治。就是這種極端形式的民族主義，使他進一步提倡將中國分成若干小國。此外，章氏所以主張聯省自治（頁 62～63）乃是因為當時政黨政治失敗。如，宋教仁被暗殺，且中央政府無能。其目的在於完全消滅權力之集中。諷刺的是，孫氏認為，此種形式之聯省自治乃是封建制度之一種變形。

章氏認為人民乃構成民族最重要的要素，因此，是最真實的；而國家只是一個概念性之結構，是較不真實的。因此，國家之區分應根據其本質而非形式。就章氏而言，只有好的政府和壞的政府（端視其是否滿足人民之利益而定）。這種強調實質勝於形式之看法，使章氏主張共和政體不必然是好的；而專制政體也不必然是不好的。

2. 章氏對西方制度之看法（頁 60～63）

章氏對現代民主制度，如，政黨、代議制及選舉權等的不信任，是與他的民族主義的性格相關連。他主張民族或國家的利益是唯一合法的；而政黨利益不僅不合法且是不道德的。他認為，代議制之設立只是增加黨派之利益，且只會產生不必要之新階級（在統治者與被統治者之間）。此外，章氏之反對不加批判地移植西方的民主制度乃是基於歷史的論證。他指出，代議制是封建制度之遺跡。章氏認為中國並無印度之種姓制度及西方資本主義社會之階級對立，因此，何必藉著代議制之設立來創造一個中國的新階級。

孫氏指出，章氏此時極為贊成孫逸仙提倡之單一稅制及耕者有其田，他們二人皆極力避免西方之資本主義病毒在中國之傳播。孫氏亦認為，章氏反對代議制之論證並不恰當，但此處的要點是章氏對政治的歷史研究中所表達的獨特性的重視。章氏主張，任何一個政治家必須考慮一個國家政治文化的獨特性，尤其對於本國的社會習俗和傳統制度必須予以尊重。此外，章氏認為，民國時期政治之所以不穩定，最主要是歸因於與過去（傳統）失聯、模仿西方及反傳統主義（五四時期之新文化運動）。甚至於在辛亥革命前，他已反對歐化之傾向。辛亥革命後，章氏繼續公然地反對西化運動和共產主義運動。章氏之政治文化觀念是完全植基於過去經驗之承續。同時，章氏對於政治之態度是強調歷史之連續性，尊重傳統及政治發展是與文化和歷史息息相關的。在章氏之政治思想中，文化和歷史是兩個最重要之範疇。

3. 章氏與保守主義（頁 64～66）

孫氏認為章氏之保守主義主要表現在政治方面。章氏主張只有獨特性是真實的；而國家並無真實性，因為它只是一個概念。只有一個民族的精神、價值系統及獨一無二之歷史才能使一個國家成為真實及富有意義。章氏亦主張漸進主義，因為他不相信價值、制度及政治形式之突然轉變而犧牲歷史之連續性。章氏與其他革命份子不同的是：後者認為民國建立是為了斬斷過去；而前者則是推翻滿清外族之入侵。無怪乎，章氏界定光復為革命，是要光復關於政治上之主權和文化獨立的歷史連續性。

章氏之保守主義，絕非一種毫無選擇的保存傳統。他對儒學之批判，預示了五四世代之反傳統主義和共產主義的出現。然而，章氏與二者不同的是，他無法接受一切過去都是邪惡的前提。很明顯的，民國時期的反傳統運動使他後悔先前對孔子的批判，然而，此亦促使他更強力地捍衛自己的保守立場。假如章氏在民國前的保守原則是一種為了推翻滿清的攻擊策略，則民國之後，就變成一種防衛的策略，其目的是要與反傳統主義取得平衡。無論如何，章氏相信要透過改革來保存傳統。的確，他對保存中國文化之關切使他投入改革或革命。章氏從未反對「變革」，只要「變革」不會斬斷與其文化的過去的聯繫。

4. 章氏對民主之看法（頁 68～69）

章氏所謂的民主觀念是與西方的民主有所不同：章氏主張代理民主（rule for the people，民享或民本），主要強調為人民謀福利；而西方之民主（rule by the people，民治）強調人民在政治上之自主性，它是基於理性的假設，認為人民確實知道他們的利益所在。章氏似乎對人民缺乏信心，他不斷地對多數暴政提出警告。或許，章氏真的對作為抽象實體的人民感到不安。

最後，孫氏認為（頁 69）章氏在政治範疇中所關心的是人民的福祉（rule for the people），而不是民主（rule by the people）。雖然如此，但是，他對西方民主政治的敵意並不至於使我們認為章氏是開放社會的敵人。因為，任何一種政治制度並不足以自動地保證良好政府的存在，或為人民帶來福祉。畢竟，人類的精神構造是較政府組織來得重要。章氏對政治思想的貢獻在於他探究人類心靈的進化及其最後的解脫。

（四）張灝：〈章炳麟〉〔註6〕本文乃張氏所寫的《中國知識分子的危機》一書中的第四章。張氏在本書中主要是以中國近代四位主要的知識份子為研究對象。他們分別是康有為、譚嗣同、章炳麟和劉師培。本書並不是他們四位的思想傳記，而是以他們四位在 1890 年至 1911 年間的思想發展為基點來探究此一轉型時期的思想變遷。張氏所以以他們作為研究的對象，主要是因為他們在這個時期扮演重要的思想角色，更重要的是，他們的世界觀反映了此一時期一個重要的思想面向。依此可知，張氏在本章中主要是根據章氏思想的形成和發展來探究其世界觀。以下試根據張氏在文中之觀點，分幾個主要方面來加以敘述：

1. 兩種生涯之抉擇（頁 104～107）

張氏指出章氏在年輕時即接受兩種不同的學術理想：一種是強調道德實踐功用的學術；另一種是與政治無關，純粹知識追求的學術。其後，章氏選擇前者，在 1896 年投身康，梁的改革陣營中。章氏之投身政治，其師俞樾並不諒解。然而，事實上，章氏終其一生，皆在結合政治之行動主義和學術的志業，亦即章氏並沒有因為參與政治而放棄學術之鑽研。

章氏在二十多歲時的學術興趣，除了大乘佛學外，諸子學對他而言，可能更為重要。他對諸子學的興趣主要來自他之前所承受的漢學的背景，其中，荀子尤其對他更有思想上之吸引力。事實上，在訄書初版中之首篇及末篇，章氏皆試圖提升荀子在儒學傳統中之地位。

2. 章氏早年思想之形成（頁 107～112）

對章氏而言，1890 年代乃其生命中一個重要的時期，因為他不僅參與政治，且擴展其學術領域。章氏超越儒學之藩籬且接觸西學。

在儒學傳統中，章氏認為荀子主張自然主義之世界觀，而孔子之所以偉大，亦在於他能超越迷信，且認為世界上並無鬼神之存在。同時，章氏亦根據此一自然主義之觀點而反對基督教之有神論及佛教之輪迴說。張氏進一步指出，荀子自然主義之觀點使章氏很容易由儒學背景轉移到西方科學的唯物論，此由其駁斥傳統天之觀念可加以證實。除科學唯物論之外，章氏從西學中亦接受了進化的宇宙論，此兩種世界觀使章氏能進一步發展出荀子的道德和社會思想。

〔註6〕 Chang Hao, *Chinese Intellectuals in Crisis:Search for Order and Meaning*, 1890~1911 (Berkeley: University of California Press, 1987), pp.104~145.

張氏認為，荀子社會組織之觀念集中於群之觀念，而後者亦是其社會和政治思想之起點。章氏發現荀子之思想與某些西方思想，尤其是社會達爾文主義有交合之處。如，荀子群之概念非常切合社會達爾文主義之世界圖像。章氏認為，群之能力不僅可以解釋何以人類能支配牛、馬等動物，且能控制所有較低等之物種。並且它可以幫助我們了解「適者生存」之法則如何在動物王國中運作。

更重要的是，群的概念使章氏更進一步了解人種間之生存競爭。章氏認為群是人類重要的能力之一，它足以決定不同種族之不同命運，如，黃種人因為達到較高之社會組織的水準，所以，優於黑、紅等種族，而白種人則優於黃種人。明顯的，章氏以荀子群的概念為出發點達到一種社會達爾文主義之世界圖像。此外，章氏認為，荀子思想有一反命論之特色。章氏發現，荀子主張個人無法控制其命運，但群體之命運則完全由其成員集體努力而決定。因此，荀子說，「一人有命，而國家無命。」

章氏之主要關切是如何整合中國使之能維持其社會政治秩序，此亦反映荀子及西方觀念對章氏思想之衝擊。整體而言，在 1890 年代晚期至 1900 年代初期之間，章氏在社會政治思想之進化方面，西學實扮演一個更重要之角色。

3. 超越種族之民族主義——一個道德之觀點（頁 112～117）

1900 年代初期，章氏以其種族之民族主義，即反滿主義而聞名於知識份子之間。表面言之，反滿主義已成為章氏群的概念最顯著的特色。簡言之，章氏之種族的民族主義圍繞一個觀念，即漢族之獨特性是植基於其血統和土地。1906 年章氏提出種族之民族主義時，他並非完全以血統和土地來說明，而是帶有強烈的道德語調。依其觀點，滿清政府之存在代表著一個由多數漢人組成之種族被少數滿人所組成之種族所統治，因此，對滿清政權之奮鬥不只是革命，即傳統上所謂的改朝換代，而主要是一種漢人之復仇行動，為的是要恢復他們集體之榮耀和尊嚴。因此，此種奮鬥並非胡亂地引發一種種族之厭惡和仇視，而是一種道德行動，此即章氏所謂之「正義之反抗」，它並不是針對所有滿人，而只是對抗滿清政府而已。

為了捍衛其種族之民族主義，章氏亦主張復仇和革命之一般原則是適用於世界上任何受到種族控制和壓迫之地區。對章氏而言，族群間之復仇是完全正當的，只要是執行對抗外族壓迫和控制的「正義之反抗」行動。依其看法，種族復仇之道德訴求與捍衛人權之革命並無不同。依此，章氏之種族復仇乃是一種普遍的種族解放之道德觀。

章氏對於未來民主秩序的概念，其最顯著的特色是反對代議制，而構成此一特色之基礎即是來自於其道德之原動力。章氏認為代議制會產生社會不平等和嚴密之階級。他指出，自從古代的封建社會沒落後，中國已是一個平等的社會。因此，為了保存中國這種社會平等的傳統，他強烈反對引進代議制之觀念，因為，他害怕中國會因此增加階級之鴻溝。

很明顯的，章氏之所以反對代議制乃是基於他對社會平等的道德關懷。這種道德關懷在他為未來民國建立時所擬思之社會綱領中甚至更為明顯。章氏認為在中國建立一個新社會有三種基本方式：（1）土地重新分配，以減少佃農和確保公平的土地所有權。（2）建立政府自己的工業，讓工人分享利益。（3）禁止財產之繼承，以避免財產集中。這些觀念明白地表達出章氏對社會公平的關切。張氏認為，就是這種對於未來的道德觀點加上章氏種族之民族主義，使他在 1900 年代由一位改革者轉變成為一位革命份子。

張氏指出，當我們檢視章氏如何達成革命之觀念時，他的道德語調甚至更為強烈。然而，或許因為他是一個觀念人（man of ideas），他的著作，整體而言，很少談到革命之手段和方法，且幾乎完全忽略革命策略和組織的問題。章氏認為，缺乏道德力量是阻礙革命之最嚴重的問題。因為，執行革命時，需要革命份子具有最堅強的道德性格。因此，章氏的種族之民族主義是富有道德之意味，且其道德觀賦予他的革命概念和革命後的秩序之概念一種特色。

4. 超越種族之民族主義——章氏邁向唯識學之路（頁 117～121）

張氏指出章氏最初是在 1890 年代經由夏曾佑及宋恕的引介而開始研究大乘佛學。但是，章氏真正嚴肅地研究佛學是在 1903 至 1906 年之間，當他因蘇報案而繫獄上海三年之時。當章氏出獄時，他已皈依佛教。因此，當他隨即赴日，在東京歡迎會上對著革命同志演說時，章氏告訴他們，宗教（指的是佛教）和保存國粹是他最重要的兩種思想關切。和當時大部分信仰佛教的知識份子一樣，章氏是唯識宗之皈依者。

張氏指出，章氏之所以在此時皈依佛教，其因有二：

（1）1900 年代是章氏生命中一個不安定的時期。他已步入中年，且繫獄三年，在獄中，他受到身體的折磨和心靈之煎熬。這些生命中之境遇，使他的心靈很容易對佛教所傳達的精神訊息有所感應。

（2）在 1900 年代，章氏大多住在上海和東京，二者乃當時中國知識份子匯聚之中心。他成為他們的領袖，並且，他們尋求章氏在思想上之指導和方向之指引。東京和上海的這些文化環境以及他在知識份子中所扮演的角色，很自然地是章氏對中國知識份子所面對的思想方向的危機感同身受。在轉型世代的章氏和其他一些知識份子（如梁任公等）一樣，他們在大乘佛學中發現一個遠景，這遠景使他們能夠結合政治行動主義和哲學去了解生命和世界。

5. 一個佛教的世界觀（頁 121～129）

章氏選擇〈齊物論〉作為他闡明佛學觀點之媒介。更重要的是，他相信莊子的思想在精神上是和唯識學相近。他知道〈齊物論〉並沒有包括在唯識教義中所使用的哲學範疇和論證。但是，他覺得這不應該隱匿二者藉著不同術語傳達相同真理和精神的事實。章氏之註解〈齊物論〉因此是藉此顯示莊子和唯識學二者之思想是相似的一種企圖，並且依據後者之系統的現象邏輯分析來詮釋前者之神祕而曖昧之觀念，依此方式來將二者之思想加以同化

〈齊物論〉之主旨是任何達到自我超越之人皆會明白「一」和宇宙萬物是普遍平等的。章氏相信，莊子之思想在唯識學中會得到反響。此正如章氏在《齊物論釋》中所說：「齊物大旨多契佛經。」張氏認為，章氏是以同化唯識思想之方式來詮釋莊子。章氏發現，莊子對世俗世界之貶抑在唯識學中得到反響。如同道家的物化觀念，在唯識學中也把現象世界視為永恆流轉，如，「六畜升沈」此一輪迴學說。而構成此一學說基礎的是「緣起」概念。此一概念，章氏認為，在精神上是與莊子之「有待」概念相近。明顯的，章氏是以大乘佛學中之「空」之概念來詮釋莊子之相對主義之世界觀。

除了著重現象世界是空的觀點外，章氏相信，唯識之世界觀亦提供另一觀點，即著重超越的終極實在之觀點。章氏在〈齊物論〉中也發現這種超越的觀點。此誠如章氏在《齊物論釋》中所概述之要點：

> 齊物者，一往平等之談，詳其實義，非獨等視有情，無所優劣，蓋
> 離言說相，離名字相，離心緣相，畢竟平等，乃合齊物之義。

依此方式，章氏再次發現莊子與唯識學具有相同的實在觀，一種萬物合一，完全包含且無分別之整體的觀點。

6. 由佛教觀點而來的文化批評者（頁 129～141）

章氏發現，唯識學不僅使他能以新的觀點來了解道家，並且，也使他發展出一種超越的生命和世界觀。他已然相信，在唯識學裡他已經發現世界上最完

美的學說。在章氏眼中，世界上大部分宗教皆有其缺失，尤其是一神論。他所批評的一神論主要是基督教。章氏指出，基督教的缺點有：（1）一神教的概念是充滿矛盾的。（2）耶和華是全知全能的描述，損害了基督教的上帝是人類創世主的概念。（3）上帝是一位先驗的、絕對的及自足的。

章氏批評一神論是因為他要證明大乘佛教是世界上最好的宗教信仰。依此觀點，唯識學並沒有一神教所具有之弱點。唯識學藉著了解在現象世界背後並沒有上帝或任何形式的神來避免一神論之陷阱，且藉由肯定阿賴耶的終極實在，來避開激進虛無主義之陷阱。因此，依章氏之見，唯識學之價值是視救贖在於個人心靈之能力，而不是來自上帝或神的力量。

由於唯識學的信念，章氏得到一個新的價值中心，此即佛教的來世觀，而來世觀解消了這個世界上存在的任何意義和價值。依此，章氏批評了唯物論、休謨的因果論及由此而來的自然律之一般觀念。尤其是，他批駁了在中國逐漸被接受的一個科學律則，即普遍的進化論。章氏指出，進化論本質上並非一個普遍現象。它或許存在於自然的有機範圍內，但並不存在於無機之領域中。因為，在無機界中，事物常以循環的方式，而不是以線性的方式發展。章氏指出，唯識學視阿賴耶識是世界之終極實在，它儲藏所有「有情」之種子。因此，它同時存在兩種狀態：清淨和雜染。在清淨的狀態，阿賴耶識只含有「本有種子」，它具有超越善惡的性格。在雜染狀態，阿賴耶識是世界上所有具體存在的根本原因。因此，阿賴耶識具有這種雜染方面，它含有「始起種子」，本身帶有善和惡的潛能。依此世界觀之架構，個人是同時具有道德的善和惡的內在傾向。因為，這種內在傾向是無可避免地表現在每個人的生命活動中，因此，進化就道德意義而言，是具有兩面性的。根據唯識學之觀點，章氏反對普遍進化論，而提出「俱分進化論」，認為世界在進化，善與惡必同時俱進，而進化亦非僅是一種進步，且必然導向一個完美的社會。

因此，根據唯識學的信念，章氏所提出之文化批判是遠較康有為和譚嗣同二人為激進。康、譚之文化批評使他們反對意識形態的傳統秩序的核心。但章氏則超越他們，他質問並挑戰不僅是當時所流行西學的一些基本假定，且是人類存在的真正意義。

7. 章氏佛教世界觀之兩面（頁 140～145）

章氏並沒有把佛教看作是一種否定的、消極的學說。因為，依大乘佛學，否定的邏輯是設計來幫助信仰者能夠超越現在世界之虛幻而達到精神的終極實在，由此，或許可以發現終極的救贖所在。並且，大乘佛學的特色是，允許在超越的世界觀之內，發展一種人類生命的肯定觀點。依此，章氏之革命理想和一個嶄新的後革命秩序的觀點就不必會與他的佛教信仰相矛盾。因此，對章氏而言，革命和新秩序之建立乃是在世界上解脫痛苦的一種悲憫的行動。因此，章氏視其政治激進主義乃世界之究極超越的必然步驟。

大乘佛學提供給章氏的，不僅是將其政治主張納入一個宇宙的視野裡的一種概念架構，而且是為了實行他革命理想所需的道德能量的來源。對章氏而言，革命是一種需要無私的承諾和最高正直的道德事業。佛教可說是具有激發革命行動動機的功能。

因此，章氏並非如有些史家所主張的，只是一個民族主義者或本土論者。尤其是 1903 年後，當章氏開始接觸大乘佛學，並使他逐漸發展出一種普世的世界觀。這種世界觀，雖然與其民族主義不必然會相矛盾，但的確章氏已超越了民族主義之藩籬。簡言之，章氏在神秘無私的理想中，發現了不僅是一個意義和認同的嶄新來源，而且是一個清新的價值核心。

（五）汪榮祖：《近代民族主義之追尋》〔註7〕本書乃美國學界第一本有關章太炎研究之專著。全書共 233 頁，計分九章，分別為：

第一章：邁向民族主義和改革之路

第二章：轉向革命

第三章：革命思想之形成

第四章：革命陣營之分裂

第五章：邁向共和政體之崎嶇之路

第六章：民主之失敗

第七章：重建民國之企圖

第八章：救國之聖戰

第九章：結論

汪氏在前言中首先說明章太炎不只是一位學者。在中國近代史中，他作出極重大之貢獻。然而，由於政治因素所衍生的一些偏見，再加上章氏思想極為複雜及行文過於古雅，在在使他的思想令人難以理解，甚至被誤解為：一位種族中心之本土論者（ethnocentric nativist），一位反共和政體者，一位政治運動

〔註7〕 Young-tsu Wong, *Search for Modern Nationalism:Zhang Binglin and Revolutionary China*, 1869~1936 (Hong Kong:Oxford University Press, 1989).

的反動者，一位文化保守主義者（cultural conservative），甚至是一位瘋子（章瘋子）。此外，有學者認為章氏在歷史上之重要性主要在於他的學術成就，而認為他的政治思想和活動不只是不重要的，且常自相矛盾。

接著，汪氏說明本書寫作目的有三：

1. 依據文化多元主義（cultural pluralism）此一文化立場來闡明章氏民族主義之性質和根源。汪氏認為章氏遭受誤解，其中一個主要原因是被扣上文化保守主義之帽子。汪氏認為，文化保守主義者很容易與種族中心之傳統主義者相混淆。章氏是一位近代中國民族主義者，他深信，民族是具有文化獨特性此一歷史主義之信念，且強烈反對文化無國界的觀念。對他而言，每一民族之歷史經驗使它具有文化之獨特性。如果沒有文化之獨特性，沒有一個國家可以維持其文化之認同。中國在近代變遷之過程中，應維持其文化和制度之特殊性。此一文化立場應不會使章氏成為一種族中心之傳統主義者。因為，他並不反對一個現代化之中國，而只是堅持它必須是在中國本身的脈絡中的變遷。質言之，他贊成具有文化承續性之變遷。因此，如果章氏被稱為一位文化多元主義之提倡者可能更為恰當。因為，他強烈主張所有個別文化之自主性，且應同時並存。章氏一生也堅持此一基本之文化立場。

2. 說明章氏之政治思想和活動之發展。汪氏以章氏乃近代民族主義者之論點來挑戰他是一位反滿之種族主義者（anti-Manchu racist）此一當時流行之觀點。汪氏指出，章氏之反滿主義（anti-Manchuism）只是在 1900 年代應用於革命運動中之一種權宜的意識形態之武器，而並不等同於他的民族主義。他的民族主義主要是對帝國主義的反應。章氏最初想要提供一個改革的架構，來幫助外來的滿清政權抵抗帝國主義之入侵。其後，他之所以放棄改革之主張，乃是因為章氏相信滿清政權沒有能力抵抗外侮。但是，章氏持續關注帝國主義之入侵，即使他已獻身反滿革命之後。而當武昌起義成功之後，章氏就放棄反滿主義，並投注其精力於反抗帝國主義之威脅。

3. 將章氏關聯於 1890 年代至 1930 年代間中國革命之脈絡中。汪氏想要透過章氏之眼光，依照年代之先後次序，去呈現中國革命之型態。

本書之主題是探討中國現代民族主義，因此，汪氏除了將此一主題關聯於1890 年代至 1930 年代間中國革命及政治變遷中加以探究外，更藉著章太炎一生之政治思想及活動之發展來彰顯此一主題。

汪氏在本書第一章一開始就敘述中國現代民族主義產生之因緣。汪氏認為，改良主義者在觀念上最大的突破是現代民族國家的發現及由之而衍生的一種民族主義的意識。

汪氏乃藉著傳統與現代之國家觀念二者作一對比來引出中國現代民族主義的誕生，以下是汪氏之論述（頁2～3）：

改良主義者不斷強調中國只不過是世界上數以百計的國家之一，這種世界觀對傳統儒家的國家觀念——天下，提出質疑。傳統意義下之國家一詞乃等同於天子之朝廷，且政治上之忠誠，主要是針對天子與朝廷而言。在帝制中國所謂的民族主義，因此是一種家長或族長式的忠誠。

直到鴉片戰爭後，由於清廷無法滿足現代化之挑戰，這種新情勢為中國本身提供了西方民族國家之模式。此一新概念無可避免的涵蘊一種忠誠重心之轉向——由天子轉向國家，或以現代民族主義之視角去間隔朝廷與國家。朝廷之安全不再被愛國主義者視為首要且唯一之關切，相對的，人民和文化之生存與否亦同樣迫切需要。

雖然如此，但是，晚清之改良主義者仍維持對朝廷之忠誠，因為，他們相信，這對於國家安全是必要的，與此同時，他們也試圖去說服清廷承認在政策及制度上革新是有其必要性，尤其當中國面臨帝國主義入侵之強大威脅時。因此，中國現代民族主義就以晚清改良主義者之一種思潮而產生。

章氏雖忝為改革派之一員，但他反對現代民族主義的普遍性（universality）。他認為，每一個民族國家，由於歷史和文化的不同，在制度上總是獨一無二的。對他而言，中國的現代命運是比世界的命運更為重要。

有關民族主義此一議題，汪氏在本書之中多所闡發，如從訄書修訂本之有關論述中，亦有此類言論，汪氏之論述如下（頁27～28）：

章氏於1920年完成《訄書》修訂本。此書被認為是第一本由現代中國作家論述革命的學術著作。在本書中，雖然充滿著章氏強烈反滿之字眼，但他不應被視為一位種族主義者（racist），因為，在達爾文主義（Darwinism）之影響下，章氏接受了此一觀點——所有種族，包括漢族和滿族皆來自相同之根源。雖然，章氏時常主要以歷史意識來界定種族，那是因為他認為民族是由歷史形成的，因此，歷史是民族的靈魂。

汪氏（頁30）認為，章氏雖提倡革命，但他既非種族中心之本土論者，亦非器量狹小之文化民族主義者。因為，當章氏論及文化之範圍時，除了自己

的文化傳統外，他也廣泛的引述日譯本之西方作者如康德（Kant）、洛克（Locke）
及達爾文（Darwin）等人之觀點來支持自己的論點。就一位文化民族主義者而
言，會稱許如此眾多的西方學者，似乎不太可能。且一位文化民族主義者亦不
會強烈的批評自己的文化傳統，而章氏本人正是如此。

至於章氏之民族主義與反滿主義二者之關係，汪氏在書中亦有論述（頁61
～64）：

章氏之反滿主義表現在以下三方面：

1. 章氏藉著譴責清廷加諸漢族之罪惡來喚醒國人之記憶——明人對國家之忠
   誠及滿清之殘酷等事實，其目的在激發國人之愛國心。

2. 章氏表達對滿族及其政府之輕蔑，把他們比作次等、野蠻及微不足道之種
   族，他們有史以來一直住在中國之邊陲地區。

3. 章氏譴責滿清政府的無能，如，義和團事變即足以證明滿清政府沒有能力
   救中國。

由於章氏對於清廷極盡攻擊之能事，傅樂詩乃為章氏貼上一些標籤，如，
種族主義者，一位大漢族主義者（a great Han chauvinist）及一位種族中心之本
土論者。但章氏此種論調乃是出於政治之理由，而非學術性之論辯。章氏所以
不遺餘力地去區分漢、滿二族，其目的是要使之成為一顯著之議題，且為了挑
戰當時流行的一種論證，即滿清政府是一合法之中國政權，因為，它已採用中
國之習俗。章氏反對任何外國政權之合法性，因為，文化有其種族之根源。雖
然，章氏反滿，但這只是政治上之宣傳武器，況且仇滿並不等同於完全消滅滿
人。章氏認為，革命乃不得已而為之，只因清廷沒有能力抵抗外國帝國主義之
入侵，而不是因為其種族之性格使然。換言之，章氏主張革命或反滿，其目的
乃為拯救國家於危亡，而非出於族群意識所使然。很明顯的，章氏之反滿主義
是與他的反帝國主義分不開的。因此，章氏乃是一位現代民族主義者，而非反
滿之種族主義者。其終極目的，是要建立一個實施共和政體形式政府的主權國
家，並排除外國勢力對中國主權之控制。

此外，民報時期，章氏使用大量大乘佛學的概念來強化他革命的論題，此
種作法常被誤解為革命運動之倒退，而馬克思主義學者亦視之為章氏由早期
及唯物思想的倒退，此外，張灝則認為此乃章氏欲建立一種佛教之世界觀
（Buddhist world view），對於此等說法，汪氏皆一一加以澄清。汪氏（頁51～
52）認為，此等判斷似乎皆未能掌握章氏之關切所在。章氏認為，中國作為一

個國家已失去其精神力量，就章氏而言，佛教之思想可以提供此種力量，如，他在上海繫獄期間，即藉由閱讀大乘佛經而來之精神力量，使他足以克服世俗之痛苦，度過人生之困境。章氏認為，大乘佛學所提供之精神力量足以為革命目的之達成提供有效之方法。因此，章氏認為革命需要宗教，尤指佛教，然而，當社會道德普遍盛行時，宗教就會消失。可見，對章氏而言，宗教或佛教只是達成其革命此一目的之手段而已。

再者，汪氏認為，章氏之文化立場乃是文化多元主義，然而，章氏之文化立場卻因為他極力主張對抗西方帝國主義之入侵而常被誤解為文化保守主義，於此，汪氏亦予以疏解（頁55～56）：

章氏由改革轉向革命、痛苦的牢獄經驗、研究佛學和西方哲學及對現代文明的挑戰等因素，促使章氏熱切提倡平等與自由。章氏之平等觀並不只是人與人之間平等，而且是文化與文化之間及民族與民族之間的平等。這種觀念實蘊涵著不同的文化應同時並存，且宜維持其獨立自主及各自之獨特性。同時，任一文化不應被任一個別之文化或現代科學文明所普遍化，此種文化觀點即是文化多元主義。

其次，章氏早年放棄學術研究而投身政治，當初是否面臨學術與政治間抉擇之困境？此一問題，汪氏在書中亦提出其看法（頁8～9）：

章氏從1890年進入詁經精舍，跟隨俞樾研讀古代經典，當章氏決定離開精舍，投入改革陣營，這無疑是章氏一生中之重大決定。汪氏認為，章氏作此決定時一點也不困難，因為，他並不打算放棄學術，誠如他日後所證明的。況且，當國家面臨危亡之秋，章氏更不能將自己侷限於象牙塔之中。

至於章氏已投身革命，且成為民報之喉舌，何以極力提倡國粹？其意義與目的為何？此等問題，汪氏亦予以疏解（頁81～83）：

雖然，章氏已投入政治且極力鼓吹排滿，然而，在革命之餘仍不忘提倡國粹之重要。章氏之提倡國粹，並非想要成為一位文化排外主義者（chauvinist）。這可以從他對外國文化之兼容並蓄及對本國傳統文化之批判來加以證實。章氏認為，每一民族皆有其獨特之文化，此一文化是由其無與倫比之歷史經驗衍生而來的。因此，文化對民族之重要性，正如靈魂之於個人。一個國家若滅亡，還有復興之機會；但是，文化若被消滅，則復興無望。章氏認為，滿清雖已統治中國近三百年，在與外族統治之奮鬥中，只要中國人固守自己的文化傳統——國魂或國粹，則中國仍有復興之希望。

此外，章氏之提倡國粹，乃針對當時二種思想危機所作之反應：

1. 章氏對當時知識份子對傳統文化所引發的懷疑主義，深感不妥。

2. 章氏不喜歡文化普遍主義（cultural universalism）此一當時流行之信仰。因為，它深深地影響當時知識份子以現代西方文化來批判自己的文化傳統。章氏認為這是更嚴重的危機，因為，此舉將導致國學之淪亡。

根據以上之論述，汪氏在本書中之主要論點可概括如下：

1. 章氏之文化立場乃是文化多元主義而非文化保守主義。

2. 章氏乃一民族主義者而非種族主義者、大漢族主義者、及種族中心之本土論者。

3. 對章氏而言，佛學僅是達成其革命目的之手段，且無意建立一佛教之世界觀。

4. 章氏主張反滿主義，僅是遂行其革命目的之手段，且不等同於其民族主義。

5. 章氏之提倡國粹，乃為維持文化之獨立自主及維護傳統文化於不墜。

6. 章氏之投身政治，並無抉擇上之困難。

7. 章氏政治思想之不一致，其意見之改變，大多順隨變化中環境之改變，且終其一生，激進及保守之因子皆呈現於其思想中。

（六）李哲賢：《章炳麟（1869～1936）：一位政治激進主義者及文化保守主義者》〔註8〕本書乃李氏根據同名之博士論文增訂而成。原論文係美國學界第一本以章炳麟為題之博士論文。全書共217頁，計分七章，分別是：

第一章：「導論」。

第二章：「章氏之早年生活及其思想背景」。一八九五年當章氏開始參與政治之時，他已經承受了包括來自本土及外來思想之廣泛影響。其中，漢學形成其學術之基礎。蓋漢學擴大章氏之學術興趣；特別是關於中國傳統文化方面。

第三章：「章氏與國粹」。此章分析章氏之國粹概念及其範圍與意義。「國粹」一詞乃是借自日本之新詞語。章氏對國粹保存之主張，不僅僅是出自於其對西力衝擊之反應所產生之文化認同上之焦慮感而已。因為，作為一位國學家，章氏非常明白保存國粹對國家存亡所具之重要性此一事實。章氏對接受國粹之態度，並非是全盤且毫無保留地接受中國之傳統文化。因為，章氏之接受中國文化乃是具批判性的；並且，他非常清楚中國文化中之那些成分是應當加以保

〔註8〕 Jer-shiarn Lee, Chang Ping-lin (1869~1936): A Political Radical and Cultural Conservative (Taipei: The Liberal Arts Press, 1993).

留的。因此，章氏之接受國粹之態度是極其審慎的。對章氏而言，國粹意指中國歷史及文化傳統特質中，那些仍舊適用於現代中國之成份或要素。

第四章：「章氏邁向革命之路」。此章分析章氏一八九五年至一九一一年間參與政治活動及促使章氏之政治立場由改革轉向革命之緣由。章氏自一八九五年以來即是革新份子。自中國在中日甲午戰爭中慘敗後，章氏即相信，要拯救中國必須提倡改革。然而，章氏支持康、梁的革新運動之真意乃是基於他對保存國粹之關切。因為，章氏認為國家生存乃是使國粹不亡之不二法門。章氏之立場之由改革轉向革命乃是由於一九〇〇年所發生之義和團事件。此一事件使中國產生極大之危機。但因滿清政府無力抵抗外力之入侵，章氏乃訴諸革命以救國。然而，對章氏而言，革命亦只是達成其保存國粹此一終極目的之手段而已。

第五章：「章氏在民國時期之活動」。在民國時期，章氏在政治上仍極其活躍。除了政治活動外，章氏則埋首於傳統學術之研究。一九一一年以後，章氏發行了「華國」月刊及「制言」半月刊此兩種刊物，且創辦「國學講習會」，經由這些媒介，章氏致力於中國傳統文化之保存與發揚。章氏致力於國粹之保存乃是他一生中最重要之使命。

第六章：「章氏與近代中國之文化保守主義」。此章將分析章氏之國粹概念與其他國粹派間之異同；並且欲對文化保守主義在近代中國思想史中之重要性及章氏在此一思潮中所扮演之角色加以評估。

第七章：「結論」。

本書主要在於探究章炳麟先生之生平與思想，特別是他對保存國粹之關切及此種關切與其參與革命之關聯。章氏一生正反映出當時知識份子中，政治革命論與文化保守主義間那種尖銳而不安之關係。本書之所以以章氏作為研究之對象，部分乃因為章氏在近代中國思想史上扮演一個極其重要之角色。然而，更重要的理由是，雖然章氏是近代中國史上一位主要思想家、學者及政治行動家，在西方之學術界中，有關章氏之研究著作卻是屈指可數。在近代中國思想研究方面，章氏之所以受到普遍的忽視，其實是有其理由的。

由於章氏行文之風格出自魏、晉，文字過於艱深古雅，加以其思想又深受西方及本土思想之多重影響，凡此皆足以使其著作令人難以理解。另一原因是，章氏之思想並不適用於「保守或激進」之分析範疇。此種範疇乃是現代歷史學者用來探究近代中國知識份子之思想的一種解釋性設計。雖然，作為一種解釋性之範疇，「保守或激進」此一區分有其解釋上或分析上之效用；然而，用來分析像章氏此一類型之思想家卻並不適用。蓋章氏雖然可稱之為保守主義者，或更精確地說，他是一位文化保守主義者；可是，在政治或政治革命之領域裡，章氏同時也是一位激進主義者。

　　即使在西方學術界，有關章氏之研究之有數著作中，對於章氏生平與思想之評估亦無法令人滿意，其中一個觀點是，章氏之思想本身充滿著矛盾。章氏曾經是康、梁改革派之擁護者，其後卻投入革命之陣營；作為一個革命份子，他卻提倡國粹不遺餘力；他是一位國學家，卻又對儒學加以抨擊；更有進者，章氏雖提倡共和政體，卻譴責代議政治。然而，這些矛盾之外觀，大部分是可以消減或甚而解消的。只要吾人了解此乃出自於章氏致力於保存國粹之結果；而保存國粹之努力又是章氏一生之思想脈絡中最首尾一貫的。因為，對章氏本人而言，所有這些表面上呈現矛盾紛紜之觀念，卻只是達成其保存國粹此一終極目的之手段而已。因此，章氏本人在政治立場或觀點上之改變，從章氏保存國粹之關切此一角度看來，就一點也不矛盾了，由於保存國粹乃是章氏思想之核心觀念及最基本且恆常之特質。因此，對於章氏生平與思想之研究當呈顯其思想中此一層面。遺憾的是，在章氏思想之研究方面，中，西學者皆普遍忽略其思想中此一核心觀念，也因此侷限了吾人對於章氏思想之理解。因此，對章氏之思想再加以評估也就有強烈之必要了。李氏希望此一研究章氏一生之英文著作能對章氏之生平及思想之進一步了解有所裨益。

　　這是一本完整研究章炳麟此一思想家之英文著作，李氏參閱所有盡可能蒐集得到之有關章氏之中文及英文的第一手及第二手之研究資料。本書主要在於探究章炳麟此一著名國學家及政治行動家之生平與思想。本書並非有關章炳麟之思想傳記，而是以思想史之方法來研究章氏。本書乃是以章氏之生平與思想做為基點來探究清末及民初中國思想之變遷。章氏之思想反映了此一時期一個重要而迄今尚未為人所研究之思想層面。章氏之生平與思想呈示出他那一代之知識份子中政治及文化理想間所產生之張力。並且，章氏終生對於保存國粹此一理念之執著，預示了近代中國思想史中最重要的思潮之一的國粹運動。此種文化保守主義在反抗民初主張全盤西化之運動中，扮演了一個非常重要之角色，甚而，新文化運動之興起亦是針對此一國粹派之文化保守主義而來。因此，李氏相信，根據中、英文之相關資料來分析章氏之生平與思想，將有助於對章氏之生平與思想獲致一較佳之理解。並且，對於此一時期之政治激進主義與文化保守主義間之關係以及文化保守主義在近代中國思想史中所扮演之角色，皆將會有一新的視野。

雖然章炳麟在辛亥革命運動中極其有名；然而，身為國學家的他卻因之而更享盛名。章氏之生平與思想反映了他那一世代之知識份子中，政治革命論與文化保守主義間那種不安之關係；並且，章氏對於保存國粹之鼓吹更為二十世紀初期影響深遠之國粹運動鋪路。本書旨在以章氏生平與思想做為基點，來探究二十世紀初期之中國知識份子中，文化與政治間之張力及文化保守主義此一思潮之重要性。

章氏對於保存國粹之關切，並不只是因為他是一位國學家；因而，深覺有擁護傳統學術之責任；而且，更是因為他相信保存國粹對於一個國家民族之存亡有其必要性。由於西力之入侵，章氏深恐本國文化受到西方文化之威脅而滅亡。為了免於中國為外人所征服，章氏相信，改革或革命對中國而言是有其必要的；並且，改革家或革命家最重要之使命即在於維護傳統文化於不墜。因此，章氏視保存國粹比保衛國家本身更具有優先性；而保護國家之所以重要，只是因為它對保存國粹而言是有其必要的。而改革或革命對救國而言，相對的，亦是必要的。

作為一位革命家，章氏卻要求維護國粹。章氏之注重國粹保存，使他明顯地有別於參與革命運動中之其他知識份子。因為，對當時大部分知識份子而言，他們所關心的並非傳統文化之維護，而是為了保衛國家此一政治實體。雖然，章氏亦關心國家之存亡；但是對章氏本人而言，國家並不僅僅是一政治實體而已；而且更是一文化實體。因之，章氏雖然仍舊關心國家富強之追求；然而，章氏之終極關切或目的卻是為了使傳統文化不因外力之入侵而亡滅。甚至當章氏主編民報——同盟會之機關報時，章氏把民報從一份通俗而激進之機關報轉變為幾乎像國粹學報那麼學術性之刊物。章氏後來並且捲入國粹運動此一文化保守主義之運動中。此種文化保守主義乃是近代中國思想史中最重要之思潮之一，其後且受到五四運動中之反傳統激進主義之挑戰。

章氏一生對保存國粹之執著，明顯地表現於他兩種不同之生涯中：一個是政治行動家；而另一個卻是國學家。民國建立之後，章氏在政治舞台上仍舊十分活躍；章氏並繼續抨擊任何足以危及中國之主權與文化之行動或個人。除了參與政治之外，章氏並獻身於傳統學術文化之教學與研究。因之，致力於國粹之保存乃是章氏一生中最前後一貫之思想脈絡。

三、章太炎研究析論

根據上述美國漢學界有關章太炎之研究，可以發現，學者在某些議題上之觀點極為分歧，底下試就幾個相關議題來加以析論：

（一）民族主義

傅文根據章氏思想中之反滿主義，宣稱章氏是一位種族中心之民族主義者，種族中心之本土論者或大漢族主義者。張文則主張章氏欲超越民族主義而建立佛教之世界觀，即普遍主義（universalism）之觀點。汪著對於此等觀點皆極力反對。汪著認為反滿主義只是章氏應用於革命運動中之手段，並不等同於他的民族主義，且章氏在革命成功之後即放棄反滿主義，並將其心力轉向反帝國主義。因此，汪著認為傅文之觀點是片面的，且是一種誤解。此外，汪著認為章氏之提倡佛學，亦只是以佛教作為達成革命之一種手段，本身並無意建立一佛教之世界觀。

實者，就民族主義此一概念加以分析，可細分為二：其一為反動的民族主義（reactive nationalism）或國家的民族主義（state nationalism），指的是反帝國主義；其二是種族之民族主義（ethnic nationalism），意指反滿主義。〔註9〕根據此一分析，可知，若傅文之觀點是片面的，則汪著之看法亦失之籠統。此外，以民族主義之概念作為解釋近代中國思想之詮釋範圍亦有其限制。誠如普萊斯（Don Price）所言，轉型世代之思想已具有普遍主義之取向，此亦民族主義此一概念所無法加以解釋的。〔註10〕當然，張文之觀點亦值得商榷。他似乎過度強調佛學尤其是唯識學在章氏思想中之支配性力量。佛學在章氏思想中當然有其重要性，但是，章氏之提倡佛學，究實而言，乃欲援佛入道，尤其是莊子，且佛學對章氏似亦具工具性之意義。此外，誠如章氏自述，當社會道德盛行時，宗教就會消失。因此，以佛教之世界觀來涵蓋章氏思想之主要歸趨，似亦值得商榷。

（二）文化立場

根據章氏主張個別文化具有獨特性、自主性及宜同時並存之觀點，汪著認為，章氏之文化立場乃是文化多元主義，而非所謂的文化排他主義、文化民族

〔註9〕 Chang Hao, Chinese Intellectuals in Crisis, p.2.

〔註10〕 Don Price, *Russia and the Roots of the Chinese Revolution* (Cambridge:Harvard University Press, 1974), pp.9~28.

主義或文化保守主義。章氏當然不是主張文化民族主義或文化排他主義，因為，章氏的確對外國文化會兼容並蓄，亦會批判自己的文化傳統。但是，即使章氏堅信文化是多元的，宜同時並存，且無排他性，此種看法與章氏之文化保守主義之立場，二者並非不可相容，或可說乃立足點有所差異而已。因為，如果「保守」意指維持其安全，使之不致受到傷害、衰微或亡失〔註11〕；而「保守主義者」意謂堅持傳統之保存比創新和改變來得重要此一態度之人。〔註12〕那麼，章氏為了抗拒文化帝國主義和西化所作的保存國粹之努力當然是一種保守主義。況且，章氏終其一生致力於國粹之保存，深恐本國文化受到西方文化之威脅而滅亡，甚至在投身政治活動之後，亦時時不忘提倡保存國粹，可知，保存國粹乃章氏之終極關懷，亦是其一生思想脈絡中最首尾一貫的核心觀念，因此，李著堅稱，章氏之文化立場乃是文化保守主義此一論點，實頗為的當。

（三）政治立場或思想之一致性

章氏之政治立場時常改變，而思想似亦前後不一致，此誠如高文所言，章氏之思想充滿矛盾。就章氏之研究而言，此一問題實極重要且必須加以解決。遺憾的是，僅高文及李著曾作此努力。高文曾引述蕭公權之說法，認為章氏思想之不一致乃出之於一深切而沉痛之抗議，高文似認同此一看法。唯高文在文中他處則說，章氏矛盾思想之唯一解釋乃是章氏之生命是一種受挫的追尋思想表現、方向及認同。不論是抗議或受挫之心靈，高文僅點出此一觀點，然並未進一步去分析。李著則從章氏保存國粹之關切此一觀點，來深入分析，並解消其思想及政治立場之矛盾之外觀。而章氏政治立場或思想中之不一致。此一問題亦獲得初步之解決，如此，對於章氏思想之把握應有其助益。

（四）保守與激進

在近代思想之研究中，保守與激進之二分法（dichotomy），常用來作為探討近代中國知識分子之詮釋性範疇。李著、汪著及高文已跳脫此二分法之窠臼，點明保守與激進之因子皆呈現於其思想中。唯後二者並未深入討論此一議題，而李著則明確區分此二因子在章氏思想中之界域，明言章氏在政治上之激進及文化上之保守，並深入予以探討。

〔註11〕C.T.Onions ed., *The Oxford Universal Dictionary of Historical Principles* (Oxford: Oxford University Press, 1955), p.375.

〔註12〕Philip P. Wiener ed., *Dictionary of the History of Ideas* (New York:Charles Scribner's Sons, 1973), v.1,p.477.

（五）革命與國粹

高文點出章氏之革命觀念來自於其保存國粹之關切。傅文明言革命最重要之使命乃保存國粹；而孫文則點明保存國粹之關切使章氏投入改革或革命，唯上述論著，於此議題並未深入探討。汪著則認為章氏之提倡國粹，是針對反傳統文化及西化等二種思想危機所作之反應，此一觀點似較忽略國粹在章氏思想中之重要性，以為章氏之提倡國粹乃出之於被動反應之一般看法。而唯李著特別抉發保存國粹之關切乃章氏思想中之核心觀念，亦是其終極關切之所在。就思想之研究而言，唯有掌握其核心思想，並以之貫串研究之主題，似乎較能全面而深入地把握思想家之思想本質。

（六）生涯之抉擇

章氏走出書齋投入政治，這無疑是章氏一生中之重大決定。汪著認為章氏在作此決定時，一點也不困難，因為，他並不打算放棄學術，誠如他日後所證明的。唯此一看法，以章氏日後之表現，來證明其當初作此生命中之重大決定時之心理層面，似有未妥。而張文亦有類似之看法。唯張文指出章氏在年輕時，已接受兩種不同的學術理想，一為強調道德實踐功用之學術；另一為與政治無關，純粹知識追求之學術。因之，章氏選擇前者而投入政治，對於章氏此時處境之抉擇，亦輕描淡寫。唯學術與政治乃兩種完全不同之領域，面對抉擇時，內心必充滿煎熬，而李著特別強調章氏在政治與學術之間抉擇之兩難（dilemma），似較能貼近章氏面對境遇困境時之心理樣貌。

（七）文化之承續性（continuity）

張文認為章氏思想雖深植於傳統，但也與傳統斷絕。張文強調章氏的思想兼具文化之持續性與非持續性，似已打破前人以此二者作為詮釋思想之解釋性範疇。而其他論著則多強調，章氏雖主張變革，但必須不能斬斷與傳統文化之紐帶。此種主張章氏思想中之文化持續性之觀點，似乎較符合章氏思想之真實樣貌。

此外，汪著以民族主義及李著以保存國粹之關切為主軸來貫串全書之主題。而張文強調章氏思想之歸趨為欲建立一佛教之世界觀，皆深具特色。孫文以章氏對政治之否定為基點來深入探討章氏之政治思想，頗有新意。高文對章氏政治生涯之轉折及政治相關議題之闡發，對章氏思想之研究有其貢獻。而傅文觸及章氏語文及學術領域之探究，頗有識見。唯過度強調章氏之種族主義之立場，亦頗有爭議。

四、結論與未來研究之展望

以上論述乃章太炎研究在美國之概況。由於篇幅所限，本文僅選擇一些較具代表性之論著作一介紹。不過，由此論述中，亦不難看出章太炎研究在美國此一研究領域之概略情形。根據上述論述，可以發現，此一研究領域在質的方面，已呈現可喜之成績。雖然，在某些議題上，學者之觀點頗為分歧，然而，多元觀點之呈現，對於章太炎思想之把握，應有正面而實質之助益。至於量的方面，則明顯不足。推其原因，可能與章氏之論著繁富、思想複雜及文字古雅艱澀有關。對於美國學者從事此一領域之研究而言，實為一重大考驗。然而，由於美國漢學界人才輩出，再加上與華語地區學術交流日趨頻仍，在此一領域之研究，一定會交出更亮麗的成績單，這應該是可以預期的。

從上述已發表之論著來看，在美國，學者對章太炎研究比較偏重章氏之政治思想和活動方面以及較為一般性之研究，這是很自然的現象。因為，自二次世界大戰以降，美國之漢學研究是以近、現代中國史為主要之研究範疇。因此，有關章太炎之研究，學者側重其政治方面之研究，亦不令人意外。且誠如汪著在其序言中所言，其研究動機之一是因為研究中國近代史之學者普遍認為章氏在歷史上之重要性主要在於其學術方面，而其政治思想及活動不僅不重要且充滿矛盾。汪氏為扭轉此情形，乃著眼於章氏之政治方面之探究。

雖然，章氏在革命運動中極為有名，然而，其聲望及盛名實多得自其國學方面之成就。實者，章氏在政治方面之貢獻不可謂之不大，然而，其在學術方面之貢獻更大，此所以章氏被稱為國學大師。況且，章氏在政治方面之觀點及靈感實大多來自其學術方面之見解。究實而言，章氏之思想實包含學術和政治兩個側面。因此，欲全面而深入地把握章氏之思想，對於這兩個側面的研究，實缺一不可。

根據上述之考察，在美國，學者對章太炎之研究多側重其政治方面之探究，或一般性之論述，而疏於對章氏國學方面之全面而深入之探討。因此，此後有關章太炎之研究，宜學術及政治兩面並重，且更應積極投入國學方面之深究。

貳、中國思想：中文篇

北宋思想家李覯之功利思想析論

一、前言

在先秦時期，孔子、孟子和荀子三人，創建了儒家主要的道德原理，提供了一個嶄新的人生理想和文化理念。這三位早期儒家的偉大人物乃儒學傳統中最具有原創性的思想家。先秦儒學之核心思想乃內聖外王之道，其中，尤以內聖之學更為根本。〔註1〕內聖即肯定人之德性是本有的，故人人經由修養自身之道德潛能，則皆能成聖。這種人人皆可以成為聖人之觀念日後乃成為儒學傳統的基本精神。

降至漢代，其時儒者之思想迥異於古代儒學，且甚而遮蔽了先秦儒學之真正特質。整體而言，儒家思想的研究在兩漢時期幾已停滯不前。有些儒者，如董仲舒（179～104B.C.）竟認為孔子是一位由天而降的神，且相信一般人是無法成聖的。蓋凡人生來並未具有如聖人之諸般能力。另外，漢儒喜歡採用陰陽學派及五行理論去詮釋儒學，他們幾乎曲解了儒學之真精神。

兩漢之後，時至魏晉（220～420），先秦之道家思想有了新的發展，學者稱之為「新道家」。此一時期，道家興盛而儒家沒落。其後至唐代（618～907），當時一流之思想家多為佛學家，蓋此一時期乃中國佛學之黃金時代。由唐至五代，佛學乃中國哲學思想之主流。雖然，儒家仍繼續維持其社會教化之影響力，然在哲學方面，並未有任何重要之發展和貢獻。

〔註1〕 T'ang Chun-l, "The Spirit and Development of Neo-Confucianism", in Arne Naess and Alastair Hannay eds., *Invitation to Chinese Philosophy* (Copenhagen: Scandinavian University Press, 1972) ,p.56.

直至宋代，當代之儒者相信一般人經由內在之自覺可以成聖，而此一觀念自漢以來已沒落了。並且他們聲稱他們在儒學傳統中已達到一新的高峰；因為，他們引進了新的內容和形式，且在儒學探究上有了新的深度〔註2〕，由此，而有所謂宋代儒學之復興，世稱「新儒學」（Neo-Confucianism）。

一般而言，新儒學一詞指的是理學（the Philosophy of Principle），它是與整個宋、明之哲學傳統相一致。在它長期及顯著之譜系中，由宋代之周敦頤、張載、二程、朱熹、陸象山，一直到明代之王陽明及劉宗周，宋、明儒者之主要關懷是追求道之實體，且主要經由哲學思辯，企圖建立儒家之道德原則。〔註3〕雖然，此種哲學思辯之形態對宋代儒學之復興而言是嶄新而令人注目的。但至少在北宋時期，理學並非當時儒學之主流，而是直到南宋時期，理學才開始取得新儒學之主要地位，並被視為正統。然而，就整體而言，理學在儒學大規模之復興中，只不過是其中之一分支而已。

在儒學傳統中，儒學包括了三個方面，即文獻研究、內聖之學與外王之學。在這三方面中，文獻研究指的是研究儒家之原始經典，且擴大到經、史、子、集等各種文獻。它被認為是保存和傳達儒家真理之媒介。「內聖」則強調經由道德之自我修養，而達成個人道德之自我實現。而「外王」則是將經世濟民之理念付諸實行。在儒學復興中，早期宋代之新儒家皆對儒學此三方面有充分之理解，因此，當熙寧二年（1069），神宗（r.1067～1085）詢問胡瑗（993～1059）之高弟劉彝（1017～1086），「胡瑗和王安石孰優」時，劉氏回答說：

> 臣聞聖人之道，有體、有用、有文。君臣、父子、仁義、禮樂，歷世
> 不可變者，其體也；詩書史傳子集垂法後世者，其文也；舉而措之
> 天下，能潤澤斯民，歸于皇極者，其用也。〔註4〕

根據劉氏之說法，聖人之道包括了三方面：一是講體，如君臣、父子、仁義禮樂，歷世不可變之體；一是講用，如何以儒學來建立社會政治秩序，即所謂經世濟民；最後是文，即指經、史、子、集等各種文獻。

「在道的三重性概念中，吾人對於宋代儒學所追求的目的有一簡明之陳

〔註2〕 Liu James, T. C., *Reform in Sung China* (Harvard University Press, 1959), p.22.

〔註3〕 Yu Ying-shih, "Rise of Ch'ing Confucian Intellectualism", *The Tsing Hua Journal of Chinese Studies* 11/1 (1975), p.121.

〔註4〕 黃宗羲：《宋元學案》，上冊（台北：河洛出版社，1975 年），頁 26。

述。依此，廣義之儒學乃由宋代學者之多元活動所發展而成的」。〔註5〕

　　就劉氏對儒家之道所明確陳述的三方面而言，體即指內聖而言，它對新儒學而言乃是最根本的。而道之體是不會改變的，此一信念使得儒者積極地追求儒道之形上基礎。〔註6〕道之用指的是外王，它主要是強調經世此一政治和社會層面而言。體和用兩者乃一體兩面，彼此互相涵攝。就此意義而言，體和用被認為是比道之文的傳統遠為重要和真實。〔註7〕其後，宋代強調儒家道之體的學者發展成為理學家，並建立新儒學之正統；而強調道之用的學者則發展成為功利思想者。

二、宋代功利思想之興起

　　宋代政治思想之重心並不在理學而是落在功利思想上。其理由是當時之政治趨向實際，而理學則較為理想化。功利思想於此是指涉一種政治學說。其特色是重心落在國家社會之實際事務方面，且反對道德原則之形上思辯。它的基本關切是為了改進人民之生活，強化軍事以對抗異族之入侵，並使國家富強。功利思想乃是反佛教及對國家軍事積弱的一種直接反應。

　　作為一種外來宗教，佛教只是當儒學衰落之際傳入中國，並在唐代開花結果，成為當時之主要思潮。自唐朝之韓愈（768～824）和李翱（774？～841？）闢佛之後，反佛亦成為宋代儒者之主要關切所在。他們反對佛學的主要目的是為了復興儒學傳統，並使之再度成為中國之支配性思想。佛學和儒學二者之根本旨趣是極其不同的。儒學之基本思想旨在關心人倫之原則、道德價值及現實人生；而佛學則極具思辯性且是出世的。中國人之思想是肯定人倫生活且是入世的；而佛學則否定現實世界，而重來世的。〔註8〕因此，作為一種宗教，佛教是與儒家之生活方式相衝突，結果，引發儒者極大之反動。

　　此外，當時學者反對佛教是基於財政和社會方面之考量。在西元1022年宋朝全國約有46萬之僧侶〔註9〕，他們的存在增加了農民之負擔，他們的宗教信仰引發整個國家的經濟和社會問題，此乃因僧侶可逃避賦稅和勞役，並

〔註5〕 Wm. Theodore de Bary,"A Reappraisal of Neo-Confucianism", in Arthur Wright ed., *Studies in Chinese Thought*(Chicago: University of Chicago Press, 1953), p.90.

〔註6〕 Yu Ying-shih.,"Rise of Ch'ing Confucian Intellectualism", p.119.

〔註7〕 Yu Ying-shih.,"Rise of Ch'ing Confucian Intellectualism", p.119.

〔註8〕 Chang Carsun, *The Development of Neo-Confucian Thought*, v.1, (New Haven: College and University Press, 1957), p.113.

〔註9〕 李攸：《宋朝事實》，卷7。

且，他們所奉行的獨身主義，中國人認為是不自然和不道德的，且亦使得婚姻和家庭的數量減少。因此，佛教僧侶之存在形成對整個社會之一種威脅。此外，佛教寺院所在之土地常極肥沃，且是免稅的，因此，宋代之反佛思潮促使學者強調的並非來世之事務，而是人間之事務，甚而是國家社會之現實事務。

至於宋代功利思想興起之最根本原因是宋代軍事之積弱不振。而軍事上之積弱乃由於宋代之開國君主太祖所建立之立國政策所致。太祖之擁有政權是由於他是一位軍事領導者。事實上，他是由將士擁立而稱帝的。然而，太祖感受到其政權為其他軍事將領所威脅；因此，在宋代建國之初，太祖即強調「重文輕武」及「強幹弱枝」之政策。〔註10〕

在軍事方面，太祖為了加強中央政府之力量，而剝奪了諸將之兵權。他以不流血之手段，用高官厚祿作為交換，達成了「杯酒釋兵權」之目的。並且，他把全國軍隊分成二類，即中央禁軍——「幹」及地方之廂軍——「枝」。中央禁軍置於首都，是軍隊之主體；而廂軍則用來防衛地方，在軍事上乃扮演輔助性之角色。此外，太祖將所有軍事，由自己直接指揮，並由文官（樞密院）而非武將來主掌軍事。雖然，太祖之軍事措施可避免國內之兵變；然而，宋代之軍隊卻不會作戰，無法抵禦外敵之入侵。此種軍事上之弱點乃反映在宋朝之軍隊常為外敵所欺之事實。〔註11〕

雖然太祖之弟及繼位者太宗曾兩度北伐，企圖收復五代時期後唐石敬塘割讓於契丹之土地——燕雲十六州，然皆無功而返。真宗即位後，遼於西元1004年侵宋，兩國並於次年達成和議，史稱「澶淵之盟」。在澶淵盟約中，兩國君主約為兄弟，宋朝承認燕雲十六州之失地，並贈與遼歲幣每年絹二十萬匹，銀十萬兩。〔註12〕此外，西夏於西元1038年建國，並開始侵宋。其後，兩國亦達成和議，宋亦贈西夏歲幣。此後，宋朝經常飽受此二外敵之武力威脅。

雖然，宋朝時常受到遼及西夏之侵擾，但宋所能作的只是付予對方歲幣以維持和平。之所以如此，主要在於宋朝軍事之積弱不振所致。在此情形下，當時之學者極其關切國家之安危，並試圖力挽國家之危亡，由此而提出諸多富國強兵之建言。因之，宋代功利思想之產生大體是由於時勢之刺激所致。

〔註10〕陶晉生：《中國近古史》（台北：東華書局，1979年），頁8～9。

〔註11〕陶晉生：《中國近古史》，頁11～12。

〔註12〕李埴：《皇宋十朝綱要》卷3，頁11。另參考陶晉生：《中國近古史》，頁63。

三、李覯（1009～1059）之生平及其功利思想

（一）李覯之生平〔註13〕

李覯字泰伯，北宋建昌南城人。李氏出身貧寒，卻喜讀書，並關心經世濟民之事務。李氏早年即沈緬於古代經籍之中，而尤好儒家學說。如同時人之所為，李氏亦企圖經由科舉而在政壇上有所作為。然而，屢次失利，並終其一生亦無緣擔任政府之重要官職。

1043年李氏應建昌軍知郡之請，出任教職。余靖屢次向朝廷推薦李氏，但皆未成；而范仲淹亦推許他為「非常儒」。最後，經由范氏之推薦，李覯被任命為「將仕郎試太學助教」。這是一個地位很低之榮譽性頭銜。後來，在1057年，李氏被任命為「太學說書」。1059年，升任「權同管勾太學」。惜僅在任一短暫時期，李氏即長眠不起。

李氏基本上是一位壯志未酬之學者，因他屢次試圖獲得一官半職以實踐其政治理想，但皆未成功。因此，他必須尋求其他途徑來使自己成名，於是，李氏轉向學術工作，並對他所處之社會作出貢獻。其主要貢獻即在學術著作上，而其作品即「直講李先生文集」。

（二）李覯之功利思想

李覯雖是儒家學者，其思想卻與孟子極其不同。孟子反對言利，在其影響下，後世儒者多有貴義輕利之說，且多以言利為恥。李氏對此極其不滿，以為聖人無不言利者。〔註14〕李氏認為儒家之道德是無法與其現實價值分離的。他說：「焉有仁義而不利者乎？」〔註15〕因之，李氏在其學說中強調利之價值。然而，李氏所謂利，究是何義？他說：

> 洪範八政，一曰食，二曰貨。孔子曰：足食足兵，民信之矣。是則治國之實，必本於財用。…是故聖賢之君，經濟之士，必先富其國焉。〔註16〕

對李覯而言，「利」即指「財用」而言。而其主要目的乃在滿足人民之慾

〔註13〕《李覯傳》及其年譜，收於《李覯集》（北京：中華書局，1981年）。另參考謝善元：《李覯》（台北：東大出版社，1991年），頁17～49。

〔註14〕蕭公權：《中國政治思想史》，下冊（台北：中國文化大學出版社，1980年），頁459。

〔註15〕《李覯集》，頁326。

〔註16〕《李覯集》，頁133。

望。李氏雖肯定欲之存在，然亦主張需以禮節之。〔註17〕由於李氏強調利、欲之價值，由此，李氏遂發展出以利、欲為中心觀念之功利思想。至於李覯之功利思想則主要表現在三方面，試分述如下：

1. 政治方面

由於李覯是一位現實主義之思想家，他渴望見到自己國家富強。李氏乃主張霸道，因它可使國家富強。在這一點上，他與孟子等儒者不同。孟子推崇王道乃治國之良方；而李覯則持論相反，力主霸道。〔註18〕他說：

> 儒生之論，但恨不及王道耳。而不知霸也，強國也，豈易及哉！管仲之相齊桓公，是霸也。外攘戎狄，內尊京師，較之於公何如？商鞅之相秦孝公，是強國也。明法術耕戰，國以富而兵以強，較之於公何如？〔註19〕

在宋代局勢危亡之際，李覯不了解當時之學者何以堅持王道乃唯一之政治理想，且忽視軍事之重要，只因它為古代所憎惡。李氏認為由於時勢不同，在達成政治秩序之穩定及使國家富強方面，霸道的確比王道更為有效。李氏並認為富國強兵之目的旨在安民；因安民乃政治之目的，亦是君主之天職。此何謂也？蓋君主乃由天所命，而「天聽自我民聽」，甚而，君主由天所命之觀念，並非為了君主之利益，而是為了千萬百姓之福祉。因之，君主有責任造福人民。若君主失去民心，則理應被推翻。〔註20〕依此，李氏主張富國強兵，與利圖霸之目的皆在安民而不在尊君，可知，李氏之功利思想乃儒家之學而非法家之學也。〔註21〕

2. 經濟及財政方面

作為一位儒家學者，李覯關心的是人民，尤其是農民之福祉及國之富強。然而，宋朝政府面臨嚴重的財政及經濟問題。此問題反映在財富分配之不均，農作生產及國家歲入之減少上。李氏認為促進百姓之福利應是成立政府之目的；而促進百姓之福利則應始於生命之維持。易言之，百姓應有足夠之糧食。所謂「生民之道食為大」。〔註22〕然當時，只有富人擁有田地，而貧者無田。

〔註17〕《李覯集》，頁6。
〔註18〕蕭公權：《中國政治思想史》，下冊，頁460。
〔註19〕《李覯集》，頁299～300。
〔註20〕《李覯集》，頁168。
〔註21〕蕭公權：《中國政治思想史》，下冊，頁462。
〔註22〕《李覯集》，頁183。

因之，富者愈富；貧者愈貧。由於窮人無法養活自己，乃被迫成為富者之佃農，或改行從事其他行業。雖然，當時可耕之地甚多，但僅有極少數用之於農業生產。加之，佃農由於土地並非己有，並未努力耕種。如此，導致農業生產及國家歲入之減少。李覯追溯此問題之原因乃是由於土地分配不均所致。而解決之道，李氏認為唯有讓農人回歸土地，限制土地擁有權及土地平均分配，始能得之。〔註23〕他說：

> 地力不盡，則穀米不多；田不墾闢，則租稅不增，理固然也。今將救之，則莫若先行抑末之術，以驅游民，游民既歸矣，然後限人占田，各有頃數，不得過制。……則一心于農。一心于農，則地力可盡矣。〔註24〕

如此，若農民有足夠之土地耕種，則就有能力繳納賦稅，而政府之歲入自然就會增加了。

至於如何使政府富足，李覯則提出一個更實際而富原創性之主張，此即「人無遺力，地無遺利」之觀念。〔註25〕此確是解決民生問題之一極高理想，蓋「充分利用人力，充分開發土地」，確是任何一位關心國家富足之君主在農業社會中永遠應該努力之目標。

李氏亦主張有效管理國家財政之重要性。然而，有效管理國家財政並非意謂政府須向人民徵收過多之賦稅，而是必須「強本而節用」。〔註26〕若政府能強本，即注重農業，則農業生產自然會增加，如此，人民就有能力繳交賦稅，而國家之歲入亦自然會增加了。由於政府之歲入乃來自賦稅，有一定之限度，因之，李氏以為政府之開支宜在歲入範圍之內，即量入為出。若政府能有效管理國家財政，則全國人民將會人人生活自足。〔註27〕

3. 軍事方面

在宋朝政府所面臨之諸多問題中，軍事之積弱不振乃李覯之主要關切所在。由於軍事之積弱，宋朝經常飽受遼及西夏之侵害。雖然宋之軍隊數量眾多，但並不可靠，且素質低落。此外，士兵在接受上級指揮之前，通常需要一段訓練時間。然而，由於將帥經常被調防，以致將帥與士兵之間彼此無法

〔註23〕謝善元：《李覯》，頁 124～125。
〔註24〕《李覯集》，頁 136。
〔註25〕《李覯集》，頁 78。
〔註26〕《李覯集》，頁 133。
〔註27〕姜國柱：《李覯評傳》（南京：南京大學出版社，1996 年），頁 161～165。

相知、相親。如此，宋之兵員雖多，但卻不必會作戰。宋代軍事積弱之另一原因是君主常懷疑將帥之忠誠，因此，想出諸多方法來節制將帥。其中之一個方法即是派遣監軍至部隊去巡視，而此等監軍通常只是宮中之太監或官階不高之官吏。〔註28〕依此，若將帥飽受懷疑，則如何發揮所長，指揮作戰？如此，作戰勢必失利。由於以上原因，宋代軍隊之積弱乃極其自然之事。而此種情形亦一直存在於宋代。

　　基本上，戰爭之勝利需要將帥與士兵之間彼此同心協力、相知、相親。因此，李氏認為將帥不應該時常調防，除非他們犯了嚴重之錯誤。由於宋兵怯懦且不擅作戰，他們需要施以一段時間之訓練，始能成為有用之兵。因之，李氏主張君主宜信任將帥，且將帥應有獨立之指揮權。將帥若能不受中央之無謂干預，如此才能全心全力發揮其指揮才能而克敵致勝。因此，李氏認為改善君主與將帥之間之關係乃君主之責任所在。〔註29〕易言之，君主宜完全了解將帥，且一旦如此，即應完全信任之，如此，始能獲致軍事上之勝利。

四、李覯之功利思想析論

　　北宋儒學雖以心性之學為主導，但究實而言，心性之學實不足以涵蓋儒學之全貌。廣義言之，儒學實包含三方面：（一）內聖──其後發展成「理學」，（二）外王──其後發展為經世致用之學，（三）經典之研究。其中以前二者較重要，蓋二者實為宋代政治思想中之二大主流也。故欲明北宋儒學復興之實況實不可忽視其經世致用之一面；且北宋時期經世致用之思想特強。兩宋經世致用之思想雖以王安石為中堅，而實廣之於李覯，蓋其立言富條理且有系統也。

　　李覯深受經世致用之學風所吸引，尤其是 1038 年趙宋受到西夏之侵害之後，此種思想即更明顯。由於李氏之思想重實用，並發展出以利、欲為中心之功利思想，因之，其思想與其他儒家學者有極大之不同。

　　宋代之功利思想重視儒家之外王此一側面。就儒學而言，內聖與外王實乃一體之兩面，然前者常被視為是「本」，而後者則是基於前者而來。因之，多數儒家學者相信內聖或成德乃經世治國之良方。然此並非意謂著他們忽略積極有為之治術。相對的，宋代以國家富強為目的之功利思想家則忽略了內聖或成德之道。因之，李覯之治術亦缺乏道德之基礎。多數其他儒者貴義賤利，並

〔註28〕謝善元：《李覯》，頁 119～121。
〔註29〕謝善元：《李覯》，頁 121～122。

以王道為治國之良方；李覯則過度重視利，並主張霸道，且甚至主張道德之價值宜以利為基礎。由於此等理由，李覯被多數儒者視為法家。但李氏辯稱他並非法家之信徒，蓋其目的乃以孔子之道來經世。李氏亦堅持他之所以強調富國乃依於孔子之以安民為目的。至於主張強兵衛國乃是獲致和平所必需。究實言之，李覯之主張富國強兵及興利圖霸，其目的乃是安民而非尊君，故李氏在本質上確是儒家而非法家。

在李氏為解決北宋問題所作之建言及辦法中，有些很新穎，亦甚有創見。他建議限制土地之擁有權及土地平均分配等皆是增加農業生產及國家歲入之良方；有效管理國家財政是使國家富足之有效方法；改善君主與將帥之間之關係則能增進軍隊之作戰能力。此等建言在當時是極其重要且可能是非常獨特的。然而，最具創見和實際之觀念則是充分利用人力和土地資源以使國家富足之主張。

五、結論

促成北宋經世致用學風之興起，其背景主要是基於對當時佛教之反動，而更重要的是由於宋代國勢之積弱不振。而在此學風中，李覯實為一特立獨行之思想家。其思想與傳統儒學，尤其是孟學有極大之不同。李氏並發展出以利、欲為中心觀念之功利思想。其所謂利乃指財用，而財用主要在於滿足人民之欲望。

本文主要就底下三方面來抉發李覯之功利思想：

一、政治方面：李氏主張霸道而非王道，蓋其認為霸道之施行方可能使宋代之國勢由積弱轉為富強。

二、經濟方面：李氏認為政府存在之目的在於解決民生問題，而最根本之方法為解決土地所有制問題，因此，李氏提出「人無遺力，地無遺利」之主張。

三、軍事方面：李氏主張皇帝須信任主帥，不得任意更換主帥，且中央不得干預練兵，並促使將、士上下一條心，如此，施以一段時間之訓練，始可應付外患之侵逼。

由於李氏在政治上並不得志，其聲望亦不高，故歷來並不受學者所重視，然其思想有系統，重實際，有遠見，而經由其著作，李氏確對其所處之社會作出貢獻。故本文特抉發之，期能對其思想有進一步之了解，且進而可對北宋儒學復興過程中之一側面（經世致用思想）之理解有所助益。

戴震之考證哲學析論〔註1〕

一、前言

　　清初，朱熹（1130～1200）學派之理學被提昇至朝廷之正統地位後，不久，朱學即成為詮釋儒家主要典籍之支配性模式。在乾嘉時期（1736～1820），雖然，朱學仍維持其影響力，但是，當時之學術潮流已開始轉而對它採取反對的態度。即使朱熹學派之學者堅稱，他們對於儒學之詮釋是完全符合儒家經典之原義，然而，許多乾嘉時期之學者則宣稱，由於他們並不了解古代聖賢之語言，且對古代典籍之詮釋在本質上是思辯的，因之，他們誤解了儒家經典之原義。由於反對理學家以哲學思辯的方式去詮釋儒學，十八世紀之學者乃從經典中去尋求客觀真理之證據，並且主張回歸古代儒學典籍本身，以便重建儒學之傳統。依此，考證學派乃於焉形成〔註2〕，而在乾嘉時期也瀰漫著復古主義（Revivalism）。〔註3〕

　　在乾嘉時期，戴震（1723～1777）是以考證學派之主要支持者而著稱。然而，戴氏與當時其他考證學者有很大的不同。前者視考證為彰顯真理之一種手段；而後者則視之為目的，亦即是為考證而考證。此外，戴氏被認為是一位哲學家而不僅僅是考證學者而已。雖然，戴氏與當時之考證學者有所不同，但是，

〔註1〕本文係 University of Ljubljana—Faculty of Arts 之邀稿之作，刊登於該校發行之 Asian and African Studies 16/1（April, 2012）.
〔註2〕「考證學」一詞，就字面上而言，是指尋求證據。它意指經由證據及藉著嚴格地採用歸納和比較之方法來詮釋和分析經典。
〔註3〕「復古」意指「回到過去」。

他和這些學者之間亦有其共同之關懷，此即，修正和重新恢復儒學傳統之原貌。

於此，我們將提出的問題是，乾嘉時期，考證學風之興起，其旨趣為何？又其與理學有何關係？

前輩學者如，胡適和錢穆二位對於此一問題之解答，很遺憾地並不夠充分。〔註4〕前者主張考證學只不過是理學之反動；而後者則堅稱考證運動是理學之延續。上述二種說法當然是值得商榷的。因為，乾嘉考證學風之興起雖與理學有關，但考證學實不應被視為僅是對宋、明理學之反動或理學之承續而已，它實代表一種自我意識之努力，乃欲恢復原始儒學之真貌，並強化儒學之傳統。此外，在全盛時期，考證學意指應用嶄新而精確的方法來評估及修正古代經典之一種經驗知識的模式。雖然，和宋、明時期相比，乾嘉時期若有所謂的哲學家和新穎理論的話，亦只是少數；而如果考證學派最偉大的哲學家戴震可視為此一時期之代表的話，那麼，乾嘉時期確有基於一更為堅實的理論和文獻基礎來重建儒學之熱切企圖。而余英時對於此一問題之觀點，亦無法令人滿意。〔註5〕因之，本文將著重於乾嘉學者，尤其是戴震在重估及檢證儒學傳統之主要典籍和概念時所作之努力，並針對戴氏之考證哲學作一析論，以明其價值及限制。本文之第一部份將說明戴震之考證哲學形成之背景，第二部分在論述戴震之思想發展，第三部分則針對戴震之考證哲學作一析論。

二、戴震之考證哲學形成之背景

清代中葉，考證學的發展臻於新的成熟階段，且終究支配了此一時期之學術界。雖然，考證學在乾嘉時期達到顛峰，但是，其根源卻可以回溯到十七世紀、北宋時期（960～1127），甚或唐代（618～907）。初唐時，孔穎達（574～648）曾編纂《五經正義》，此書日後且成為科舉考試之標準參考本。〔註6〕但

〔註4〕 胡適：《戴東原的哲學》（台北：商務印書館，1971年）；及錢穆：《中國近三百年學術史》（台北：商務印書館，1976年）。

〔註5〕 余英時：〈清代思想史的一個新解釋〉，收於《歷史與思想》（台北：聯經出版社，1978年），頁121～156。

〔註6〕 實際上，《五經正義》並非孔氏一人所獨力編纂，而是由他及其他唐代學者所合力編成。據說，原來有六經，其中《樂經》在西元前三世紀前亡佚。所謂五經是指《詩經》、《書經》、《易經》、《禮經》或《儀禮》及《春秋》。而孔氏之《五經正義》乃是作為唐代明經科考試之標準教科書。在唐代，明經科乃科舉考試中之一類，其重要性僅次於進士科。參見 Charles O. Hucker ed, *A Dictionary of Official Titles in Imperial China* (Stanford: Stanford University Press, 1985), p.333.

是，不久之後，卻出現了一種文獻校勘之新趨勢來挑戰孔氏正統注疏之權威。
與此趨勢相關之學者倡導回歸經典本身，以之作為了解聖賢真義之基礎。雖然，
這些學者敢於對傳統提出質疑，但是，他們在這方面的成就不大。雖然如此，
但是，重要的是，他們的確企圖透過經典而非依賴注疏來獲得真理。〔註7〕

　　雖說，考證學並非宋代（960～1279）學者之主要關切所在，但是他們在
這方面的努力卻獲致重要的成果。〔註8〕宋代學者追隨其唐代前輩之腳步在
仁宗慶曆（1042～1048）年間，開始摒棄孔穎達為官方所認可之《五經正義》。
他們寧可回歸經典本身，並試圖以其自身之觀點來詮釋儒家經典。依此精神，
孫復（992～1057）直接研讀春秋經而非三傳。〔註9〕在研究《春秋》時，孫
氏「試圖以最簡單的詞語來表達它的主要意義，而不去考慮各種不同且令人
混淆之傳疏。」〔註10〕王安石（1021～1086）研究三經並加上其個人之注解
〔註11〕，此注本後來成為北宋科舉考試之標準參考本。王氏在注釋經典時，
強調其通義而非字面上之詮釋。〔註12〕隨著十一世紀理學之興起，宋代理學
家在經典的研究上則更往前推進一步，他們偏好以哲學或義理之方法來詮釋
經典，亦即強調道德原理之理解而非字面上之意義。他們加入其強調哲學概
念之注解，但有時不免悖離經典之字義。〔註13〕

　　在十一世紀時，尤其是在1025到1100年之間，與此同時並行發展的是
關於經典真偽的懷疑主義之滋長。在宋代學者中，歐陽修（1007～1072）對
經典提出嚴正之質疑。他懷疑《周禮》、《易經》之某些部分及〈詩序〉等之
真實性。蘇軾（1036～1101）對《周禮》和《尚書》提出質疑。司馬光（1019

〔註7〕 Edwin Pulleyblank, "Neo-Confucianism and Neo-Legalism in T'ang Intellectual
　　　　Life, 755~805", in Arthur Wright ed, *The Confucian Persuasion*(Stanford: Stanford
　　　　University Press, 1960), pp.77~114. See also Benjamin A. Elman, *From Philosophy
　　　　to Philology*(Cambridge: Harvard University Press, 1984), pp.40~41. 另參見馬宗
　　　　霍：《中國經學史》（台北：商務印書館，1979年），頁107～126。

〔註8〕 Winston W. Lo, "Philology, An Aspect of Sung Rationalism", *Chinese Culture* 17/4
　　　　（Dec.,1976），pp.1～26.

〔註9〕 皮錫瑞：《經學歷史》（台北：藝文印書館，1966年），頁202；See also Wing-
　　　　tsit Chan, "Chu Hsi's Completion of Neo-Confucianism", in Wing-tsit Chan, *Chu
　　　　Hsi: Life and Thought*(Hong Kong: The Chinese University Press, 1987), p.130.

〔註10〕 Wm. Theodore de Bary, "A Reappraisal of Neo-Confucianism", in Arthur Wright
　　　　ed, *Studies in Chinese Thought*(Chicago: University of Chicago Press, 1953), p.92.

〔註11〕 三經是指《詩經》、《尚書》和《周禮》，See Chan, "Chu Hsi's Completion of Neo-
　　　　Confucianism", p.132.

〔註12〕 de Bary, "A Reappraisal of Neo-Confucianism", p.102.

〔註13〕 Chan, "Chu Hsi's Completion of Neo-Confucianism", p.132.

～1101）及李覯（1009～1059）二人皆對《孟子》一書之可靠性有所懷疑。
朱熹甚至對經典之外的其他典籍亦提出質疑。而這種針對經典而來的懷疑主
義之精神則延續到元（1279～1368）、明（1368～1644）時期。如，元代之吳
澄（1247～1331）和明代之梅鷟（約 1513 年時在世）二人皆斷定《古文尚
書》是偽造的。〔註 14〕

　　雖然，理學，尤其是王陽明（1472～1529）學派支配了明代之思想界，
但是，在此一時期，王學卻無法完全加以壟斷。至少，明代一些學者，如楊
慎（1488～1559）、陳第（1541～1617）及焦竑（1541～1620）等則將經學重
新加以定位，即由哲學之詮釋轉向文獻之分析、考證。楊慎乃一著名之考證
學者，他試圖藉由古籍之研究來重建古音；陳第則企圖透過詩經韻腳之分類
來界定古音。〔註 15〕其古音研究之方法其後被清初學者顧炎武（1613～1682）
所採用。〔註 16〕焦竑反對經典之正統注疏及詮釋，認為它們有時會模糊經典
之真義。因此，焦氏建議當時之學者，宜直接回歸經典本身而不必先行參考
注疏。他主張以一種語言學或考證學的方法來研究經典。〔註 17〕此等經學研
究之新方向預示了日後清初考證學之發展，並為其奠定基礎。在十七世紀時，
顧炎武和閻若璩（1636～1704）〔註 18〕等人激烈地反對明代正統之經學——
其研究取向是哲學的，創造了一種新的學術風氣及一種新的思想模式，因此，
在性質上似更具學術性。〔註 19〕而顧、閻二氏則強調經典研究宜基於文本研
究及文獻考證。閻氏在嚴謹考察古代典籍時，表現出一種強烈的懷疑主義之
精神。身為一位經學家，閻氏之主要貢獻在於《尚書古文疏證》一書。雖然，

〔註 14〕　皮錫瑞：《中國經學史》，頁 202；See also Chan, "Chu Hsi's Completion of Neo-
　　　　　Confucianism", pp.132~134；James T. C. Liu, *Ou-yang Hsiu: An Eleventh-Century
　　　　　Neo-Confucianist* (Stanford: Stanford University Press, 1976), p.94.

〔註 15〕　陳新雄：《古音學發微》（台北：文史哲出版社，1975 年），頁 25～32 及頁 34
　　　　　～44。See also Elman, *From Philosophy to Philology*, pp.215～216.

〔註 16〕　Arthur W. Hummel ed., *Eminent Chinese of the Ch'ing Period* (1644～1912) (此
　　　　　後本書引為 ECCP) (Washington: Government Printing Office, 1943～1944), v.1,
　　　　　pp.421～426.

〔註 17〕　Edward T. Ch'ien, "Chiao Hung and the Revolt against Ch'eng-Chu Orthodoxy", in
　　　　　de Bary ed., *The Unfolding of Neo-Confucianism* (New York: Columbia University
　　　　　Press, 1975), pp.287～291, and Edward T.Ch'ien, *Chiao Hung and the
　　　　　Restructuring of Neo-Confucianism in the Late Ming* (New York: Columbia
　　　　　University Press, 1986), pp.181～182.

〔註 18〕　*ECCP*, v.2, pp.908～910.

〔註 19〕　Elman, *From Philosophy to Philology*, pp.43～44.

在閻氏之前，《尚書》之真偽，長久以來已廣為學者所研究，但是，大致上，它仍被視為是真本。閻氏則應用經驗的方法去分析原典，且根據文獻考證，而斷定《古文尚書》乃是後人所偽造。此一結論被當時大多數考證學者所接受。〔註 20〕

另一重要人物是顧炎武。顧氏通常被認為是考證學派之創立者，因為，他發展了一種新的研究方法學。雖然，顧氏從事研究之主要目的是經世致用，但是，他的確強調，文獻校勘和考證對經典研究而言是不可或缺的，顧氏且界定出適用於各種不同學術分支領域之研究方法。因之，顧氏所建立之方法學的確標示了經學研究之新方向，且為清朝中葉之考證學的興起鋪路。〔註 21〕「考證」一詞，並非一新詞，它曾被宋代學者王應麟（1223～1296）所使用，然而，考證學卻是一直到十七世紀時才開始風行。〔註 22〕

此一時期之學者之所以轉向考證學乃是基於一種基本理由，即欲恢復儒家經典之真貌，並將之由前人錯誤之詮釋中加以解放。彼等聲稱宋代理學之致命弱點有二，其一是雜染了佛、道二家之思想〔註 23〕；另一則是宋代理學家之知識不足或缺乏考證學之訓練和嚴謹性〔註 24〕，以致彼等對經典所作思辯式之詮釋，乃建立在錯誤或偽造之儒家典籍之版本上。為了避免此等問題，乾嘉時期之考證學者主張回到過去，以便重建原始儒學之真貌。並且，欲以此方式而以考證學來取代哲學或理學。〔註 25〕

此一復古或回到過去之導向表現出一種欲恢復及檢證儒學真理之企圖。同時，為了達成此一目的，考證學者在從事研究時所依據的是較宋代為早，亦即那些漢代之典籍，以便克服宋代理學家在認知上之限制。因此，他們將其注意力轉向漢代解經之作。此等作品，被認為是可信的，因為，在時間上，漢代是與古代較為接近。〔註 26〕由於乾嘉學者強調漢代學術及其研究目的之關聯性，因此，十八世紀之考證學通常被稱為漢學。

漢學家強調經典之詳細的考證分析，而與宋代理學家之著重思辯式之研

〔註 20〕 *ECCP*, v.2, pp.909～910.

〔註 21〕 *ECCP*, v.1, pp.423～424.

〔註 22〕 Elman, *From Philosophy to Philology*, p.45.

〔註 23〕 戴震：《孟子字義疏證》，收於《戴東原先生全集》（本書此後引為《全集》）（台北：大化書局），頁 305。

〔註 24〕 戴震：〈與某書〉，收於《全集》，頁 1100。

〔註 25〕 「哲學」一詞，清代學者意指形上學和宇宙論之系統思想而言。

〔註 26〕 梁啟超：《清代學術概論》（台北：商務印書館，1972 年），頁 33。

究有所不同。在恢復儒家文化之精華之使命上，考證學不僅是一種輔助工具，而且是一種必備且嚴格要求之學科。因此，考證學者將他們新近建立之學科應用到所有與古典傳統相關之文獻資料上，並且，包括語言學、音韻學、史學、天文學、數學、水利工程學、地理學、制度、金石學、校勘學及輯佚學等各種不同之領域上。他們的座右銘是「實事求是」和「無徵不信」。而其學術成果是經典之注釋及校訂，其後則收於《皇清經解正編》〔註27〕及《皇清經解續編》〔註28〕二書中。而在此一時期之考證學者中，惠棟（1697～1758）和戴震二人被認為是最傑出的。

蘇州・元和之惠棟被認為是吳派或蘇州學派之創立者，並且，他也促使漢學盛行於蘇州地區。惠氏治學之基本精神是「凡古必真；凡漢皆好。」〔註29〕他聲稱漢代經學家之觀點是與經典本身具同等之地位。〔註30〕依此，惠氏試圖將漢學提昇至經典之地位。他推崇漢學，以之作為有關經典詮釋之最後權威，由此，確立十八世紀漢學學派之方向。然而，或許惠氏對漢學之推崇太過輕率，其學術目的似乎是在保存漢學，而非在發現可檢證之真理。因此，戴震批判其治學方法，並思有以超越漢學之藩籬。

三、戴震之思想發展

戴震可能是清代最偉大之哲學家及學者。戴氏之主要關切在於恢復並保存儒學傳統。戴氏曾明白指出，其為學之目的是為了獲致儒家真理。〔註31〕戴氏曾說，他之所以研究經典乃是為了使聖人之微言大義，能存續下去。〔註32〕當他意欲尋求儒家真理或道時，戴氏自己即轉向考證學。他對考證學之描述如下：

> 經之至者，道也，所以明道者，其詞也，所以成詞者，未有能外於小學文字者也。由文字以通乎語言，由語言以通乎古聖賢之心志。
> 〔註33〕

因此，考證學即成為戴氏欲恢復儒家真理時，所選擇之方法學。由於戴氏

〔註27〕 本書為阮元所編纂，原刻本 296 冊，補刊本 360 冊，計 1400 多卷。
〔註28〕 本書乃王先謙（1842～1918）所編，凡 320 冊，並於 1886～1888 年間出版。
〔註29〕 梁啟超：《近代中國學術論叢》（香港：崇文書店，1973 年），頁 68。
〔註30〕 梁啟超：《清代學術概論》，頁 33。
〔註31〕 戴震：〈與某書〉，收於《全集》，頁 1100。
〔註32〕 戴震：〈與姚姬傳書〉，收於《全集》，頁 1099。
〔註33〕 戴震：〈古經解鉤沈序〉，收於《全集》，頁 1102。

了解考證學乃恢復古代聖賢原義之必要手段，因此，在他早年之研究中即著重考證學之技術，且其盛名即得之於考證學。

　　雖然，戴震成為一位考證學家乃是基於個人自我之抉擇，但是，他和大多數其他漢學家有所區隔。戴氏並不像多數考證學家那樣將考證學本身視為一種目的〔註34〕，而只是將之視為一種顯現儒家真理之手段而已，戴氏之主要目的是空所依傍地尋求真理，且不為他人甚或他自己所迷惑；而多數漢學家則為學派之教條和傳統所拘限。依據此一治學方法，戴氏試圖維持一種高度之客觀性，研究事實而無所依傍，因此，戴氏成功地將漢學研究之水準提昇至一新的高峰。

　　戴震並沒有將自己侷限在古代哲學典籍之研究。他也將考證學之方法應用到許多其他學科之研究，諸如，音韻學、數學、曆法、天文學、科技和水文學等。在戴氏之眾多學術成就中，下列著作特別顯著：《考工記圖注》、《聲韻考》、《原象》及《水經注》。

　　雖然，戴氏因其考證學方面之成就及博學而為錢大昕（1728～1804）及朱筠（1729～1781）等漢學家之讚賞；但是，戴震卻相信考證學本身並不即是其目的，且更相信哲學研究之重要性。由於不滿多數考證學家之眼光狹隘，戴氏晚年即超脫考證學之藩籬，並發展出自身之哲學。在這方面，戴氏之哲學著作即反映出他試圖以自己的哲學來取代宋代之理學。

　　戴氏之哲學觀點主要表現於下列三部著作中：（一）、《原善》：1766 年完成改訂本。〔註35〕（二）、《緒言》：完成於 1772 年。（三）、《孟子字義疏證》：1777 年完成。〔註36〕此三部作品具體表現出戴氏對宋代理學及其自身哲學觀點之不同態度。

　　在他第一部哲學論著《原善》中，戴氏對宋代理學，並未明白地加以批判。當時，他似乎仍接受宋代主要思想家對儒家經典詮釋之權威性。〔註37〕在他第二部著作《緒言》中，戴氏對宋代理學家之主要觀點已逐漸產生懷疑。雖然如此，但是，尤其是在他的最後一部作品《孟子字義疏證》中，戴氏反對宋代理

〔註34〕戴震：〈答鄭用牧書〉，收於《全集》，頁 1099。

〔註35〕本書之英文譯本，見 Chung-ying Cheng, *Tai Chen's Inquiry into Goodness* (Hawaii: University of Hawaii Press, 1971).

〔註36〕本書之英文譯本，見 Ann-ping Chin and Freeman Mansfield, *Tai Chen on Mencius: Explorations in Words and Meaning* (New Haven: Yale University Press, 1990).

〔註37〕Carsun Chang, *Development of Neo-Confucian Thought* (New York: Bookman Associates, 1962), v.2, p.346.

學家之觀點最為明顯。在戴氏對理學之批判中，包含了一種還原儒家經典中之主要術語或用語之原義的渴望。因為，此等詞語已被理學家所誤解或誤用。而《孟子字義疏證》一書所採用之書名及批判之方法在在說明了考證思想對基本哲學問題之衝擊。〔註38〕在本例中，戴氏所選擇之書名非常明白地強調他的目標是：他認為研究哲學最好的方法是透過考證學，並且，他把他在這方面的努力看作是考證運動之一部分。因此，戴氏在考證學的研究和他的哲學興趣二者是不可分的，且是互補的。〔註39〕戴氏研究《孟子》所採用的方法是在於確定書中主要用語之精確意義。他相信這種方法將提供一種更精確地理解《孟子》一書及駁斥理學家主觀地詮釋儒家經典之基礎。〔註40〕

從戴震之學術生涯中可以看出戴氏之思想發展是由考證學走向哲學。戴氏似乎很早就對哲學產生興趣，但是，直到他寫作《原善》之後，哲學才成為其研究之重心。這是因為戴氏在早年並未發展其自身之哲學。此外，戴氏相信，研究哲學最好的方法宜植基於考證學上；並且，任何人必須花費長時間之研究才有可能精通考證學。戴震是直到晚年才開始建立其自身之哲學且完成其主要之哲學著作。雖然，戴氏對其哲學作品深感滿意；但是，當時之學者並不看重其哲學，且甚而聲稱戴氏根本不需要撰述那些哲學著作。〔註41〕雖然，戴氏之哲學作品在當時並不受歡迎；但是，戴氏認為其哲學方法極為重要且深具意義；因為，它足以駁斥宋代理學家對經典詮釋之主觀的研究方法。

四、戴震之考證哲學析論

誠如前文所指出，戴震哲學研究之基本方法是嚴密考證儒家傳統中之主要典籍。戴氏對此種特殊的哲學方法很早就有興趣。他在晚年寫給其弟子段玉裁（1735～1815）之信中曾提到：

> 僕自十七歲時，有志聞道，謂非求之六經、孔、孟不得，非從事於字義、制度、名物，無由以通其語言。為之三十餘年，灼然知古今治亂之源在是。〔註42〕

雖然，考證學及哲學乃分屬不同之學術領域，但是，對戴氏而言，兩者乃相輔

〔註38〕Elman, *From Philosophy to Philology*, p.19.
〔註39〕Wing-tsit Chan, *A Source Book in Chinese Philosophy* (Princeton: Princeton University Press, 1963), p.709.
〔註40〕Elman, *From Philosophy to Philology*, p.19.
〔註41〕章學誠：《文史通義》（台北：史學出版社，1974 年），頁 57。
〔註42〕段玉裁：《戴東原先生年譜》（香港：崇文書店，1971 年），頁 5。

相成的，他說：

> 經之至者道也，所以明道者其詞也，所以成詞者字也。由字以通其
> 詞，由詞以通其道，必有漸。求所謂字，考諸篆書，得許氏《說文
> 解字》，三年知其節目，漸睹古聖人制作本始。又疑許氏於故訓未能
> 盡，從友人假《十三經注疏》讀之，則知一字之義，當貫群經，本
> 六書，然後為定。〔註43〕

因此，考證學乃戴氏所以選擇用來恢復儒家真理之方法學。

雖然，戴氏思想之主要信念是與反對理學密切相關，但是，似乎除了批判理學外，戴氏早年即曾表現出其對真正的儒學義理之關切。因此，在《原善》中，戴氏並未明白地批評理學，而在《孟子字義疏證》一書中，戴氏則就其所理解之理學，直率地予以批判其哲學上之缺失。此種對理學之批評，說明了戴震對正確地理解儒學之主要用語的關切。

戴氏之哲學著作說明了考證學對哲學議題之衝擊。戴氏所採用之方法學主要是一種語言學之方法，亦即訓詁之方法。〔註44〕例如，《孟子字義疏證》一書，包含釋「理」者凡十五條；釋「天道」者四條；釋「性」者凡十三條；釋「道」者四條；釋「仁」、「義」、「禮」、「智」者各兩條。戴氏首先將上述每一詞語作詳細之訓詁。為了確定這些詞語之精確意義，戴氏乃追溯其原義或本義。例如，戴氏解釋「理」字之原義或本義是分理，由此而有文理、肌理、腠理等義，此一意義乃源自許慎（58～147）之《說文解字》。除了解釋每一詞語之原義外，戴氏並引用《易經》、《孟子》、《中庸》及《樂記》等古書中之例句來說明其用法。此一程序足以說明此等解釋並非根據個人之臆想，而是有其經典上之根源。此種訴諸語源學之方法，戴氏相信，將使他足以駁斥宋代理學家對儒學中主要詞語之曲解。戴氏認為，宋代理學家注釋儒家經典之所以有誤，乃是因為他們受到佛、道二家思想之影響；並且，缺乏正確的考證學之專門知識。〔註45〕因之，其對經典之理解乃恃胸臆為斷。戴氏說：「宋以來，孔、孟之書盡失其解，儒者雜襲老、釋之言以解之。」〔註46〕此外，戴氏亦云：「宋以來，儒者以己見硬坐為古聖賢立言之意，而語言文字實未之知。」〔註47〕由

〔註43〕戴震：〈與是仲明書〉，收於《全集》，頁1098。

〔註44〕Elman, *From Philosophy to Philology*, p.19.

〔註45〕戴震：〈與某書〉，收於《全集》，頁1100。

〔註46〕戴震：〈孟子字義疏證〉，收於《全集》，頁305。

〔註47〕戴震：〈與某書〉，收於《全集》，頁1100。

於戴氏之主要關切乃是欲恢復原始儒學之真理，因此，他試圖嚴格地區分儒家及佛、道二家之教義。〔註48〕

依此，戴震之考證哲學的建立，主要乃針對宋、明理學家之詮釋儒學而來。由於不滿宋、明學者以哲學思辨之方式研究儒學典籍，而未能把握原始儒學之真貌，戴震乃轉而以考證之方式來研究儒家之原典。戴震此種欲植基於一更為堅實之理論和文獻基礎來重建儒學之自我意識之努力，其目的在於恢復儒家典籍之本來面目，建立對原始儒學之客觀知識。要之，此種努力實有其積極之意義及一定之價值。

戴震之哲學的主要關切在於欲恢復原始儒學之真理或原貌，此實與其反理學有關。此由戴震在《孟子字義疏證》一書中對於宋明理學在哲學上之缺失所作之批評可知。戴震認為，宋明學者對儒家經典之詮釋所以恃胸臆以為斷，乃是因為他們缺乏正確的考證學之專門知識，並因此而曲解儒學典籍中之主要詞語之意義。因之，戴震乃採用考證學作為彰顯儒學本來面目之方法學。

戴震所採用之方法學主要是一種語言學或訓詁之方法。如，戴震為《孟子》一書所作之詮釋，戴氏係將《孟子》書中之主要詞語作詳細訓詁，並追溯其原義。戴氏認為，藉由訓詁字義之方法或語源學之方法，恢復「性」、「理」等詞語之字義，如此，足以駁斥宋明理學家對儒家經典中主要詞語之曲解。

戴震所發展出的研究方法確是對宋明理學家方法論之一種改進，同時，可用來釐清傳統之哲學問題。此種方法學之價值在於能追溯經典中主要詞語之原義，並對傳統儒學真貌之理解具有重要之參考。

然者，此一「以語言學之觀點解決思想史中之問題」的方法，實有待商權。如，戴震為《孟子》一書作詮釋，其方法不外乎詳考孟子時代之日常語言，並將《孟子》中之主要詞語轉為當代之通行語。〔註49〕然而，戴震可能忽略了一大問題，亦即孟子立說時，所用語言未必符合當時之日常語言用法。蓋一哲學家試圖建立一學說或理論時，他既無法任意創造一套語言以表述其學說，則唯有使用已有之語言，而賦以新義，其作法是對所使用之特殊用語下定義，以表明此一詞語之新義，由此遂形成其學說中之專有術語。〔註50〕此種實例在中、西哲學史中比比皆是。

〔註48〕戴震：〈答彭進士書〉，收於《全集》，頁1088。
〔註49〕勞思光：《新編中國哲學史》(廣西：廣西師範大學出版社，2005年)，頁608。
〔註50〕李哲賢：〈論荀子思想之矛盾〉，《興大中文學報》第12期（2007年），頁169。

　　就中國哲學史而論，如，孟子所用之「性」字，道家所用之「生」字或佛教初傳中國時所用之「空」字等，皆與當時之日常語言之意義不符。〔註51〕因此，當吾人在理解哲學理論之文獻時，若以為此文獻中之一切詞語必與當時日常語言中之用法相同，則大謬矣。

　　依此，戴震欲採用訓詁之方法，恢復《孟子》中主要詞語之原義，並以此批駁宋儒，甚或欲恢復原始儒學之原貌，此勢必有所不殆。而更遑論欲以此方法論建立其考證哲學，並取代宋、明理學。

五、結論

　　在佛、道二家之影響下，宋代儒者傾向於直觀地詮釋儒家學說而非訴諸古代經典之嚴密考證。由於不滿此一情況，乾嘉學者乃回歸漢代之解經方式來矯正宋代理學家之主觀研究方法。此種學問意謂著不僅是對理學之反動，而且是一種希望恢復儒家傳統真理之自我意識之努力。毫無疑問的，乾嘉學者是把重新檢證古代典籍此一需求視為其首要任務，為了達成此一目的，他們採用考證學方法作為恢復儒家真理之主要工具。

　　雖然，經典研究是乾嘉學者之主要重心所在；但是，他們的研究領域卻幾乎擴展到文化傳統之每一側面。如，音韻學、史學、地理學、數學和天文學等〔註52〕，經由他們的努力，無論是經學、訓詁學、音韻學、史學、方志、地理學、數學、金石學、辨偽及輯佚等皆作出貢獻，尤其是在辛勤的經典詮釋方面。〔註53〕乾嘉學者對古籍之詳密考證及注釋，其對字句之解釋皆較過去更為完善。凡此，皆說明乾嘉學者在古代學術方面之主要成就。〔註54〕

　　雖然，古籍已重新檢證，並加以修正，但是，乾嘉時期並未創造出新的思想潮流，亦未建立新的哲學學派，乾嘉學者乃古代文化之辛勤詮釋者，而非思想之原創者。〔註55〕此外，當他們專注於考證學研究時，他們對於傳統儒學所關切之議題，如，社會現實或經世致用等並不關心。

　　戴震被認為是當時主要之考證學家。因為，他的研究方法客觀而可靠，且

〔註51〕　勞思克：《新編中國哲學史》，頁609。
〔註52〕　梁啟超：《清代學術概論》，頁49～62。
〔註53〕　Chang, *Development of Neo-Confucian Thought*, v.2, p.339.
〔註54〕　Chang, *Development of Neo-Confucian Thought*, v.2, p.339.
〔註55〕　梁啟超：《清代學術概論》，頁33～55；See also Immanuel C. Y. Hsü, *The Rise of Modern China*（New York: Oxford University Press, 1975），p.89.

學問亦極為淵博。戴震學術研究之目的在於檢證古代經典而非保存漢學，在這方面，他已跳脫漢學之藩籬，此由其對考證方法、音韻學、曆算和水利學等皆有令人印象深刻之貢獻，足為明證。

戴震在當時被認為是一位獨特之思想家，並且，他認為考證學本質上並非即是目的，而只是顯現真理之一種手段而已。戴氏所發展出之研究方法代表著對宋代理學家方法論之一種改進，同時，可用來釐清傳統之哲學問題。此種方法學之價值在於它能精確地界定經典中主要詞語之原義，並且，依次地，對於理解傳統儒學之真貌亦是一重要之分水嶺。要之，戴震藉由此一考證之方法學來建立其考證哲學，並企圖以之來取代宋明理學。

然者，戴震「以語言學之觀點解決思想史中之問題」的方法，實有其限制。蓋一哲學家試圖建立一學說或理論時，其所使用之主要詞語或專有術語與當時之日常語言或通行語並不一致，因此，戴震採用語源學之方法來追溯經典中主要詞語之原義，並由此建立其考證哲學以恢復原始儒學之原貌，此勢必不可行。

戴震之哲學信念在當時並不為人所接受；然而，在十九世紀時，阮元（1764～1849）及焦循（1763～1820）採用和戴氏相同的方法去重建儒學中主要概念之意義。〔註56〕在二十世紀前，戴氏之思想並不為人所理解；而他的哲學亦受到忽視。直到二十世紀，戴震在中國思想史上之地位首先被章太炎（1869～1936）所認同，並使之為大眾所知曉。〔註57〕

〔註56〕阮元：《性命古訓》；焦循：《孟子正義》；See also Elman, *From Philosophy to Philology*, p.21.

〔註57〕章太炎：〈釋戴篇〉，收於上海人民出版社編：《章太炎全集》（上海：人民出版社，1985 年），第 4 冊，頁 122～124；also Elman, *From Philosophy to Philology*, p.21.有關章太炎之英文論著，見 Jer-shiarn Lee, *Chang Ping-lin（1869～1936）: A Political Radical and Cultural Conservative*（台北：文史哲出版社，1993 年）。

論章太炎及其終極關切——保存國粹

一、前言

在辛亥革命之歷史中，雖然章太炎〈1869～1936〉是以他在中國革命運動中所扮演的角色而知名，但他卻是一位獨特的思想家。章氏與同盟會中其他的領袖人物，如孫逸仙、黃興等人所不同的是：後者是在政治、軍事及組織工作方面扮演領導的角色；而章氏由於他是一位著名的古典學者，他的貢獻主要在於意識型態此一方面。也正是由於這種思想的獨特性，使得一般人們難以理解他，且時常對他產生誤解。同時，由於他思想的複雜性，這可以追溯到他思想的各種不同來源——由古代中國到近代西方，因此，他的思想，整體而言，似乎是與他本人及其世界有所衝突。

章氏由於在幼年時期讀過晚明遺老之著作而引發他的反滿情感。〔註1〕然而，這些情感並未使他立即成為一位革命者。事實上，儘管章氏反對康有為〈1858～1927〉對儒學所作之詮釋〔註2〕，但是，在1895年至1899年之間，章氏卻是康、梁改革運動之堅定擁護者。章氏是一直到1900年義和團事變爆發後，才改變他的政治立場，而由改革走向革命。到了1903年，章氏成為一位激進的革命者，並開始批評康有為之政治意識型態及其對儒學之詮釋方式，且甚而譏諷光緒皇帝為一小丑。〔註3〕結果，致使章氏在1903年6月捲入著

〔註1〕章太炎：〈我的平生與辦事方法〉，收於《章太炎的白話文》（台北：藝文印書館，1972年），頁88。

〔註2〕章太炎：《太炎先生自訂年譜》（台北：文海出版社，1972年），頁516。

〔註3〕章太炎：〈駁康有為論革命書〉，收於上海人民出版社編：《章太炎全集》，第四冊（上海：人民出版社，1985年），頁173～184。

名之蘇報案，並因此入獄三年。

1906 年 6 月，章氏出獄。不久，即成為同盟會之機關報——民報之主編、發行人及其主要撰文者。〔註4〕然而，在 1906 年至 1911 年之間，章氏卻變成一位溫和而非激進之革命者。他甚至批評胡漢民及汪精衛二人之觀點，認為他們在民報上所刊登之文章中，對於梁啟超〈1873～1929〉改革主張之攻擊過於激烈。〔註5〕同時章氏作為一位革命運動之發言人，他在民報上所發表之文章，其重心並不在對抗康有為之保皇或改革之觀念上，而是大多著重於處理中國國粹之保存方面。更有甚者，章氏是一位儒家學者，卻反對儒家之道德，甚至輕視儒家之一些觀念〔註6〕；並且，章氏是共和運動之領導者，但他卻譴責代議政治。〔註7〕章氏之觀念，整體而言，似乎與他自己與他的世界相衝突。

雖然，蕭公權及 Michael Gasster 兩位學者在他們的著作中皆曾指出章氏思想中似乎存有自相衝突之處〔註8〕，但是，他們在章氏思想之相關研究之中，並未能解答上述之問題。此外，我們從張玉法及朱浤源兩位學者之著作中，亦無法獲得滿意的解釋。〔註9〕

雖然，表面上，章氏之思想似乎是自相矛盾，但是，事實上卻一點也沒有不一致。由於章氏是一位著名的古典學者及同盟會之喉舌，並且，他的終極關切是保存國粹於不墜，而此亦是其觀念之所以貌似自相衝突之所自。究實而言，章氏思想中之不一致僅是表面如此，而非真實的。

本文主要就一八九五年至一九一一年間，章氏思想之轉變、矛盾之思想外觀及其與章氏之保存國粹此一終極關切間之關係做一考察，期能對章氏此一時期之思想有一相應而深入之理解。

〔註4〕 章太炎所主編之民報係由第七號至第十八號及第二十三號至二十四號。

〔註5〕 《太炎先生自訂年譜》，頁 11。

〔註6〕 《章太炎的白話文》，頁 91～92。

〔註7〕 章太炎：〈代議然否論〉，收於《章太炎全集》，第四冊，頁 300～311。

〔註8〕 蕭公權：《中國政治思想史》，下冊（台北：中國文化大學出版部，1980 年），頁 867～898 及 Michael Gasster, *Chinese Intellectuals and the Revolution of 1911:the Birth of Modern Chinese Radicalism*(Seattle:University of Washington, 1969), pp.190～227.

〔註9〕 張玉法：〈章炳麟〉，收入王壽南編：《中國歷代思想家》，第十冊（台北：商務印書館，1978 年），頁 5995～6059 及朱浤源：〈民報中的章太炎〉，《大陸雜誌》第 68 卷 第 2 期（1984 年 2 月），頁 14～43。

本文主要分成四部分：

（一）說明章氏對於保存國粹之關切，此亦章氏思想中之核心觀念。

（二）分析章氏在 1895 年至 1899 年間，作為一位改革者之生涯。

（三）說明章氏由改革至革命，此種政治立場改變之原因。

（四）分析章氏 1906 年至 1911 年間，其思想所呈現之衝突，並試著予以消滅甚或解除之。

二、章氏對於保存國粹之關切

雖然，章氏自 1895 年至 1899 年之間是一位改革者，並且，之後，他全心全意地支持革命，但是，保存國粹卻是章氏一生中最重要之使命。所謂國粹，章氏意指中國歷史和文化特質中仍適用於近代中國的那些要素。

章氏的教育和家庭環境造就他成為中國傳統文化之傳承者。在幼年時期，章氏曾先後受教於他的外祖父及父親。〔註 10〕他們教導他有關中國古代經典和歷史之知識。在他 23 歲時，章氏在一位著名的國學家——俞樾所主持的杭州詁經精舍繼續接受考證、歷史和經典方面之洗禮。〔註 11〕章氏在 28 歲前，在國學方面之造詣已非常深入。雖然，章氏並不願意在滿清統治之下參加科舉考試〔註 12〕，但是，他已經發展出他在考證及古代經典的終身興趣。甚而，在他從事改革及革命等政治活動的生涯中，章氏亦深深地沉潛於國學之研究中，並出版了許多他在國學方面最重要的著作。〔註 13〕1911 年後，章氏陸續發行了華國月刊〔註 14〕和制言半月刊〔註 15〕，並創立一所私人學校——章氏國學講習會〔註 16〕，藉此，章氏企圖保存中國文化於不墜。

作為一位國學家，章氏確信他一生負有保存中國文化的責任。他曾說，他一生的理想就是尊重國史和保存中國獨特的語言文字。〔註 17〕1903 年因蘇報案入獄時，章氏嘆道：「上天以國粹付余，……國故民紀，絕於余手，是則余

〔註 10〕 《太炎先生自訂年譜》，頁 2。

〔註 11〕 《太炎先生自訂年譜》，頁 3～4。

〔註 12〕 《太炎先生自訂年譜》，頁 2；頁 53。

〔註 13〕 這些著作分別是：《春秋左傳讀》、《新方言》、《莊子解故》、《文始》、《國故論衡》及《齊物論釋》。

〔註 14〕 《太炎先生自訂年譜》，頁 50。

〔註 15〕 《太炎先生自訂年譜》，頁 50。

〔註 16〕 《太炎先生自訂年譜》，頁 50。

〔註 17〕 張玉法：〈章炳麟〉，頁 6048。

之罪也。」〔註18〕章氏甚至在獄中所寫的家書中感傷地說:「吾死以後,中夏文化亦亡矣。」〔註19〕他認為國與國之間的不同就在於它們的歷史與語言文字。因此,當中國受到外國勢力入侵時,章氏必須捍衛中國歷史及語言文字於不墜。

　　雖然,章氏極力強調保存國粹之重要性,但是他對中國文化之態度並非全盤接收,而是以批判之方式加以取捨,並且,他非常確定文化中之那些要素是必須保存的,因此,章氏之接受中國文化是經由深思熟慮之選擇並予以去蕪存菁的。就章氏而言,國粹並非意指康有為所主張之孔教〔註20〕,而是指中國歷史。〔註21〕章氏所謂之歷史乃就廣義而言,其中又可分為三項:〔註22〕

（一）**語言文字**:藉著語言文字,人們能夠閱讀古書,並了解中國之歷史。因之,章氏甚至認為語言文字實乃人禽之辨之主要依據。他說:「且人類所以殊于鳥獸者,惟其能識往事,有過去之念耳。國粹盡亡,不知百年以前事,人與犬馬當何異哉?」〔註23〕

（二）**典章制度**:章氏認為「我們今日崇拜中國的典章制度,只是崇拜我們的社會主義。那不好的,雖要改良;那好的,必定應該頂禮膜拜。」〔註24〕他認為均田制是中國最特別優長之制度,是歐美各國所萬不能及的,且合於社會主義的制度。〔註25〕因為中國施行均田制度使得自魏晉至唐代「貧富不甚懸絕,地方制度容易施行。」〔註26〕至於中國極不好的制度,章氏亦略舉兩項:其一是刑名法律;另一則是科場選舉。章氏認為「中國法律雖然近於酷烈,」〔註27〕但是,法律之前卻是人人平等的。而章氏亦認為科舉制度原亦是最惡劣之制度,但是科舉制度之施行,貧人才有做官的希望。〔註28〕章氏認為「這兩件事,本是極不好的,

〔註18〕章太炎:〈癸卯獄中自記〉,收於《章太炎全集》,第四冊,頁144。
〔註19〕湯國梨編:《章太炎先生家書》(台北:文海出版社,1966年),頁101。
〔註20〕《章太炎的白話文》,頁96。
〔註21〕《章太炎的白話文》,頁96。
〔註22〕《章太炎的白話文》,頁96。
〔註23〕章太炎:〈印度人之論國粹〉,收於《章太炎全集》,第四冊,頁366。
〔註24〕章太炎:〈東京留學生歡迎會演說辭〉,收於湯志鈞編:《章太炎政論選集》,上冊(北京:中華書局,1977年),頁278～279。
〔註25〕章太炎:〈東京留學生歡迎會演說辭〉,頁278。
〔註26〕章太炎:〈東京留學生歡迎會演說辭〉,頁278。
〔註27〕章太炎:〈東京留學生歡迎會演說辭〉,頁278。
〔註28〕章太炎:〈東京留學生歡迎會演說辭〉,頁278。

尚且帶幾分社會主義的性質。」〔註29〕簡言之，章氏認為所有中國的制度都傾向於社會主義且能平等地適用於所有人。

（三）人物事跡：章氏認為中國人物，「其中最可崇拜的，有兩個人：一是晉末受禪的劉裕，一是南宋伐金的岳飛，都是用南方兵士打勝胡人，可使我們壯氣。」〔註30〕至於學問上的人物，章氏則特別推崇中國哲學上的周秦諸子〔註31〕，認為他們是中國最有學問的人。總之，章氏自云，提倡國粹意味著國人宜珍視自己的歷史。〔註32〕很明顯的，章氏之國粹概念指的是中國文化中之精粹。

章氏對於保存國粹之關切並不只是因為他是一位國學家，且是因為他認為保存國粹對國家之存亡有其重要性。在西方列強船堅砲利的威脅下，章氏恐怕中國文化會因之滅亡。為了避免外國勢力之征服，章氏相信，在中國實行改革或革命的措施都是必要的，而改革或革命最重要的使命是維護中國文化於不墜。因此章氏認為保存國粹較國家本身具有優先性。亦即國家之所以重要只是因為它對國粹之保存有必要性，並且，依次地，改革或革命對拯救國家之生存有其必要性。

三、維新時期之章太炎

從 1895 年開始，章氏已經是一位改良主義者。當中國在中日戰爭〈1894～1895〉中遭受挫敗後，章氏相信，中國在政治上必須採取改革措施才足以拯救國家於危亡。1895 年章氏加入一個維新組織——強學會，它是由康有為發起而成立的。〔註33〕1896 年，章氏進入時務報，這是由梁任公所創立的。〔註34〕據說，章氏在當時是一位維新運動之堅定支持者。甚至在康、梁維新運動失敗後，章氏仍未改變其支持維新之政治立場。章氏是一直到 1900 年義和團事件爆發後，才放棄他的維新立場而邁向革命之路。

雖然，章氏在幼年時期即已孕育反滿思想，但是，他之所以支持康、梁之改革乃是因為其主要關切在於國粹之保存。當中國面對西方列強勢力之入侵，

〔註29〕章太炎：〈東京留學生歡迎會演說辭〉，頁 278。
〔註30〕章太炎：〈東京留學生歡迎會演說辭〉，頁 279。
〔註31〕章太炎：〈東京留學生歡迎會演說辭〉，頁 279。
〔註32〕《章太炎的白話文》，頁 96。
〔註33〕馮自由：《中華民國開國前革命史》，上冊（台北：世界書局，1954 年），頁 112。
〔註34〕《太炎先生自訂年譜》，頁 5。

章氏希望滿清政府能抵禦外侮。章氏認為一次成功的改革將會強化政府捍衛國家之能力。因此，他說：「彼瀛國之既俘，永曆魯監國之既墜，而支那曠數百年而無君也，如之何其可也。」〔註35〕然而，吾人應該明白的是，章氏之所以支持改革，其目的並非想要維護滿清之政權，而是要拯救中國於危亡，並且他將國家之生存視為保存國粹之唯一方法。

　　甚至在1898年，康、梁之維新運動失敗後，章氏仍然獻身於改革運動，這主要是因為章氏認同康氏採用中國文化來進行改革，且其目的亦是為了保存中國之文化傳統。然而，章氏與康氏不同的是，康氏是今文學派之擁護者，其觀點是來自公羊傳；而章氏卻是古文學派之支持者，且在春秋經之詮釋上，章氏主張左傳優於公羊及穀梁二傳。雖然，據說章氏很早就已經反對康氏對於儒學之詮釋觀點，但是此種反對並未影響章氏在1895年加入強學會，且其後支持康、梁之維新運動。這是因為章氏在當時尚非古文學派之堅定支持者，在他當時的一些著作中，亦曾採用今文學派之觀點〔註36〕，而非全然採用古文學派之觀點。並且，章氏亦曾寫過一篇文章來捍衛康氏詮釋儒學之觀點。〔註37〕當時章氏反對康氏對於儒學之詮釋並不是很強烈，同時這也只是顯示章氏對於儒學之基本了解與康氏不同而已。章氏一直要到1900年之後才開始淨化中國文化之要素，確定自己的學術立場，並反對康氏之觀點。很明顯的，章氏在1895年至1899年間之所以支持康氏之改革，主要是因為康氏採用中國文化來進行改革，同時，也是因為康氏和他一樣，都是藉著改革來達成其目的：保存中國文化傳統於不墜。

四、章太炎邁向革命之路

　　促使章氏之政治立場由改革轉向革命的是1900年發生之義和團事變。這次事件升高了滿清政府之危機，因為八國聯軍在6月16日佔領大沽，並且清廷在6月21日向聯軍宣戰。〔註38〕由於義和團事變所帶來之危機，章氏乃參加由康有為之弟子——唐才常所組織之「國會」。〔註39〕此次國會之主要宗旨是：「一、保全中國自主之權，創造新自立國；二、決定不讓滿清政府有統治

〔註35〕湯志鈞編：《章太炎政論選集》，上冊，頁87。
〔註36〕湯志鈞：《章太炎年譜長編》，上冊（北京：中華書局，1979年），頁41～42。
〔註37〕湯志鈞編：《章太炎政論選集》，上冊，頁87～89。
〔註38〕蕭一山：《清代通史》，第四冊（台北：商務印書館，1962年），頁196～198。
〔註39〕馮自由：《中華民國開國前革命史》，下冊，頁76。

中國之權；三、清光緒皇帝復辟。」〔註40〕由於此會之宗旨曖昧，章氏於會中「當場批判了唐才常不當一面排滿，一面勤王，既不承認滿清政府，又稱擁護光緒皇帝，實屬大相矛盾，絕無成事之理，宣言脫社，割辮與絕。」〔註41〕由於辮子乃漢人臣服滿清統治之象徵，此種行動表現出章氏與滿清政府之最後決裂。章氏此時深信，中國之存亡絕不能依賴滿清之政權，因此，滿清政府必須加以推翻。他說：「滿州弗逐，欲士之愛國，民之敵愾，不可得也。浸微浸削，亦終為歐美之陪隸已矣。」〔註42〕自此而後，章氏明顯地即成為一位反滿之革命份子。

由於滿清政府無法抵抗外國勢力之入侵，章氏乃訴諸革命來拯救自己的國家。然而，對章氏而言，革命只是達成其終極目標之一種手段而已，而此目標乃是保存中國國粹。他說，若國人不知國粹，則將步入印度人之後塵，而為外人所統治。〔註43〕並且，章氏主張國人應由中國文化中去發掘革命之靈感，且利用國粹去激勵種性和增進國人之愛國熱情。〔註44〕章氏並且表達他進一步且更基本的信念──保存國粹乃一個國家之所以存在之使命及意義所在。他說：「且人類所以殊於鳥獸者，惟其能識往事，有過去之念耳。國粹盡亡，不知百年以前事，人與犬馬當何異哉？人無自覺，即為他人陵轢，無以為生；民族無自覺，即為他民族陵鑠，無以自存。然則抨彈國粹者，正使人為異種役耳！」〔註45〕很顯然地，章氏獻身革命主要是認為革命乃是維護中國文化並保證中國文化及學術傳統能繼續傳承下去的一種手段而已。

五、章太炎思想中之衝突

在 1906 年至 1911 年間，章氏之思想異常複雜，並且他的思想，整體看來，似乎與他自己及其世界相衝突。作為一個革命分子，章氏卻提倡國粹不遺餘力；他是一位國學家，卻又對儒學加以抨擊；更有進者，章氏雖提倡共和政體，卻又譴責代議政治，諸如此類，不一而足。究竟章氏思想中之不一致是真實如此，抑或祇是表象而已呢？

〔註40〕馮自由：《中華民國開國前革命史》，下冊，頁 77。
〔註41〕《太炎先生自訂年譜》，頁 7。
〔註42〕《章太炎全集》，第三冊，頁 120。
〔註43〕湯志鈞編：《章太炎政論選集》，上冊，頁 307。
〔註44〕《章太炎的白話文》，頁 91。
〔註45〕《章太炎全集》，第四冊，頁 366。

　　儘管章氏是革命運動中之一位領袖人物，他卻呼籲保存國粹。當 1906 年 6 月，章氏出獄時，隨即受到同盟會成員之熱烈歡迎，其後並為他們作了一次演說。〔註46〕然而，在這次的演說中，章氏並未暢論有關革命及政治方面之議題，卻大談國粹之重要。其後，在他主持民報期間，除了盡到主編之責任外，章氏大多沉浸於國學之研究及教學上。在這期間，章氏也出版了許多他在國學研究方面最重要的一些著作。作為一位革命家，章氏卻要求維護國粹。章氏之注重國粹保存，使他明顯地有別於參與革命運動之其他成員，且甚而與他自己的革命立場有所衝突。因為對當時大部分之成員而言，他們所關心的並非傳統文化之維護，而是為了保衛國家此一政治實體。雖然，章氏亦關心國家之存亡，但對章氏本人而言，國家並不僅僅是一政治實體而已，而且更是一文化實體。因之，章氏雖然仍舊關心國家富強之追求；然而，章氏之終極關切或目的卻是為了使傳統文化不致因外力之入侵而亡滅。因此，當滿清政府無力抵抗外力之入侵時，章氏乃訴諸革命以救國。然而，對章氏而言，革命或救國皆只是達成其保存國粹此一終極目的之手段而已。因此，從章氏對保存國粹之關切此一角度看來，就一點也不矛盾了。

　　另一看似衝突的觀念是：章氏是一位儒家學者，卻反對儒家之道德。〔註47〕因為，就章氏而言，「儒家之病，在以富貴利祿為心。」〔註48〕並且「用儒家之道德，故艱苦卓厲者絕無，而冒沒奔競者皆是。」〔註 49〕儘管儒學有此缺失，但是，章氏亦推崇孔子是古代之良史〔註50〕，且稱許他對中國教育及歷史之貢獻。〔註51〕況且，儒家在章氏所提倡之國粹中亦扮演重要之角色。例如，孔子、孟子及荀子皆是章氏在其國粹範疇中推崇之周秦諸子。由於章氏接受國粹之態度並非是全盤且毫無保留地接受傳統文化，而是批判性地接納中國文化。而在章氏眼中，儒學並非毫無瑕疵，其缺失即在誘使人追求祿利。因此，根據章氏保存國粹之關切此一角度而言，章氏稱許儒學中之精華，而批判其缺失，就不足為奇了。

〔註46〕沈延國：《記章太炎先生》（台北：文海出版社），頁 29～30。
〔註47〕湯志鈞編：《章太炎政論選集》，上冊，頁 289～291。
〔註48〕《章太炎的白話文》，頁 92。
〔註49〕章太炎：〈諸子學略說〉，收入湯志鈞編：《章太炎政論選集》，上冊，頁 289～291。
〔註50〕章太炎：〈訂孔〉，收入《章太炎全集》，第三冊，頁 135。
〔註51〕章太炎：〈駁建立孔教議〉，收入《章太炎全集》，第四冊，頁 196～197。

此外，章氏宣稱共和政體乃目前最進步之政體〔註52〕，但是，他卻譴責代議政體。〔註53〕這是因為章氏認為代議政體乃封建制度之遺跡〔註54〕，且不適用於平等之社會。他說：「代議政體非能伸民權，而適墬鬱之，蓋政府與齊民才有二階級耳。橫置議士於其間，即分為三。政府誠多一牽制者，齊民亦多一抑制者。代議者，封建之變形耳。君主立憲，其趣尤近。上必有貴族院，下必審諦戶口土田錢幣之數，至纖至悉。非承封建末流弗能。……去封建遠者，民皆平等；去封建近者，民有貴族黎庶之分。」〔註55〕由上可知，代議政體之特色是其上議院乃由貴族階級所組成〔註56〕，且是封建制度之遺制，是不適用於平等之社會。因此，章氏主張中國不宜採行代議政體，蓋其不適用於中國。

根據章氏國粹之概念，一個良好的制度應能平等地適用於社會人群，章氏之所以譴責代議政體，實因此制度是與平等不相容，且是封建之遺跡，更重要的是，此一制度是與章氏之國粹概念相違背的。

總之，章氏思想中所呈現之矛盾外觀，大多是可以消滅甚至解消的，只要吾人了解此乃出自章氏致力於保存國粹之結果所致；而保存國粹之努力又是章氏一生之思想脈絡中最首尾一貫的。因為，對章氏本人而言，所有這些表面上所呈現之矛盾紛紜之觀念，皆只是達成其保存國粹此一終極目的之手段而已。因之，章氏本人在政治立場或觀點上之改變或不一致，從章氏保存國粹之關切此一角度而言，就一點也不矛盾了。

六、結論

雖然，章氏在革命運動中極其有名；然而身為國學家的他卻因而更享盛名。在章氏一生之經歷中，參與維新或革命皆只是他生命中的插曲，而致力於國粹保存卻是他畢生之使命。因此，致力於保存國粹之努力乃章氏一生思想脈絡中最首尾一貫的。當中國受到外力侵逼之危機時，章氏深恐中國文化會遭此威脅而滅亡。為了維護國粹，章氏乃訴諸改革和革命以救之。然而，對章氏而言，改革和革命皆只是保存國粹之一種手段而已。

章氏乃同盟會之領袖之一。然而，章氏注重國粹保存卻使他明顯地與其他

〔註52〕 章太炎：《章太炎的白話文》，頁94。
〔註53〕 章太炎：〈代議然否論〉，頁456～470。
〔註54〕 章太炎：〈代議然否論〉，頁456。
〔註55〕 章太炎：〈代議然否論〉，頁456。
〔註56〕 章太炎：〈代議然否論〉，頁456。

成員有所區隔。並且由於他的思想極其複雜，整體看來，似乎自身充滿矛盾。但是，所有這些表面上呈現之矛盾觀念，皆只是達成其保存國粹此一目的之手段，因此，從此一角度看來，他的思想就一點也不矛盾了。

雖然，章氏提倡中國文化不遺餘力，除了致力於國學之教學與研究外，他也參與革命等政治活動。蓋作為一位知識份子，他應當關心國事，尤其是當中國面臨危亡之秋。章氏乃中國傳統知識分子之典型，他對自己國家的責任從不敢或忘。並且，他不僅致力於國學研究，且將他的理念付諸實踐。

學術與政治之間——
論章太炎及其生涯抉擇之兩難

一、前言

　　章太炎（1869～1936）乃近代中國史上一位主要之思想家、學者及政治行動家。由於章氏行文之風格出自魏、晉，文字過於艱深古雅，加之其思想又深受西方及本土思想之多重影響，凡此皆足以使其思想令人難以理解。

　　雖然章炳麟在 1911 年之辛亥革命中極其有名；然而，身為國學家的他卻因之而更享盛名。章氏之生平與思想反映了他那一世代之知識分子中，徘徊於學術與政治間那種不安之關係；並且章氏對於保存國粹之鼓吹更為二十世紀初期影響深遠之國粹運動鋪路。

　　章氏自幼即深受清代漢學之薰習，日後且成為清季古文學派之最後一位大師。由於漢學傳統強調為學術而學術之精神，並且學術與政治須分離。因此，當章氏於 1895 年開始參與政治活動時，即使他處於學術與政治間抉擇之兩難；而章氏如何解決此一困境呢？

　　雖然，張灝和汪榮祖兩位學者在其著作中〔註1〕，皆對章氏早年放棄學術研究而投身政治，當初是否面臨學術與政治間抉擇之困境此一問題，提出其看法，然而，從其在章氏思想之相關研究中，實無法獲得令人滿意之解釋。

〔註1〕 Chang Hao, *Chinese Intellectuals in Crisis: Search for Order and Meaning, 1890～1911*(Berkeley: University of California Press, 1987); Wong Young-tsu, *Search for Modern Nationalism: Zhang Binglin and Revolutionary China, 1869～1936*(Hong Kong: Oxford University Press, 1989).

張灝指出,章氏在年輕時即接受兩種不同的學術理想:一種是強調道德實踐功用的學術;另一種是與政治無關,純粹知識追求的學術。其後,章氏選擇前者,在 1896 年投身康、梁的改革陣營中。章氏之投身政治,其師俞樾並不諒解。然而,事實上,章氏終其一生,皆在結合政治之行動主義和學術的志業,亦即章氏並沒有因為參與政治而放棄學術之鑽研。〔註2〕

而汪榮祖則認為,章氏從 1890 年進入詁經精舍,跟隨俞樾研讀古代經典,當章氏決定離開精舍,投入改革陣營,這無疑是章氏一生中之重大決定。汪氏認為,章氏作此決定時一點也不困難,因為,他並不打算放棄學術,誠如他日後所證明的。況且,當國家面臨危亡之秋,章氏更不能將自己侷限於象牙塔之中。〔註3〕

實者,章氏走出書齋而投入政治,這無疑是章氏一生中之重大決定。汪氏認為,章氏在作此決定時,一點也不困難,因為,他並不打算放棄學術,誠如他日後所證明的。唯此一看法,以章氏日後之表現,來證明其當初作此生命中之重大決定時之心理層面,似有未妥。而張氏亦有類似之看法。唯張氏指出,章氏在年輕時,已接受兩種不同的學術理想,一是強調道德實踐功用的學術;另一為與政治無關,純粹知識追求的學術。因之,章氏選擇前者而投入政治,張氏對於章氏此時處境之抉擇,亦只是輕描淡寫。唯學術與政治乃兩種完全不同之領域,面對抉擇時,內心必充滿煎熬,而本文則特別強調章氏在政治與學術之間抉擇之兩難(dilemma),似較能貼近章氏面對困境時之心理樣貌。依此,本文試圖從章氏之終極關切——保存國粹此一側面來探究章氏如何解決其所面對之上述困境,冀能對其思想有一相應而深入之理解與把握。

二、章太炎之終極關切——保存國粹

雖然,章太炎自 1895 年至 1899 年之間是一位改革者,並且,之後,他全心全意地支持革命,但是,保存國粹卻是章氏一生中最重要之使命。所謂國粹,章氏意指中國歷史和文化特質中仍適用於近代中國的那些要素。

章氏的教育和家庭環境造就他成為中國傳統文化之傳承者。在幼年時期,章氏曾先後受教於他的外祖父及父親。〔註4〕他們教導他有關中國古代經典和

〔註2〕Chang, pp.105～106.
〔註3〕Wong, pp.8～9.
〔註4〕章太炎:《太炎先生自訂年譜》(台北:文海出版社,1972年),頁2。

歷史之知識。在他 23 歲時，章氏在一位著名的國學家─俞樾所主持的杭州詁經精舍繼續接受考證、歷史和經典方面之洗禮。〔註 5〕章氏在 28 歲前，在國學方面之造詣已非常深入。雖然，章氏並不願意在滿清統治之下參加科舉考試〔註 6〕，但是，他已經發展出他對考證及古代經典的終身興趣。甚而，在他從事改革及革命等政治活動的生涯中，章氏亦深深地沉潛於國學之研究中，並出版了許多他在國學方面最重要的著作。〔註 7〕1911 年後，章氏陸續發行了《華國》月刊〔註 8〕和《制言》半月刊〔註 9〕，並創立一所私人學校─章氏國學講習會〔註 10〕，藉此，章氏企圖保存中國文化於不墜。

作為一位國學家，章氏確信他一生負有保存中國文化的責任。他曾說，他一生的理想就是尊重國史和保存中國獨特的語言文字。〔註 11〕1903 年因蘇報案入獄時，章氏嘆道：

> 上天以國粹付余，自炳麟之初生，迄於今茲，三十有六歲。鳳鳥不
> 至，河不出圖，惟余亦不任宅其位，肇素王素臣之迹是踐，豈直抱
> 殘守闕而已，又將官其財物，恢明而光大之！懷未得遂，纍於仇國，
> 惟金火相革歟？則猶有繼述者。至於支那闊碩壯美之學，而遂斬其
> 統緒，國故民紀，絕於余手，是則余之罪也。〔註 12〕

章氏甚至在獄中所寫的家書中感傷地說：「不死於清廷購捕之時，而死於民國告成之後，又何言哉！吾死以後，中夏文化亦亡矣。」〔註 13〕他認為國與國之間的不同就在於它們的歷史與語言文字。因此，當中國受到外國勢力入侵時，章氏必須捍衛中國歷史及語言文字於不墜。

雖然，章氏極力強調保存國粹之重要性，然而，章氏何以要提倡國粹呢？他說：

〔註 5〕章太炎：《太炎先生自訂年譜》，頁 3～4。

〔註 6〕章太炎：《太炎先生自訂年譜》，頁 2。

〔註 7〕這些著作分別是：《春秋左傳讀》、《新方言》、《莊子解故》、《文始》、《國故論衡》及《齊物論釋》。

〔註 8〕湯志鈞編：《章太炎年譜長編》，下冊（北京：中華書局，1979 年），頁 727。

〔註 9〕湯志鈞編：《章太炎年譜長編》，下冊，頁 959。

〔註 10〕湯志鈞編：《章太炎年譜長編》，下冊，頁 947。

〔註 11〕張玉法：〈章炳麟〉，收入王壽南編：《中國歷代思想家》，第十冊（台北：商務印書館，1978 年），頁 6048。

〔註 12〕章太炎：〈癸卯獄中自記〉，收於上海人民出版社編：《章太炎全集》，第四冊（上海：人民出版社，1985 年），頁 144。

〔註 13〕湯國梨編：《章太炎先生家書》（台北：文海出版社，1966 年），頁 101。

為甚提倡國粹？不是要人尊信孔教，只是要人愛惜我們漢種的歷史。
這個歷史，是就廣義說的，其中可以分為三項：一是語言文字，二
是典章制度，三是人物事迹。近來有一種歐化主義的人，總說中國
人比西洋人所差甚遠，所以自甘暴棄，說中國必定滅亡，黃種必定
勦絕。因為他不曉得中國的長處，見得別無可愛，就把愛國愛種的
心，一日衰薄一日。若他曉得，我想就是全無心肝的人，那愛國愛
種的心，必定風發泉湧，不可遏抑的。〔註14〕

但是他對中國文化之態度並非全盤接收，而是以批判之方式加以取捨，並
且，他非常確定文化中之那些要素是必須保存的，因此，章氏之接受中國文化
是經由深思熟慮之選擇並予以去蕪存菁的。就章氏而言，國粹並非意指康有為
所主張之孔教〔註15〕，而是指中國歷史。〔註16〕

章氏對於保存國粹之關切並不只是因為他是一位國學家，且是因為他認
為保存國粹對國家之存亡有其重要性。在西方列強船堅砲利的威脅下，章氏恐
怕中國文化會因之滅亡。為了避免外國勢力之征服，章氏相信，在中國實行改
革或革命的措施都是必要的，而改革或革命最重要的使命是維護中國文化於
不墜。因此，章氏認為保存國粹較國家本身具有優先性。亦即國家之所以重要
只是因為它對國粹之保存有其必要性，並且，依次地，改革或革命對拯救國家
之生存有其必要性。

三、章太炎生涯抉擇之兩難

從 1895 年開始，章氏已經是一位改良主義者。當中國在中日戰爭〈1894
～1895〉中遭受挫敗後，章氏相信，中國在政治上必須採取改革措施才足以
拯救國家於危亡。此次挫敗帶給中國人之衝擊遠較之前任何一次中國敗在外
強手中來得更大。〔註17〕這次戰爭也相對地證實了在中國已經實行二十多年
的自強運動是徹底失敗的。〔註18〕而更令大多數中國人震驚和憤怒的是中國

〔註14〕 湯志鈞編：《章太炎年譜長編》，上冊，頁 213。
〔註15〕 章太炎：《章太炎的白話文》（台北：藝文印書館，1972 年），頁 96。
〔註16〕 章太炎：《章太炎的白話文》（台北：藝文印書館，1972 年），頁 96。
〔註17〕 Chang Hao, "Intellectual Change and the Reform Movement, 1890～8", in Denis
Twitchett and John Fairbank eds., *The Cambridge History of China* (Cambridge:
Cambridge University Press, 1980), v. 11, p.291.
〔註18〕 Immanuel C.Y. Hsu, "Late Ch'ing Foreign Relations, 1866～1905," in *The
Cambridge History of China,* v.11, pp.106～107.

此一泱泱大國竟然會敗給向來被認為在文化上和國力上皆遠遠不如中國的落後國家——日本。〔註19〕此次的挫敗也因此將大多數中國人從美夢中喚醒——原來以為只要採用西方之科技，中國即可經由自強運動而成為一個強國。〔註20〕因此，許多中國知識分子開始意識到，除非中國在政治上進行根本的改革，否則中國的生存將令人堪憂。而康有為之改良主義於此知識變動之際，就顯得非常突出。

雖然，康有為在 1888 年就已經向清廷上書，並提出中國在政治上有其改革之必要，然而，卻都徒勞無功。〔註21〕直到 1895 年中國戰敗後，大規模的改革才開始推展。1895 年春，康有為趁著在北京應試的機會，聯合各省應試舉人一千三百多人發動「公車上書」，聯合抗議馬關條約，並向清廷提出改革之請願。八月，康氏在北京籌設強學會，目標在於政治改革。兩個月之後，康氏於上海設立強學會之分會。〔註22〕

當章太炎仍在詁經精舍潛心向學時，他得知中國於 1894 年甲午戰爭中慘敗於日本。章氏注意到中國正處於飄搖欲墜之情境，此誠如他所說：「雖然，目睹其支體骨肉之裂而不忍，去之而不可，則惟強力忍詬以圖之。」〔註23〕當中國面臨列強瓜分之危機時，章氏再也無法忍受，他必須挺身而出。因此，原來過著書齋式寧靜生活之章太炎，受到甲午戰爭戰敗和國家危亡之刺激以及康、梁維新變法運動之影響，再也無法壓抑內心之激動，於是，章氏決定走出書齋，投身政治活動中。當章氏獲悉上海成立強學會分會時，他即寄出會費，申請入會。1896 年，章氏離開詁經精舍，並獲邀擔任時務報之撰述。〔註24〕

當章太炎決定離開詁經精舍而投身政治時，此舉令其師俞樾深感不悅。〔註25〕俞氏認為，章氏此一作法係背離漢學學派之傳統。蓋漢學傳統強調為學術而學術之精神，且學術必須與政治完全分離。因之，章太炎之離開學術而投身政治，確使他陷入學術與政治抉擇之兩難。對於此一問題，張灝和汪榮祖二

〔註19〕 Chang Hao, "Intellectual Change and the Reform Movement, 1890～8", p.291.
〔註20〕 Leung Man-kam, "Chang Ping-lin: His Life and Career", *Lien-ho shu-yuan hsueh-pao 8* (1970), p.97.
〔註21〕 湯志鈞編：《章太炎年譜長編》，上冊，頁 9～10。
〔註22〕 湯志鈞編：《章太炎年譜長編》，上冊，頁 25。
〔註23〕 章太炎：〈明獨〉，收入姜義華編：《章太炎選集》（上海：人民出版社，1981 年），頁 7。
〔註24〕 《太炎先生自訂年譜》，頁 5。
〔註25〕 《太炎先生自訂年譜》，頁 5。

位學者皆提出其看法。張灝指出，章氏之投身政治，其師俞樾並不諒解，然而，章氏終其一生並未因參與政治而放棄學術之鑽研。因之，章氏之投入政治，張灝對於章氏此時處境之抉擇，亦只是輕描淡寫。至於汪榮祖雖然認為，章太炎走出書齋而投身政治係章氏一生中之重大決定。但汪氏以為，章氏作此決定時一點也不困難，蓋章氏並不打算放棄學術，誠如其日後所證明的。

　　張灝和汪榮祖二位學者對於章氏面對此一人生之重大決定時，似乎並不認為章氏之內心有任何之煎熬、掙扎。唯學術與政治乃兩種完全不同之領域，章氏選擇後者而放棄前者，此無疑是章氏一生中之重大決定，因之，當他對此生命中之重大關卡作出決定時，內心想必充滿煎熬。尤其，章氏自幼即接受清代漢學之薰習，日後且成為清末古文學派之最後一位大師，因此，當他選擇放棄學術而投身政治時，其內心能不充滿掙扎與壓力？更何況中國學術傳統，尤其是漢學傳統特別強調家法、師道，章太炎之選擇投身政治，不僅不為其本師俞樾所諒解，且其師甚而感到極其不悅，謂其背棄漢學傳統，蓋漢學傳統強調純粹知識之追求，且與政治完全無涉。依此，當章氏選擇投身政治時，一者，他是放棄其當時藉以安身立命之漢學；再者，他的決定是違背師命及漢學傳統，因之，作此生命中重大決定之章太炎，確是令其處於學術與政治間抉擇之兩難，然則，章太炎如何解決此一困境呢？

　　實者，章太炎自幼即深受清代漢學之薰習，其後，進入清代漢學大師俞樾所主持之詁經精舍深造，接受俞氏之教誨，章氏日後且成為清末古文學派之最後一位大師。依此，中國傳統文化或漢學係章氏一生安身立命之所在。因之，章氏曾極自負地說，「上天以國粹付余」〔註26〕，並說，「吾死以後，中夏文化亦亡矣。」〔註27〕可知，章氏心中念茲在茲的乃保存國粹或維護傳統文化於不墜，尤其是中國受到外國勢力之侵襲時。而保存國粹乃章氏一生之職志或終極關切。因此，章氏特別強調國粹或國學之重要性。他指出，國粹或國學乃國家所以成立之源頭，國粹係國家所以存在之必要條件，且若國家不幸衰亡，而國粹不絕，則國家仍有復興之希望。〔註28〕依此，章氏所秉持之保存國粹足以挽救國家於危亡此一信念似乎為其所面對之困境提供一解答。

　　當然，作為一個知識分子，章太炎深知國家興亡，匹夫有責之道理。因之，

〔註26〕章太炎：〈癸卯獄中自記〉，頁144。
〔註27〕湯國梨編：《章太炎先生家書》，頁101。
〔註28〕湯志鈞編：《章太炎年譜長編》，上冊，頁215；頁295。

當中國受到外國勢力入侵而面臨危亡之秋，深處書齋之中的章氏，其心裡勢必極為焦慮，希望也能投入政治，為國家盡一份心力。然而，身為一位學者，學術乃其一生之志業，尤其，從事漢學研究，學術必須與政治完全切割。若離開書齋而投身政治活動，章氏深知此舉等於是背棄師門，且背離漢學學派之傳統，其內心之掙扎、煎熬及壓力何其之大。因之，當章氏面對此一生命中之重大決定時，確是使其處於學術與政治間抉擇之兩難。

然而，章氏認為，在外國列強船堅砲利之威脅下，中國文化恐怕會因之而滅亡。為了避免外國勢力之征服，並進而使中國文化因而衰亡，章氏相信，在中國進行政治改革之措施是必要的，蓋一次成功的改革將會強化政府捍衛國家之能力，而從事改革最重要之使命是維護中國文化於不墜。因之，章太炎深信，保存國粹較國家本身具有優先性，亦即，國家之所以重要只是因為它對國粹之保存有其必要性，並且，依次地，改革對拯救國家之生存有其必要性。因之，章氏雖然參與政治，他卻從未放棄其漢學研究，蓋章氏相信國家之生存有賴於國粹之保存，並且保存國粹可以強化國家之生存能力。

雖然，章氏在幼年時期即已孕育反滿思想，但是，他之所以支持康、梁之改革乃是因為其主要關切在於國粹之保存。當中國面對西方列強勢力之入侵，章氏希望滿清政府能抵禦外侮。章氏認為，一次成功的改革將會強化政府捍衛國家之能力。因此，他說：「彼瀛國之既俘，永曆魯監國之既墜，而支那曠數百年而無君也，如之何其可也。」〔註29〕然而，章氏之所以支持改革，其目的並非想要維護滿清之政權，而是要拯救中國於危亡，並且他將國家之生存視為保存國粹之唯一方法。

甚至在 1898 年，康、梁之維新運動失敗後，章氏仍然獻身於改革運動，這主要是因為章氏認同康氏採用中國文化來進行改革，且其目的亦是為了保存中國之文化傳統。然而，章氏與康氏不同的是，康氏是今文學派之擁護者，其觀點是來自公羊傳；而章氏卻是古文學派之支持者，且在春秋經之詮釋上，章氏主張左傳優於公羊及穀梁二傳。雖然，據說章氏很早就已經反對康氏對於儒學之詮釋觀點，但是此種反對並未影響章氏在 1895 年加入強學會，且其後支持康、梁之維新運動。這是因為章氏在當時尚非古文學派之堅定支持者，在他當時的一些著作中，亦曾採用今文學派之觀點〔註30〕，而非全然採用古文學

〔註29〕湯志鈞編：《章太炎政論選集》，上冊，頁 87。
〔註30〕湯志鈞：《章太炎年譜長編》，上冊，頁 41～42。

派之觀點。並且,章氏亦曾寫過一篇文章來捍衛康氏詮釋儒學之觀點。〔註31〕
當時章氏反對康氏對於儒學之詮釋並不是很強烈,同時這也只是顯示章氏對
於儒學之基本了解與康氏不同而已。章氏一直要到 1900 年之後才開始淨化中
國文化之要素,確定自己的學術立場,並反對康氏之觀點。很明顯的,章氏在
1895 年至 1899 年間之所以支持康氏之改革,主要是因為康氏採用中國文化來
進行改革,同時,也是因為康氏和他一樣,都是藉著改革來達成其目的:保存
中國文化傳統於不墜。

綜言之,1895 年章氏加入一個維新組織──強學會,它是由康有為發起而
成立的。〔註32〕1896 年,章氏進入時務報,這是由梁任公所創立的。〔註33〕
據說,章氏在當時是一位維新運動之堅定支持者。甚至在康、梁維新運動失敗
後,章氏仍未改變其支持維新之政治立場。章氏是一直到 1900 年義和團事件
爆發後,才放棄他的維新立場而邁向革命之路。

四、章太炎邁向革命之路

當章太炎仍是一位改良主義者時,他認為一次成功之改革可以強化滿清
政府抵禦外國勢力入侵之能力。然而,章氏指出,若滿清政府無法抵抗列強之
入侵,他將放棄滿清而投入革命之陣營。對章氏而言,選擇改革或革命之方式
完全在於何者可以拯救中國於危亡。因之,若改革無法救中國,則唯一之選擇
就只有訴諸革命了。

促使章氏之政治立場由改革轉向革命的是 1900 年發生之義和團事變。這
次事件升高了滿清政府之危機,因為八國聯軍在 6 月 16 日佔領大沽,並且清
廷在 6 月 21 日向聯軍宣戰。〔註34〕由於義和團事變所帶來之危機,章氏乃參
加由康有為之弟子──唐才常所組織之「國會」。〔註35〕此次國會之主要宗旨
是:「一、保全中國自主之權,創造新自立國;二、決定不讓滿清政府有統治
中國之權;三、清光緒皇帝復辟。」〔註36〕由於此會之宗旨曖昧,章氏於會中
「當場批判了唐才常不當一面排滿,一面勤王,既不承認滿清政府,又稱擁護

〔註31〕湯志鈞:《章太炎年譜長編》,上冊,頁 87~89。
〔註32〕馮自由:《中華民國開國前革命史》,上冊(台北:世界書局,1954 年),頁 112。
〔註33〕《太炎先生自訂年譜》,頁 5。
〔註34〕蕭一山:《清代通史》,第四冊(台北:商務印書館,1962 年),頁 196~198。
〔註35〕馮自由:《中華民國開國前革命史》,下冊,頁 76。
〔註36〕馮自由:《中華民國開國前革命史》,下冊,頁 77。

光緒皇帝，實屬大相矛盾，絕無成事之理，宣言脫社，割辮與絕。」〔註37〕由於辮子乃漢人臣服滿清統治之象徵，此種行動表現出章氏與滿清政府之最後決裂。章氏此時深信，中國之存亡絕不能依賴滿清之政權，因此，滿清政府必須加以推翻。他說：「滿州弗逐，欲士之愛國，民之敵愾，不可得也。浸微浸削，亦終為歐美之陪隸已矣。」〔註38〕自此而後，章氏明顯地即成為一位反滿之革命份子。

　　由於滿清政府無法抵抗外國勢力之入侵，章氏乃訴諸革命來拯救自己的國家。然而，對章氏而言，革命只是達成其終極目標之一種手段而已，而此目標乃是保存中國國粹。他說，若國人不知國粹，則將步入印度人之後塵，而為外人所統治。〔註39〕並且，章氏主張國人應由中國文化中去發掘革命之靈感，且利用國粹去激勵種性和增進國人之愛國熱情。〔註40〕章氏並且表達他進一步且更基本的信念─保存國粹乃一個國家之所以存在之使命及意義所在。他說：

> 且人類所以殊於鳥獸者，惟其能識往事，有過去之念耳。國粹盡亡，不知百年以前事，人與犬馬當何異哉？人無自覺，即為他人陵轢，無以為生；民族無自覺，即為他民族陵轢，無以自存。然則抨彈國粹者，正使人為異種役耳！〔註41〕

　　很顯然地，章氏獻身革命主要是認為革命乃是維護中國文化並保證中國文化及學術傳統能繼續傳承下去的一種手段而已。

五、民國時期之章太炎

　　中華民國建立之後，章太炎在政治舞台上仍極其活躍。除了參與政治活動外，章氏並繼續抨擊任何足以危及中國之主權與文化之行動或個人。

　　1912 年中華民國成立後，孫中山先生宣誓就任臨時大總統。章太炎應中山先生之邀請，擔任總統府樞密顧問。其後，袁世凱接任大總統，並任命章氏為總統府高等顧問，是年冬天，章氏接受袁氏任命為東三省籌邊使。1917 年中山先生就任軍政府海陸軍大元帥，章氏受任命為軍政府秘書長。1920 年應

〔註37〕湯志鈞：《章太炎年譜長編》，上冊，頁 108。
〔註38〕湯志鈞：《章太炎年譜長編》，上冊，頁 111。
〔註39〕湯志鈞編：《章太炎政論選集》，上冊，頁 307。
〔註40〕《章太炎的白話文》，頁 91。
〔註41〕章太炎：〈印度人之論國粹〉，收入《章太炎全集》，第四冊，頁 366。

譚延闓邀請，共同推行「聯省自治」運動。其後，章氏並繼續抨擊任何足以危及中國主權與文化之行動或個人。1924年，他公開反對國共合作，1926年，章氏通電反對北伐。1931年，918事變發生，章氏對時局多所建言，並呼籲抗日，號召青年拯救國家於危亡之秋。〔註42〕

　　章太炎除參與政治活動外，並獻身於傳統學術文化之教學與研究。章氏弟子於1912年發起國學會，並請章氏擔任會長。1913年起，章氏開始講學，直至其去世前。章氏之提倡國粹，推動國學之研習不遺餘力。此外，章氏並發行了《華國》月刊及《制言》半月刊此兩種學術刊物，經由這些媒介，章氏致力於中國傳統文化之保存與發揚。因之，致力於國粹之保存乃是章氏一生中最前後一貫之思想脈絡，且是他一生中最重要之使命。

六、結論

　　章太炎乃近代中國史上一位主要之思想家、學者及政治行動家。雖然，章炳麟在1911年之辛亥革命中極其有名；然而，身為國學家的他卻因之而更享盛名。章氏之生平與思想反映了他那一世代之知識分子中，徘徊於學術與政治間那種不安之關係；並且章氏對於保存國粹之鼓吹更為二十世紀初期影響深遠之國粹運動鋪路。

　　章氏自幼即深受清代漢學之薰習，日後且成為清季古文學派之最後一位大師。由於漢學傳統強調為學術而學術之精神，並且學術與政治須分離。因此，當章氏於一八九五年開始參與政治活動時，即使他處於學術與政治間抉擇之兩難；而章氏如何解決此一困境呢？實者，章氏所秉持之保存國粹足以挽救國家於危亡此一信念似乎為其所面對之困境提供一解答。

　　章氏認為，在外國列強船堅砲利之威脅下，中國文化恐怕會因之而滅亡。為了避免外國勢力之征服，並進而使中國文化因而衰亡，章氏相信，在中國進行政治改革之措施是必要的，蓋一次成功的改革將會強化政府捍衛國家之能力，而從事改革最重要之使命是維護中國文化於不墜。因之，章太炎深信，保存國粹較國家本身具有優先性，亦即，國家之所以重要只是因為它對國粹之保存有其必要性，並且，依次地，改革對拯救國家之生存有其必要性。對章氏而言，改革或革命只是達成其保存國粹此一終極關切之手段而已。

〔註42〕何成軒：〈章太炎生平大事年表〉，收於《章太炎評傳》（河南：教育出版社，1990年），頁350～360。

　　章氏一生對保存國粹之執著，明顯地表現於他兩種不同之生涯中：一是政治行動家；而另一則是國學家。民國建立之後，章氏在政治舞台上仍舊十分活躍；章氏並繼續抨擊任何足以危及中國之主權與文化之行動或個人。除了參與政治之外，章氏並獻身於傳統學術文化之教學與研究。因之，致力於國粹之保存乃是章氏一生中最前後一貫之思想脈絡，且是他一生中最重要之使命。

參、中國思想：英文篇

On Li Kou's Utilitarian Thought in Northern Sung

I. Introduction

In the Pre-Ch'in dynasty (221~206 B.C.), Confucius, Mencius and Hsun Tzu, orginally proposed all the main Confucian ideals of life and culture, and the central Confucian view of the universe. These three great figures in early Confucianism were the most original and creative contributors to the Confucian tradition. The central core of Confucian thought, which was laid down by these ancient Confucians, was the ideal of human life as a life of sagehood[1], which implied that every man could become a sage through cultivating his own moral potentiality. This idea remained as a fundamental spirit in Confucian tradition.

In the Han dynasty (206B.C.~220A.D.), since Confucian scholars expressed their thoughts very differently from those of ancient Confucians, and even concealed the true character of ancient Confucianism, the study of Confucian thought on the whole ceased to make any significant progress. Some Han scholars, such as Tung Chung-shu (179~104 B.C.), regarded Confucius as a god decended from Heaven, and believed that sagehood was beyond an ordinary man because he was not born with the abilities as those of the sages. In addition, since Han scholars applied the

---

1 T'ang Chun-I, "The Spirit and Development of Neo-Confucianism", in Arne Naess and Alastair Hannay eds., *Invitation to Chinese Philosophy* (Copenhagen: Scandinavian University Press, 1972), p.56.

ideas of Yin-Yang school and the theory of Five Elements to interpret the Confucian thought, they almost misinterpreted the spirit of Confucianism.

After the Han dynasty, there came a noticeable revival of Taoism called "Neo-Taoism" in the Wei-Chin dynasty (220~420). And in the T'ang dynasty(618~907), most of the great thinkers were Buddhist monks, for this was the golden age of Buddhism in China. From the T'ang to the Five Dynasties, Buddhism was the main current of Chinese philosophical thought. Although Confucian scholars continued to exist, they did not make any significant innovations in Confucian philosophy.

Down to the Sung dynasty (960~1279), Sung Confucians believed that an ordinary man could become a sage from within, an idea which had been lost to Confucianism since the Han dynasty. Moreover, they claimed that they had reached a new height in the Confucian tradition, for they introduced new contents, new formulation, and investigated new depths in Confucianism.[2] So there came the revival of Confucianism called "Neo-Confucianism" in Sung times.

In general, the term "Neo-Confucianism" referred to the Philosophy of Principle (Li-hsueh) which was identified with the entire Sung-Ming philosophical tradition. The Neo-Confucian philosophers in the long and distinguished genealogy, from Chou Tun-i, Chang Tsai, the two Ch'eng brothers,. Chu-Hsi, and Lu Hsiang-shan in Sung times all the way to Wang Yang-Ming and Liu Tsung-chou in the Ming dynasty (1368~1644), were primarily concerned with the quest for the substance of Tao and sought to establish, chiefly through metaphysical speculations, Confucian moral principles.[3] Although this type of metaphysical speculation was essentially new and remarkable to the Sung revival of Confucian learning, at least in Northern Sung times the Philosophy of Principle was not the main stream of Confucianism. It was not until the Southern Sung times when the Philosophy of Principle began to occupy the central place of Neo-Confucianism, and was accepted as the orthodoxy. In the Northern Sung, while the revival of Confucianism was on a large scale, the Philosophy of Principle was nothing but a branch.

2　Liu James, T.C., *Reform in Sung China* (Cambridge: Harvard University Press, 1959), p.22.

3　Yu Ying-shih, "Rise of Ch'ing Confucian Intellectualism", *The Tsing Hua Journal of Chinese Studies* 11/1(1975), p.121.

In the broad frame of the Confucian heritage, the Confucian Tao (Way) might be divided into three major categories: classical studies, inner sageness (nei-sheng), and outer kingliness (wai-wang). Of these three aspects, classical studies referred to the Confucian Classics, which were considered as a medium for preserving and communicating the Confucian truth in all its forms. The "inner sageness" meant to emphasize on the moral self-cultivation leading to personal self-realization; however, the "outer kingliness" meant to put the idea of governing and benefiting the people into practice (ching-shih chi-min). These three aspects of Confucian Tao were conceived by the early Sung Neo-Confucians in the revival of Neo-Confucianism. So in 1069 Liu I (1017~1086),a leading disciple of Hu Yuan (993~1059), explained the Confucian Tao to Emperor Shen-tsung (r.1067~1085), as follows:

> It is said that the Way (Tao) of the sages has three aspects: substance (t'i) , function (yung), and literary expression (wen). The bond between prince and minister and between father and son, benevolence, righteousness, rites and music-these are things which do not change through the ages; they are the substance of Tao. The Books of Poetry and Documents, the dynastic histories, the writings of the philosophers and the works of men of letters-these perpetuate the right example down through the ages; they are the literary expression of Tao. To initiate this substance and put it into practice throughout the empire, enriching the lives of the people and ordering all things to imperial perfection-this is the function of Tao.[4]

A modern scholar makes this observation:

> In the threefold conception of the Tao---, we have a concise statement of the aims of the Sung school in their most general terms ---- suggesting the broad line along which it was to be developed by the manifold activities of Sung scholars.[5]

Of the three aspects of Liu's formulation of the Confucian Tao, the t'i or

---

4　Sung-Yuan hsueh-an, v.1, p.26.
5　Wm. Theodore de Bary, "A Reappraisal of Neo-confucianism", in Arthur Wright ed., *Studies in Chinese Thought* (Chicago: University of Chicago Press, 1953), p.90.

substance, identified with the aspect of "inner sageness", was the most fundamental to Neo-Confucianism. It was precisely the belief, which the substance of Tao was not subject to change, that led Neo-Confucians to search intensively for the metaphysical foundations of the Confucian Tao.[6] The function of Tao, referred to the aspect of "outer kingliness", was essentially of the political and social kind, which stressed "practical statesmanship". Substance and function were but two sides of the same coin, and the two implied each other. In this sense, then the aspects of substance and function were regarded as far more important and real than its literary (including classical or, more appropriately, scriptural) traditions.[7] Later on, the Sung Neo-Confucians, those who emphasized the substance of Confucian Tao, developed to be the Philosophers of Principle and established the orthodoxy of Neo-Confucianism, while those who stressed the function of Confucian Tao led toward utilitarians.

II. The Rise of Utilitarian Thought in Sung Times

During Northern Sung times, the center of gravity in political thought was not in Philosophy of Principle, but in utilitarian thought. The reason was that politics tended to be practical, while philosophy was inclined to be idealized. Utilitarian thought as understood here was a political theory. Utilitarian thought was characteriized by its emphasis upon the practical affairs of state and society, and rejected the metaphysical speculations on moral principles. Its basic concern was to improve the people's livelihood, to strengthen military defenses against the barbarian menace, and to enrich the country. It was a direct reflection of anti-Buddhism and a response to the military weakness of the state.

Buddhism, as a foreign religion, was introduced into China at the time of the decline of orthodox Confucianism, and became dominant thought during the T'ang dynasty. Since Han Yu (768~824) and Li Ao (774?~841?) argued against Buddhism during T'ang times, anti-Buddhism was the main concern of Confucian scholars during Sung times. Their major purpose for arguing against Buddhism was to restore

---

6 Yu Ying-shih, p.119.
7 Yu Ying-shih, p.119.

Confucian tradition, and make it the dominant thought again in China, because Buddhist thought was very different from Confucianism. The basic thought of Confucianism was concerned mainly with principles of human relationships, moral values and concrete life, while Buddhist thought was highly speculative and other-worldly. Chinese thought affirmed ethical life and the world; however, Buddhist thought negated them.[8] Therefore Buddhism as a religion and an institution was in conflict with the Confucian pattern of life, and consequently there was much opposition to it.

Other reasons for anti-Buddhism were financial and social. In 1022, there were 458, 854 monks in the state.[9] Their existence increased the burden of peasants, and their religious belief caused both economic and social problems for the state. For the monks avoided their share of taxes and corvee labor and their practice of celibacy, which the Chinese felt, was unnatural and immoral, reduced the numbers of marriages and families, therefore the existence of Buddhist monks became a menace to the society as a whole. Moreover, the rich holdings of the great Buddhist monasteries were often fertile and yet tax exempt. Thus, the trend of anti-Buddhism in Sung times urged the Sung scholars to emphasize not other-worldly affairs, but human affairs, and even the practical affairs of society and state.

Actually, the most fundamental reason for the rise of utilitarian thought of the Sung was the military weakness of the state. The military weakness was owing to the founding principle established by Emperor T'ai-tsu (r.960~976), the founder of the dynasty.

Emperor T'ai-tsu gained the throne by his personal ability as a military leader. In fact, he was made emperor by his soldiers. However, Emperor T'ai-tsu felt threatened by other militarists. At the very beginning of the Sung dynasty, Emperor T'ai-tsu emphasized civil administration at the expanse of national defense.

He made the generals retire with proper rewards or transferred them to minor positions. In addition, he divided all the army units in the country into two categories:

---

8 Chang Carsun, *The Development of Neo-Confucian Thought* , v.l (New Haven: College and University Press, 1957), p.113.

9 Li YU. Sung-ch'ao shih-shih, v.7

the imperial army of the central government and the militia of the local government. The main body of the imperial army was placed in the capital, while the militia units under the prefectual commanders merely played an auxiliary role.[10] And he placed all the military forces directly under the control of the emperor. In addition to the emperor's direct control of the armies, Emperor T'ai-tsu also followed a policy of replacing militaristic governors with civil officials. Although Emperor T'ai-tsu's military policies could prevent rebellions within the country, his troops could not guard against foreign powers, because of the military weakness of the state. The military weakness of the dynasty was reflected in the Sung army being defeated by foreign powers.

Although Emperor T'ai-tsung (r.976~998), Emperor T'ai-tsu's younger brother and successor, twice campaigned northward in attempts to recover the prefectures dominated by the Liao, but was beaten off. After the war of Shan-yuan in 1004, the Sung ruler even made a peace agreement with the Liao ruler in Shan-yuan. In the treaty of Shan-yuan, the ruler of the Liao agreed to treat the Sung emperor as an elder brother, the Sung acknowledged the permanent loss of sixteen prefectures, which were lost during the Five Dynasties (907~960), and promised to give the Liao an annual tribute of 200,000 bolts of silk, and 100,000 taels of silver.[11] Moreover, in 1038 the Tanguts had proclaimed a Chinese-style state of their own, called Hsi Hsia or Western Hsia, and started to invade the Sung. Then, peace was arranged when the Sung also agreed to give Hsi Hsia annual tribute. Later on, the Sung was frequently threatened by these two foreign states.

Although the Sung often suffered from the invasions by Hsi Hsia and the Liao, what the Sung could do was to maintain peace by paying them tributes. This was because the military weakness existed in the country. Under the circumstances, the scholars were concerned with the crisis, and tried to save their country by making proposals for enriching the state and strengthening the military force. Therefore the rise of utilitarian thought was the response of the time and circumstances.

---

10 Miyazaki Ichisada, "The Centralized Policy," in James T.C. Liu and Peter J. Golas eds., *Change in Sung China* (Lexington, Mass.: Heath, 1969), p.61.

11 Li Chih ed., *Huang-Sung shih-ch'ao kang-yao* (Essential annals of the first ten reigns of the Sung dynasty), v.3, p.11.

Among the Confucian utilitarians in early Sung times, Li Kou(1009~1059) was considered as a scholar whose thought was especially systematic, realistic, and broad-minded.

III. The Life and Utilitarian Thought of Li Kou[12]

(I) The Life of Li Kou

Li Kou, whose courtesy name was T'ai-po, came from Nan-ch'eng in the military prefecture of Chien-ch'ang. He was born into a poor family; however, he enjoyed studying and contemplation, and was concerned with the significant affairs of society and state. At an early age, Li concentrated his attention on the Classics, and was particularly interested in Confucianism. Like other young men in his day, Li earnestly intended to become a civil servant by taking the government examinations. However, he failed the examinations again and again, and did not become an important official in his life time.

In 1043, he took a teaching post in the district school in Nan-ch'eng. Li was repeatedly recommended for promotion by Yu Ching, and Fan Chung-yen, who regarded him as an outstanding scholar (fei-ch'ang-ju) in the country. The recommendation was effective at last. Li was appointed as a Teaching Assistant at the National University (Chiang shih-lang t'ai-hsueh chu-chiao), which was a low and honorary rank without subatantive appointment. Later, in 1057 Li became a Lecturer at the National University (T'ai-hsueh shuo-shu), and in 1059, he was provisionally in charge of the University (ch'uan-t'ung kuan-kou t'ai-hsueh).

Li was basically a frustrated scholar, since he repeatedly failed to win a government position, by which he could carry out his political ideals. Therefore, he had to seek other ways to obtain a reputation for himself. He turned toward intellectual work to make a contribution to the society in his day. His writings were known as Chih-chiang Li-hsien-sheng wen- chi (Collected Works of Li Kou).

---

12 Cf. "Li Kou chuan" (Biography of Li Kou) and the "Nien-p'u" (A Chronological Biography) which are in his collected works, *Chih-chiang Li hsien-sheng wen-chi* (Hereafter cited as *LWC*) (Peiking: Chung-hua Bookstore Press, 1981). For a study of Li Kou, see Hsieh Shan-yuan, *The Life and Thought of Li Kou* (San Francisco: Chinese Materials Center, INC. Press, 1979).

(II)Li Kou's Utilitarian Thought

Although Li Kou was a Confucian scholar, his thought was very different from that of Mencius, who objected to discussing advantage (li) in his doctrine. Under the influence of Mencius, Confucian scholars seldom failed to prize righteousness and despise advantage, and were even ashamed of discussing advantage thereafter. Li Kou disagreed with this idea. He thought that no Confucian virtue could be separated from its practical value. "How can benevolence (jen) and righteousness (i) work to the exclusion of advantage?"[13] So Li Kou stressed the value of advantage in his thought. However, what did advantage mean to Li Kou? He said:

> Of the eight methods of government in the (chapter of) Hung-fan (Great Rule), the first concerns food, and the second money, and (when Tzu-kung inquires what is essential in the government of a country,) Confucius says, There must be sufficient food for the people; an efficient army; and confidence of the people in their ruler. So the substance of governing a nation is that it must be based on effective management of the country's finances----That is why sage kings and capable statesmen give priority to the enrichment of the country.[14]

To Li Kou, advantage referred to the country's finances, and the main purpose of it was to satisfy the people's desires. Li affirmed the existence of desires, which were human nature; however, the desires should be refined and regulated by propriety (li).[15] Since Li Kou's thought was focused on the desires and advantage, they were considered as the central idea in his utilitarian thought. As for Li Kou's utilitarian thought, they are stated as follows :

1. The Aspect of Politics

Since Li Kou was a practical thinker, he was eager to see his own country become militarily strong. Unlike other Confucian scholars, who praised kingly way (wang-tao) as a good method of governing, Li Kou advocated the way of hegemony (pa-tao), which could make a country strong and powerful. He said:

---

13 *LWC*, p.326.
14 *LWC*, p.133.
15 *LWC*, p.6.

The Confucian scholars usually have the point of view that they regret not to see the wang-tao put into practice. They do not know that the practice of the pa-tao can make a state strong. How can it be easily reached? When Kuan Chung was the prime minister of Duke Huan, the state of Chi was hegemon. It repelled barbarian invasions from the north and the west and hornored the Chou ruler in the capital. How does that compare with the existing situation today? When Shang Yang was the prime minister of Duke Hsiao, the Ch'in state was a powerful country. It formulated laws and regulations and encouraged both farming and fighting. By these means, the state of Ch'in became rich and their army strong. How does that compare with the existing situation today?[16]

Under the urgent circumstances in Sung times, he did not understand why scholars should insist on the kingly way as the only ideal and disregard military power just because the latter was abhorred by ancient Confucians. Since circumstances differed, Li Kou thought, the way of hegemony was more effective than the kingly way to achieve a stable order, and make a country strong and powerful. Moreover, Li Kou thought that the purpose of making a state hegemonic, enriching the state and strengthening the military force was to pacify the people, since pacification of the people was the end of politics and of the ruler's duty. The reason why the welfare of the people was the ruler's duty was that the ruler was established by Heaven, and "the people were the agents of Heaven through whom Heaven sees and hears." Moreover, the idea of Heaven's establishing the ruler was not for the interest of the rulers but for the interest of millions of people. A ruler thus had the duty to nurture the people. If a ruler lost the support of the people, then he would be banished from the throne.[17]

2. The Aspect of Economy and Finance

Li Kou, as a Confucian scholar, was concerned with the welfare of the people, especially of the farmers, and the enrichment of his country. However, the Sung government faced serious problems in economy and finances, which were reflected

---

16 *LWC*, pp.299~300.
17 *LWC*, p.168.

in the unequal distribution of wealth and the reduction in agricultural productivity, and in revenues. Li Kou thought that the welfare of the people should be the end of the government. The welfare of the people should begin with the assurance of their survival, which meant they should be provided with adequate food, since "the reason that a man is a man is that he has enough food to eat."[18] Only the rich owned lands; the poor were landless. Therefore, the rich became richer, while the poor became poorer. Since the poor could not support themselves, they were forced to become tenant farmers for the rich, or to devote themselves to other occupations. Although there were vast lands to be tilled, too few tenants were engaged in agriculture. In addition, the tenants did not work hard in tilling lands, because the lands did not belong to them. The consequence was the reduction in agricultural productivity and in revenues. Li Kou traced the cause of reduction in productivity and in revenues to the unfair distribution of lands. The remedy, Li Kou thought, was to make the peasants back to the lands, to limit the amount of lands to be occupied, and to equalize the distribution of lands:

> The remedy is first to follow the method of restraining the secondary occupations, such as commerce and industry in order to drive the peasants back to the lands. When the peasants return to the land, then the government should limit the amount of land to be occupied by each person. Each would have a definite number of hectares and no one should be permitted to own more than that stipulated by the regulations. Once the peasants are driven back to the land and the annexation of lands are not to be allowed, then the price of land will certainly become cheap. When the price of land becomes cheap, then land will be easily obtainable. If the land is easily obstainable and there is no way either to be engaged in secondary occupations or to have the opportunity of eating without working, then the peasants will devote themselves wholeheartedly to agriculture. If the peasants devote themselves wholeheartedly to agriculture then the resources of lands can be fully exploited.[19]

---

18 *LWC*, p.183.
19 *LWC*, p.136.

If the peasants had enough land to cultivate, then they could pay taxes to the government, and the revenues would probably increase.

Moreover, Li Kou made an even more realistic and original proposal. To enrich the country, the government should make "Each man engages himself in tilling lands and no land left underdeveloped"[20] in the country. Indeed, this proposal was a great ideal to solve the problems of people's livelihood. However, if a ruler concerned with the enrichment of the country, he would make full use of man power and the land resources in an agricultural society.

Li kou also maintained the importance of the effective management of the country's finances. However, to manage the finances of the country efficiently did not mean levying excessive taxes on the people, but rather "strengthening the foundation (agricultural productivity) and cutting down expenses."[21] If the government strengthened the foundation, the agricultural productivity would increase. Therefore, the people would be capable of paying taxes, and there would certainly be an increase in revenues. But, since the revenues of the government, which came from taxation, would have a definite limit, Li Kou was convinced that the government should spend within the limit of its revenues. If the government could manage efficiently the finances of the country, then everyone in the country would have enough.

3. The Military Aspect

Among the problems in Sung times, the military weakness of the country was probably Li Kou's primary concern. Because of the military weakness, the Sung was frequently suffered from the invasions by the Hsi Hsia and the Liao. Although the Sung army was characterized by its large size, it was unreliable, because the soldiers were poorly trained. Moreover, since military commanders and soldiers were constantly rotated so that the two could not identify with each other, the soldiers did not have a period of training before they willingly obeyed their commanders. Another factor which contributed to the weakening of the Sung army was that the Sung rulers were distrustful of their generals and thought of various devices to put

---

20 *LWC*, p.78.
21 *LWC*, p.133.

checks on military commanders. If the ministers who commanded armies could be suspected, how could they improve the fighting ability of the army? Thus, it was natural that the weakening of the army existed in Sung times, and in turn, the military weakness throughout the dynasty.

Basically, the success in warfare required a feeling of unity between commanders and soldiers, and. the two should identify with each other. Thus, Li Kou thought that generals should not be constantly replaced, unless they committed very grave mistakes.

Since Sung soldiers were weak and timid, they should be given a period of training in military matters. A thorough training in strategy and cavalry warfare, Li Kou thought, could make good soldiers. Moreover, Li Kou maintained that the ruler should trust his generals, and generals should be independent. If a general did not have any interference from the central government, he could devote himself wholeheartedly to military matters and improve the fighting ability of the army. So Li Kou was conceived that it was the ruler's duty to improve the relationship between him and his generals. The ruler should know the ability of generals fully, and once he knew them, then he should trust them.[22]

IV. On Li Kou's Utilitarian Thought

In his day, Li Kou was attracted by practical matters of society and state. After the Sung empire was invaded by the Hsi Hsia in 1038, this emphasis on practicality was even more obvious. Since his thought was too practical, and then led toward utilitarian thought, it was very different from that of other Confucian scholars.

Utilitarian thought in Sung times stressed the aspect of outer kingliness in Confucian Tao. Among the Confucian Tao, inner sageness and outer kingliness were but two sides of the same coin; however, the former was considered as the most fundamental, and the practice of outer kingliness should be based on that of inner sageness. So most Confucian scholars believed that in the way of governing a nation the virtue of self-cultivation and moral excellence was considered as a means of ordering society. But, those who emphasized self-cultivation were not all indifferent

22 *LWC*, p.160.

to the institutional setting of society or the proper policies of state. However, the utilitarians in Sung times, whose goal was a wealthy and powerful state, were indifferent to moral self-cultivation. Therefore, Li Kou's practice of statecraft (chih-shu) was also lacking in moral foundation. Most other Confucian scholars did not emphasize advantage, instead, they praised the kingly way as a good method of governing. Li Kou over-emphasized advantage, advocated the way of hegemony, and even maintained that the value of morality should be based on advantage. For these reasons, Li Kou was considered, by many other Confucian scholars, as a Legalist. However, he argued that he was not a Legalist since his end was to "order society" in terms of that of Confucius. He also maintained that his emphasis on wealth referred to the Confucian goal of assuring the people's livelihood, and that the defense of the nation was necessary to the achievement of peace and harmony. Since Li Kou's goal was to pacify the people, not to honor the ruler, he was not a Legalist but was indeed a confucian in essence.

Among the suggestions Li Kou made for the solution of Northern Sung problems, some were fresh and original. He recommended that the limit on the ownership of lands and equal distribution of lands were the efficient way to increase agricultural productivity and revenues, that the effective management of the country's finances was a good means to enrich the country, and that the improvement of the relationship between the ruler and his generals could advance the fighting ability of the army. These recommendations were important and possibly unique in his day. However, the most original and realistic concept was to make full use of man power and of land resources as a means of enriching the country.

V. Conclusion

During Northern Sung times, the center of gravity in political thought was not in Philosophy of Principle, but in utilitarian thought. The rise of utilitarian thought was a direct reflection of anti-Buddhism and a response to the military weakness of the state.

Among the Confucian utilitarians in early Sung times, Li Kou was considered as a scholar whose thought was especially systematic, realistic, and broad-minded.

Since Li Kou's thought was focused on the desires and advantage, they were considered as the central ideas in his utilitarian thought.

This paper is mainly to explore Li Kou's utilitarian thought, which consists of three aspects: the aspects of politics, economy and finance, and the military aspect.

Although Li Kou was not successful in his political career, and was not a man of great reputation, he was a systematic, realistic and broad-minded scholar, and through his works, he did make a contribution to the society in his day.

Tai Chen and Revivalism during the Ch'ien-lung and Chia-ch'ing Eras

I. Introduction

After the Neo-Confucianism of Chu Hsi (1130~1200) school was elevated to the position of state orthodoxy in the early Ch'ing, it soon became the dominant mode in the interpretation of the key Confucian texts. During the Ch'ien-Chia era(1736~1820), it remained as an influential force, however, the tide of scholarship had turned against it. Although the scholars of the Chu Hsi school maintained that their interpretations accorded fully with the Confucian Classics, many scholars in the Ch'ien-Chia era held that, instead, they misinterpreted the Classics because they did not really understand the language of the ancient sages, and that their readings of the ancient texts were speculative in nature. Rejecting the philosophical speculations of Neo-Confucianism, scholars in the eighteenth century searched for evidence of objective truth in the Classics, and favored a return to the ancient Confucian sources in order to reconstruct the classical tradition. In this way, the school of evidential research (k'ao-cheng, lit. "search for evidence", means the interpretation and analysis of the Classics through evidence and by employing critically the inductive and comparative methods) came into being. And revivalism (that is,"return to the past") pervaded the Ch'ien-Chia era.

During the Ch'ien-Chia era, Tai Chen (1723~1777) was known as a leading proponent of the k' ao-cheng school, however, he differed in an important way from other k'ao-cheng scholars of his time. Unlike his contemporaries, who pursued k'ao-cheng scholarship for its own sake, Tai Chen regarded it as primarily a means of revealing the truth. Moreover, he was regarded as a philosopher rather than as merely a k'ao-cheng scholar. Although Tai Chen distinguished himself from others in this particular regard, he shared their concern, that is, the need to correct and reinvigorate the Confucian tradition.

The question which will be addressed here is about the rise of k'ao-cheng scholarship during the ch'ien-chia era. What is its aim and its relationship with Neo-Confucianism?

Previous examinations of this question by Hu Shih [1] and Ch'ien Mu[2] unfortunately do not suffice. The former argued that k'ao-cheng scholarship represented no more than a reaction against Neo-Confucianism, while the latter held that the evidential research movement was a continuation of Neo-Confucianism. It is surely incorrect to say that k'ao-cheng scholarship, however, was merely a simple reaction to or a continuation of Neo-Confocianism, for it actually represented a self-conscious effort to restore the objective truth of the Confucian Classics, and to strengthen the Confucian tradition. Moreover, at its best it represented a mode of empirical scholarship that employed new and precise methods by which to evaluate and correct the ancient classical texts. Although there were few, if any, great philosophers or novel theories as compared to the Sung (960~1279) and Ming(1368~1644) dynasties, if Tai Chen, the greatest philosopher of the k'ao-cheneg school, can be taken as representative, there was nevertheless an earnest attempt to re-establish Confucianism on a more solid theoretical and textual foundation. The published views of Yu Ying-shih on this matter also weren't close reexamination.[3] Thus my paper will focus on the attempt of Tai Chen and his contemporaries to reevaluate and verify key texts and concepts belonging to the Confucian

---

1 Hu Shih, *Tai Tung-yuan ti che-hsueh* (The Philosophy of Tai Chen) (Taipei: Shang-wu yin-shu kuan, 1971).
2 Ch'ien Mu, *Chung-kuo chin san-pai-nien hsueh-shu shih* (A History of Chinese Scholarship during the Last 300 Years) (Taipei: Shang-wu yin-shu kuan, 1976).
3 Yu Ying-shih, "Ch'ing-tai ssu-hsiang-shih ti i-ko hsin chieh-shih" (A New Interpretation of the Intellectual History of the Ch'ing Period), in *Ssu-hsiang yu li-shih* (Thought and History) (Taipei: Lien-ching ch'u-pan she, 1978), pp.121~156.

tradition.The first section deals with revivalism in the Ch'ien-Chia era. The second section analyzes Tai Chen's personal intellectual development. Section three deals with Tai Chen's approach to philosophy and his key philosophical beliefs.

II. Revivalism in the Ch'ien-Chia Era

During the mid-Ch'ing, the practice of evidential research reached a new level of maturity and eventually dominated the intellectual world of the time. Although k'ao-cheng scholarship reached its zenith during the Ch'ien-Chia era, its roots could be traced back to the seventeenth century or indeed to Northern Sung times(960~1127) or even to T'ang (618~907). In early T'ang times, K'ung Ying-ta(574~648) had edited the Standard Commentaries on the Five Classics (Wu-ching cheng-i)[4] , which was later established as the standard reference for the civil service examinations.[5] However, a new trend in the textual criticism emerged to challenge the authority of K'ung's orthodox commentaries. Scholars associated with this movement advocated a return to the classics themselves as a basis for understanding the true meaning of the sages. Although these scholars dared to call tradition into question, they did not go far enough in questioning that tradition. However, most importantly they did attempt to get at the truth by emphasizing the Classics and relying less on the commentaries.[6]

---

4 Actually, the *Wu-ching cheng-i* was not edited by K'ung alone, but by him and other T'ang scholars. It is said that originally there were Six Classics, one of which, the *Book of Music* (*Yueh- ching*) was lost before the third century B.C. The so-called Five Classics were the *Book of Songs* (*Shih-ching*), the *Book of Documents* (*Shu-ching*), the *Book of Changes* (*I-ching*), the *Book of Ceremony and Ritual* (*Li-ching* or *I-li*) and the *Spring and Autumn Annals* (*Ch'un-ch'iu*). However, in K'ung's *Wu-ching cheng-i*, the *Book of Ceremony and Ritual* was replaced by the *Book of Rites* (*Li-chi*).

5 K'ung's orthodox commentaries was used as the standard text for the *ming-ching k'o* (Classicist Category), one of several categories in the regular civil service examination system. In T'ang, the ming-ching examinations were highly popular and among the regular examinations second only to the *chin-shih* (presented scholars, that is highest examination graduates) examinations in prestige. See Hucker, Charles, O., ed., *A Dictionary of Official Titles in Imperial China* (Stanford: Stanford University Press, 1985), p. 333.

6 Edwin Pulleyblank, "Neo-Confucianism and Neo-Legalism in T'ang Intellectual Life, 755~805", in Arthur Wright ed., *The Confucian Persuasion* (Stanford: Stanford University Press, 1960), pp. 77~114. See also Elman, Benjamin A., *From Philosophy to Philology* (Cambridge: Harvard University Press, 1984), pp. 40~41; and Ma Tsung-huo, *Chung-kuo ching-hsueh shih* (A History of Chinese Classical Studies)(Taipei: Shang-wu yin-shu kuan, 1979), pp. 180~200.

Although philology was not the major concern of Sung (960~1279) scholars, their labors in this field did result in important gains.[7] Following their T'ang predecessors, Sung scholars, after the Ch'ing-li era (1042~1048) of Jen-tsung (r.1023~1063), began to discard K'ung's officially accepted interpretations of the Five Classics. They preferred instead to go back to the Classics themselves and seek their own interpretations. In this spirit, Sun Fu (992~1057) studied the Spring and Autumn Annals instead of its three commentaries.[8] In his study of the Annals, Sun "sought to express its essential meaning in the simplest terms, without regard to the diverse and confusing commentaries on the work."[9] Wang An-shih (1021~1086) studied the three Classics and added his own commentaries[10], which later became the standard references for civil service examination candidates in Northern Sung times. Wang, in his commentaries of the Classics, emphasized their general meaning instead of literal interpretations. [11] With the rise of Neo-Confucianism in the eleventh century, Sung Neo-Confucians went even further in their studies of the Classics. They favored a philosophical (i-li) approach to the Classics, which stressed the apprehension of moral principles instead of literal meaning. They added their own commentaries emphasizing philosophical concepts sometimes going far afield of the literal meaning of the texts.[12]

Parallel with this development was the growth of skepticism concerning the authenticity of the Classics in the eleventh century, especially during the years 1025~1100. Among Sung scholars, Ou-yang Hsiu (1007~1072) raised serious doubts about the Classics. He questioned the authenticity of the Rituals of Chou (Chou-li), of portions of the Book of Changes, and of the prefaces to the Book of Songs (Shih-

---

7   Winston W. Lo, "Philology, An Aspect of Sung Rationalism", *Chinese Culture* 17/4(Dec., 1976), pp. 1~26.

8   P'i Hsi-jui, *Ching-hsueh li-shih* (History of Classical Studies) (Taipei: I-win yin-shu kuan, 1966), p. 202. See also Chan Wing-tsit , "Chu Hsi's Completion of Neo-Confucianism", in Chan Wing-tsit, *Chu Hsi: Life and Thought* (Hong Kong: The Chinese University Press, 1987), p. 130.

9   de Bary, "A Reappraisal of Neo-Cofucianism", in Arthur Wright ed., *Studies in Chinese Thought* (Chicago: University of Chicago Press, 1953), p. 92.

10 These three Classics are the Book of Songs, the Book of Documents, and the *Rituals of Chou*. See Chan, "Chu Hsi's Completion of Neo-Confucianism", p. 132.

11 de Bary, "A Reappraisal of Neo-Confucianism", p. 102.

12 Chan, "Chu Hsi's Completion of Neo-Confucianism", p. 132.

hsu). Su Shih (1036~1101) raised questions concerning both the Rituals of Chou and the Book of Documents. Both Ssu-ma Kuang (1019~1101) and Li Kou (1009~1059) were skeptical of the reliability of the Mencius (Meng-tzu). Chu Hsi even cast doubts upon many other books besides the Classics. And the spirit of this kind of skepticism toward the Classics was carried on by scholars during the Yuan (1279~1368) and Ming periods. For instance, Wu Ch'eng (1247~1331) of the Yuan and Mei Tsu(fl. ca.1513) of the Ming, among others, concluded that the Ancient Text chapters of the Book of Documents were forgeries.[13]

Although the intellectual world of the Ming was dominated by Neo-Confucianism, especially by the Wang Yang-ming (1472~1529) school, it was not entirely monopolized by the school. At least, since mid-Ming, scholars such as Yang Shen (1488~1559), Ch'en Ti (1541~1617), and Chiao Hung (1541~1620), and others reoriented classical scholarship from philosophical interpretation to philological analysis. Yang Shen, a famous philologist, attempted to reconstruct the ancient pronunciation of Chinese by the study of ancient rhyme schemes. Ch'en Ti attempted to define ancient phonetics by classifying and comparing rhyme words in the Book of Songs.[14] His method in phonetical research was later adopted by the early Ch'ing scholar, Ku Yen-wu (1613~1682).[15] Chiao Hung rejected orthodox commentaries and interpretations of the Classics, arguing that they sometimes obscured the true meanings of the Classics. He, therefore, suggested that scholars go back directly to the Classics without first referring to the commentaries. He advocated a linguistic or philological approach to the Classics.[16] These reorientations in classical scholarship anticipated and laid the ground-work for later developments in evidential research in

---

13 P'i, p. 202. See also Chan, "Chu Hsi's Completion of Neo-Confucianism", pp. 132~134; James T. C. Liu, *Ou-yang Hsiu: An Eleventh-Century Neo-Confucianist* (Stanford: Stanford University Press, 1976), p. 94.

14 Elman, pp. 215~216.

15 Hummel, Arthur W., ed., *Eminent Chinese of the Ch'ing Period* (1644~1912)(hereafter cited as *ECCP*)(Washington: Government Printing Office, 1943~44), v.1, pp. 421~426.

16 Edward T. Ch'ien, "Chiao Hung and the Revolt against Ch'eng-Chu Orthodoxy" in Wm. Theodore de Bary ed., *The Unfolding of Neo-Confucianism* (NewYork: Columbia University Press, 1975), pp. 287~291 and his *Chiao Hung and the Restructuring of Neo-Confucianism in the Late Ming*(New York: Columbia University Press, 1986), pp. 181~182.

early Ch'ing times.

During the seventeenth century, Ku Yen-wu, Yen Jo-chu (1636~1704)[17] and others reacted vigorously against the orthodox classical scholarship of the Ming,which had been philosophical in its approach and created a new climate of learning as well as a new mode of thought, thus more scholarly in nature.[18] They emphasized the study of the Classics based on textual research and extensive evidence. Yen Jo-chu exhibited a strong spirit of skepticism in his critical examinations of the ancient texts. His major achievement as a classical scholar is the Shang-shu ku-wen shu-cheng (Evidential Analysis of the Ancient Text [Version of the] Book of Documents). While the authenticity of the Book of Documents, which had been studied by scholars for ages, had been questioned by scholars before Yen's time, it was generally accepted as a valid work. Yen employed empirical methods to analyze the text, and based on extensive philological evidence concluded that the Ancient Text chapters were a later forgery. This conclusion was later accepted by most k'ao-cheng scholars of the time.[19]

Another important figure was Ku Yen-wu. Ku is generally regarded as the founder of the school of evidential research, for he developed a new research methodology. Although the main purpose of his study was the practical application of knowledge to society, Ku did stress that textual criticism and philological investigation were indispensable for the study of the Classics, and defined research methods appropriate to the various branches of study. Thus, the research methodologies which Ku originated, did signal a reorientation in classical scholarship and paved the way for the rise of the k'ao-cheng school in mid-Ch'ing times.[20] The term k'ao-cheng was not a neologism ; instead, it was a term which had been used by the Sung scholar Wang Ying-lin (1223~1296). However, it only came into vogue during the seventeenth century.[21]

---

17 *ECCP*, v. 2, pp. 908~910.
18 Elman, pp.43~44.
19 *ECCP*, v. 2, pp. 909~910.
20 *ECCP*, v. 1, pp. 423~424.
21 Elman, p.45.

The scholars of this era turned to this new kind of textual scholarship for one basic reason: to authenticate the Confucian Classics and rescue them from what they believed to be the misinterpretations of their predecessors. They asserted that Sung Neo-Confucianism suffered from two deadly weaknesses: first, it was contaminated by Buddhist and Taoist ideas [22]; and second, it was the Sung philosophers' intellectual inadequancies or lack of philological training and rigor[23], that their speculative interpretations of the Classics were based on incorrect or forged versions of the Confucian texts. In order to avoid these problems, they favored a return to the past in order to reconstruct the authentic truth of original Confucianism, and in this way philology became a kind of substitute for philosophy.[24]

This fu-ku(return to the past) orientation represented an attempt to revive and verify Confucian truth, and in order to accomplish these goals, scholars of the k'ao-cheng persuasion based their studies on texts older than the Sung --- that is, those of the Han period --- in order to overcome perceived limitation in Sung Neo-Confucianism. Thus, they turned their attention to the study of Han dynasty exegetical works, which were considered authentic because the Han was closer in time to antiquity.[25] In stressing the relevance of Han dynasty scholarship to their own purposes, evidential research scholarship in the eighteenth century was commonly referred to as Han Learning.

Han Learning scholars placed a primary emphasis on a detailed philological analysis of the classical texts as opposed to the mainly speculative approach of the Sung Neo-Confucians. Philology was not simply an auxiliary tool but a required and demanding discipline in the task of recovering the essentials of Confucian culture.Thus, k'ao-cheng scholars brought their newly perfected discipline to bear on all textual data relating to the classical tradition, and involving the separate

---

22 Tai Chen, *Meng-tzu tzu-i shu-cheng* (Evidential Analysis of the Meanings of Terms in the Book of Mencius), in *Tai Tung-yuan hsien-sheng ch'uan-chi* (Complete Works of Mr. Tai Chen) (hereafter cited as *Ch'uan-chi*)(Taipei: Ta-hua shu-chu), p. 305.

23 Tai Chen, "Yu mou shu" (A Letter to Someone), in *Ch'uan-chi*, p. 1100.

24 By philosophy, Ch'ing scholars meant metaphysical and cosmological systems of thought.

25 Hui Shih-ch'i, *Li shuo*(On Ritual), See quote in Liang Ch'i-ch'ao, *Ch'ing-tai hsueh-shu kai-lun* (An Introduction to the Scholarship in the Ch'ing Period) (Taipei: Shang-wu yin-shu kuan, 1972), p. 33.

disciplines of linguistics, phonetics, history, astronomy, mathematics, hydraulic engineering, geography, institutions, bronze and stone inscriptions, the collation of texts, the assembling of lost texts, etc. Their mottoes were to get at the truth through concrete proof (shih-shih ch'iu" shih) and to hold no belief without solid evidence (wu-cheng pu-hsin). The products of their academic labors were the commentaries on and emendations to the Classics later collected in such compendia as the Huang Ch'ing ching-chieh cheng-pien[26] and its continuation, the Hsu-pien.[27] Among the k'ao-cheng scholars of this era, Hui Tung (1697~1758), and Tai Chen were considered to be the most outstanding.

Hui Tung of Yuan-ho, Soochow, was widely recognized as the founder of the so-called Wu or Soochow school, and he was responsible for making the Han Learning movement popular in the Soochow area. The fundamental spirit of his approach to learning was that "that which is of the ancient times must be authentic and that which is of the Han times must be good. "[28] He held that the views of the Han classical scholars were equal in standing to the Classics themselves.[29] In this way, Hui Tung attempted to elevate the views of the Han classical masters to the rank of the Classics. His respect for Han scholarship as the final authority in matters pertaining to the Classics consolidated the orientation of the Han Learning school in the eighteenth century. But, perhaps too credulous in revering Han Learning, the main goal of his scholarship seems to have been the preservation of Han Learning rather than the discovery of verifiable truth. Therefore, Tai Chen criticized this approach to learning, and attempted to go beyond Han Learning.

III. Tai Chen's Intellectual Development

Tai Chen was probably the greatest thinker and scholar of the Ch'ing dynasty. His primary concern was to restore and retain the Confucian tradition. On one

---

26 This collection, containing more than 360 volumes totaling 1400-odd chuan, was edited by Juan Yuan (1764~1849).

27 This work was compiled by Wang Hsien-ch'ien (1842~1918) and published between 1886~1888.

28 Liang Ch'i-ch'ao, *Chin-tai Chung-kuo hsueh-shu lun-ts'ung* (Essays on Modern Chinese Scholarship) (Hong Kong: Ch'ung-wen shu-tien, 1973), p. 68.

29 Hui Tung, "Chiu ching ku-i shuo shu" (Preface to the Ancient Meanings of the Nine Classics), See quote in Liang, *Ch'ing-tai hsueh-shu kai-lun*, p.33.

occasion, he stated that his intention was to get at the Confucian truth.[30] Tai Chen also said that he studied the Classics because he attempted to keep alive the suggestive sayings of the sages.[31] In his search for the Confucian truth, or the truth of Tao, Tai Chen oriented himself toward philology. He described the discipline of philology as follows:

> The eternal truth embodied in the Classics is the Tao. The Tao is expressed through words (tz'u). The words are formed on the basis of philological studies. From [the study of] primary and derived characters, we can then understand the true meaning of words. Through the understanding of the true meaning of words, we can then comprehend the mind and will of the ancient sages and virtuous men.[32]

Thus, philology became his chosen methodology to restore the Confucian truth. Since Tai Chen realized that philology was the requisite means to recover the pristine meanings of the ancient sages, early in life he focused his studies on the techniques of philology, and it was in this field of scholarship that his great reputation rested.

Although Tai Chen became a philologist by choice, he differed from most other Han Learning scholars. Tai Chen viewed philology not as an end in itself, as many Han Learning scholars tended to do, but only as a means to reveal the Confucian truth. His primary objective in this wise was to seek the truth without any kind of dependence (k'ung so i-pang)[33], and not be deluded by anyone, including himself, whereas most proponents of Han Learning were bound by school tenets and traditions. Since in his approach to scholarship he sought to maintain a high degree of objectivity, and to investigate the facts without dependence, he succeeded in raising the standards of research to a new height in his time.

Tai Chen did not limit himself to the study of the primary philosophical texts of antiquity. He also applied k'ao-cheng techniques to the study of phonetics,

---

30 Tai Chen, "Yu mou shu", in *Ch'uan-chi*, p. 1100.
31 Tai Chen, "Yu Yao Chi-chuan shu" (A Letter to Yao Chi-chuan), in *Ch'uan-chi*, p. 1099.
32 Tai Chen, "Ku ching chieh kou ch'en hsu" (Preface to Someone's Fishing for the Sunken in Explanation of the Ancient Classics), in *Ch'uan-chi*, p. 1102.
33 Tai Chen, "Ta Cheng Yung-mu shu" (A Reply to Cheng Yung-mu's Letter), in *Ch'uan-chi*, p. 1099.

mathematics, calendrical science, astronomy, technology, water-ways, and many other subjects. Among his numerous scholarly accomplishments, the following works are particularly noteworthy : Annotation with Illustrations of the Chapter on Technology in the Rites of Chou (K'ao-kung chi t'u chu), A Study of Phonetics (Sheng-yun k'ao), An Inquiry into the Origins of Astronomy. (Yuan-hsiang), and Commentary on the Water Classic (Shui-ching chu).

Although Tai Chen was admired by Han Learning scholars, such as Ch'ien Ta-hsin (1728~1804) and Chu Yun (1729~1781), for his accomplishments in philology and his extensive learning, Tai Chen was convinced that exegetical research was not an end in itself. He also acknowledged the importance of philosophical inquiry. Dissatisfied with what he regarded as the narrowness of vision of most k'ao-cheng scholars, late in life Tai Chen went beyond the realm of evidential research to evolve a philosophy of his own. In this respect, his philosophical writings reflect an attempt to substitute his own philosophy for the Sung Philosophy of Principle (li-hsueh).

Tai Chen's philosophical views are chiefly embodied in three works: first, the book Yuan Shan (Inquiry into Goodness)[34], which reached its present form in 1766; second, a work entitled Hsu-yen(Prolegomena), completed in 1772; and finally, the work Meng-tzu tzu-i shu-cheng (Evidential Analysis of the Meanings of Terms in the Book of Mencius)[35], which was completed in 1777. These three titles embody Tai Chen's different attitudes towards Sung philosophy and his own philosophical views.

In his first philosophical treatise, Yuan Shan, Tai Chen expressed no explicit criticism of Sung Neo-Confucianism. He seems still to have accepted at that time the authority of the major Sung thinkers in their philosophical interpretations of the Confucian Classics.[36] In his second work, Hsu-yen, there is evidence of his growing doubts concerning the key principles of the Sung philosophers. However, it is

---

34 For an English Translation of this work, see Cheng Chung-ying, *Tai Chen's Inquiry into Goodness* (Hawaii: University of Hawaii Press, 1971).

35 For the English Translation of this work, see Chin Ann-ping and Mansfield Freeman, *Tai Chen on Mencius: Explorations in Words and Meaning* (New Haven: Yale University Press, 1990).

36 Chang Carsun, *Development of Neo-Confucian Thought* (New York: Bookman Associates, 1962), v. 2, p.346.

especially in his last work, the Meng-tzu tzu-i shu-cheng, that his opposition to those principles is most evident. Tai Chen's critique of Neo-Confucianism comprised a desire to restore the original meanings of key Confucian terms that had been misunderstood and misused by Neo-Confucian adherents. Both the title of his last work and the critical approach adopted in it demonstrate the impact of k'ao-cheng thinking on fundamental philosophical issues.[37] Tai's choice of title in this instance underscored his aim of making it plain that in his opinion the best approach to philosophical considerations was through philology, and that he saw his efforts as part of the evidential research movement. Therefore, his philological studies and his philosophical interests were inseparable, for they reinforced each other.[38] The k'ao-cheng method he chose in his approach to the Mencius was to determine the precise meanings of key terms in the text. This approach, he believed, would provide a basis for a more precise understanding of that work and the refutation of the subjective interpretations of the classics by the Neo-Confucianists.[39]

From Tai Chen's intellectual life, it indicated his intellectual development from philology to philosophy. It seemed that Tai Chen had an earlier concern with genuine philosophical observations, however, he did not focus his studies in philosophy in his early life until he wrote Yuan Shan. This was because during his early life, Tai Chen had not evolved his own philosophy. Moreover, Tai Chen believed that the best approach to philosophy should be based on the study of philology, and that one could not become familiar with philology until one had spent long years of study. It was not until in his late life that Tai Chen started to establish his own philosophy and complete his major philosophical studies. Although Tai Chen was satisfied with his philosophical works, his contemporaries esteemed his philosophy very lightly. They even claimed that Tai Chen need not have written these philosophical works.[40] While his philosophical writings were unpopular in his day, Tai Chen thought that

---

37 Elman, p. 19.
38 Chan Wing-tsit, *A Source Book in Chinese Philosophy* (Princeton: Princeton University Press, 1963), p. 709.
39 Elman, p. 19.
40 Chang Hsueh-ch'eng, *Wen-shih t'ung-i* (General Meaning of Literature and History) (Taipei: Shih-hsueh ch'u-pan she, 1974), p. 57.

his approach to philosophy was significant, because it could refute the subjective approach to the Classics by Sung philosophers.

IV. Tai Chen 's Philosophical Beliefs and Approach

Tai Chen's basic approach to the study of philosophy was, as I have already indicated above, through a rigorous philological examination of key texts belonging to the Confucian tradition. His interest in that particular approach developed quite early. In a letter written late in life to his disciple, Tuan Yu-ts'ai(1735~1815), he remarked :

> Since I was seventeen, I have had the intention to get at the truth and believed that Tao can be found only in the Six Classics and the works of Confucius and Mencius. However, if we are not engaged in the study of the meanings of words, institutions, and terms and objects [in the Classics], we can not understand the language of these Classics.[41]

Although separate branches of study, philology and philosophy were for him complimentary undertaking, with one reinforcing the other. He said :

> The eternal truth embodied in the Classics is the Tao. What illuminates the Tao is the words. The words are constructed of characters. Through the characters we may know the words. And by knowing the words we may comprehend the Tao. These are successive steps. Thus, we must know the characters first.[42]

Thus, philology was the methodology chosen to restore the Confucian truth.

Although the main tenets of his beliefs were closely related to his reaction against Sung Neo-Confucianism, it seems that, aside from his criticisms of Neo-Confucianism, he had earlier expressed concern for authentic Confucian principles. Therefore, in his first published work, the Yuan Shan, he did not criticize Neo-Confucian ideas explicitly. On the other hand, his last published work, the Meng-tzu tzu-i shu-cheng, forthrightly criticized the philosophical shortcomings of Neo-

---

41 Tuan Yu-ts'ai, *Tai Tung-yuan hsien-sheng nien-p'u* (A Chronological Biography of Mr. Tai Chen) (Hong Kong: Ch'ung-wen shu-tien, 1971), p. 5.

42 Tai Chen, "Yu Shih Chung-ming shu" (A Letter to Shih Chung-ming), in *Ch'uan-chi*, p. 1098.

Confucianism as he understood them. This critique of Neo-Confucianism demonstrated his concern to correct the understanding of key Confucian terms.

Tai Chen's philosophical writings indicate the impact philology had on philosophical issues. The methodology Tai Chen adopted was essentially linguistic, that is, hsun-ku(etymology, lit., "glossing").[43] For example, his Meng-tzu tzu-i shu-cheng consists of fifteen notes on the term li (reason, principle), four notes on the word t'ien-tao (the way of heaven), thirteen notes on hsing (human nature), four notes on tao (the way), and two notes on jen, i, li, and chih (the four cardinal virtues) respectively. He began with careful glosses of each of these terms. In order to determine their precise meanings, Tai Chen traced them back to their origins. For example, he explains the earliest meaning of the term li as the texture or fibre of things. This definition takes its origin in Hsu Shen's (58~147) Shuo-wen chieh-tzu (Analysis and Explanation of Primary and Derived Characters). In addition to an explanation of the root meaning of each term, examples of usage are cited from the ancient Classics, such as the I-ching (The Book of Changes), the Meng-tzu (the Book of Mencius), the Chung Yung (The Doctrine of the Mean), and Yueh Chi (The Record of Music). This procedure sufficed to indicate that these explanations were not based on personal considerations but had their origin in the Classics. This appeal to etymology, Tai Chen believed, would enable him to confute the misinterpretations of key Confucian terms by earlier thinkers. Tai Chen asserted that Sung Neo-Confucianists erred in interpreting the Confucian texts because they were negatively influenced by Buddhism and Taoism and lacked proper philological expertise.[44] Therefore, their understanding of the Classics characterized by private opinion. He stated, "Since the Sung, the works of Confucius and Mencius were misinterpreted completely, for Confucian scholars adopted ideas from Buddhism and Taoism to interpret these Classics."[45] Elsewhere he argued:

> Although Confucian scholars since the Sung claimed that their interpretations of the Classics accorded fully with what the ancient sages

---

43 Elman, p. 19.
44 Tai Chen, "Yu mou shu", p. 1100.
45 Tai Chen, *Meng-tzu tzu-i shu-cheng*, in Ch'uan-chi, p. 305.

and virtuous men intended to say, they did not really understand the language of these classical works.[46]

Since Tai Chen's primary concern was to recover the essential truth of classical Confucian teachings, he sought to distinguish sharply the teachings of Confucianism from those of Buddhism and Taoism.[47]

V. Conclusion

Operating under the influence of Taoism and Buddhism, Sung dynasty Confucian scholars tended to interpret Confucian doctrines intuitively rather relying on close textual examination of the ancient canons of their tradition. Dissatisfied with this state of affairs, k'ao-cheng scholars of the Ch'ien-Chia era turned back to the exegetical studies of the Han dynasty as a corrective to the subjective approach of their Neo-Confucian predecessors. This kind of scholarship represented not only a reaction against certain Neo-Confucian interpretations of doctrine, but also a conscious effort to recover essential truth of the tradition. Unquestionably, they saw as their first task a need to reexamine and verify the ancient texts. In order to do this, they adopted philological methods as their primary tool.

Although the primary focus of their efforts remained the Classics, they extended their activities into nearly every aspect of the cultural heritage, such as, phonetics, history, geography, mathematics and astronomy.[48] Through these efforts, obscure passages in ancient texts were clarified, lost texts were restored from a variety of sources, forgeries were exposed, and new commentaries on the Classics were written.[49] This effort by k'ao-cheng scholars to subject the ancient texts to close analysis and emendation represented a major achievement.[50]

Although the ancient texts were re-examined and corrected, no new currents of thought were created or major schools of philosophy founded. These men were diligent interpreters of the ancient culture, however, they were not creative

---

46 Tai Chen, "Yu mou shu", p. 1100.
47 Tai Chen, "Ta P'eng chin-shih shu" (Reply to *Chin-shih* P'eng's Letter), in *Ch'uan-chi*, p. 1088.
48 Liang Ch'i-ch'ao, *Ch'ing-tai hsueh-shu kai-lun*.
49 Chang Carsun, v.2, p. 339.
50 Chang Carsun, v.2, p. 339.

builders.[51] Moreover, as they were preoccupied with their philological studies, little interest was taken in current social realities or questions of public morality, matters of traditional Confucian concern.

Tai Chen was regarded as the leading k'ao-cheng scholar of his time because his research methods were objective and reliable and his learning was broad. The goal of his scholarship was to verify the classical texts rather than to preserve Han Learning as such, and in this regard, his scholarship exceeded the scope of Han Learning. This is evident from his contributions to such diverse fields as philological methodology, phonetics, calendrical computations and mathematics, and hydrology, all of which were impressive.

In the context of his time, Tai Chen was a unique thinker and he saw that k'ao-cheng scholarship was not an end in itself, but simply a means to reveal certain truth. The research methods he developed represented improvements upon the work of his predecessors and served to clarify and correct traditional philosophical issues. The merit of this methodology was its precision in defining the meaning of key terms in the Classics, and this in turn had important ramifications for the understanding of the traditional systems of belief.

Tai Chen's own philosophical beliefs were not well received in his day. However, in the nineteenth century, Juan Yuan and Chiao Hsun (1763~1820) adopted the same scholarly procedures in reconstructing the meanings of Confucian concepts.[52] Before the twentieth century, Tai Chen's ideas were not understood and his philosophy was ignored. It was not until the twentieth century that his place in the Chinese intellectual history was first recognized by Chang Ping-lin (1869~1936)and made public.[53]

---

51 Liang Ch'i-ch'ao, *Ch'ing-tai hsueh-shu kai-lun*, pp. 33~55.
52 Juan Yuan, *Hsing-ming ku-hsun* (Ancient Glosses on Nature and External Necessity); Chiao Hsun, *Meng-tzu cheng-i* (Orthodox Meaning of the Book of Mencius).
53 Chang Ping-lin, "Shih Tai p'ien"(Interpretation of Tai Chen's Thought), in *Chang T'ai-yen ch'uan-chi* (Complete Works of Chang T'ai-yen) (Shanghai: Jen-min ch'u-pan she, 1985), v. 4, pp. 122~124; For a study of Chang Ping-lin, see Jer-shiarn Lee, *Chang Ping-lin (1869~1936): A Political Radical and Cultural Conservative* (Taipei :Wen-shih-che ch'u-pan she, 1993).

Chang Ping-lin and His Concern for the Preservation of the National Essence (Kuo-ts'ui 國粹), 1895~1911

I. Introduction

In the history of the Revolution of 1911, although Chang Ping-lin (1869~1936) was known for his role in the Chinese revolutionary movement, he was a unique thinker. Unlike his comrades in the Revolutionary Alliance (T'ung-meng hui), such as Sun Yat-sen (1866~1925) and Huang Hsing (1874~1916) who played leading roles in political, military and organizational tasks, Chang Ping-lin, a prominent classical scholar, made his contributions in the ideological field. It was this very uniqueness that made it difficult for people to understand him and has often caused him to be misunderstood. Moreover, with the complexity of his thought, which could be traced to a variety of sources, from ancient China to the modern West, his ideas, taken together, seemd to be contradictory and in conflict with his world.

Chang's anti-Manchu sentiments were inspired by the writings of late Ming loyalists which he read during his boyhood[1], however, these sentiments did not make him an instant revolutionary. In fact, in spite of his opposition to K'ang Yu-wei's

---

1 Chang Ping-lin, "Wo ti p'ing-sheng yu pan-shih fang-fa" 我的平生與辦事方法 (My Life and the Method for Accomplishing Things), in *Chang T'ai-yen ti pai-hua wen* 章太炎的白話文(The Writing in Vernacular Chinese by Chang T'ai-yen), (Hereafter cited as *CTYTPHW*)(Taipei: I-wen yin -shu-kuan, 1972), p. 88.

interpretation of Confucianism[2], Chang was a firm supporter of the reform movement from 1895 to 1899. Chang did not change his position from reform to revolution until after the outbreak of the Boxer Uprising in 1900. In 1903, Chang became a radical revolutionary and began to attack K'ang's political ideology and even ridiculed the Kuang-hsu emperor (1871~1908).[3] Subsequently, he became involved in the well-known Su-pao (Kiangsu Daily) case in June 1903, and was imprisoned for this for three years. On 29 June 1906, Chang was released from prison and soon became a chief editor of and a major contributor to Min-pao (People's Journal), the principal journal of T'ung-meng hui.[4] However, from 1906 to 1911, he became a moderate revolutionary instead of a radical. He even criticized the views of Hu Han-min and Wang Ching-wei, who, in their articles published in Min-pao, attacked Liang Ch'i-ch'ao (1873~1929) too bitterly.[5] Moreover, although Chang was a spokesman for the rising revolutionary movement, his Min-pao articles did not strongly attack K'ang's rationale for protecting the Kuang-hsu emperor or his reform ideas, but dealt mostly with the preservation of the Chinese national essence. Also paradoxically, he was a Confucian scholar, who rejected Confucian morality and denounced some Confucian ideas[6]; he was a leader of the republican movement, who condemned representative government.[7] His ideas, put together, seemed in conflict with himself and his world. Despite the apparent inconsistency in Chang's thought, his ideas, in fact, were not inconsistent at all. Since Chang was an outstanding classical scholar and a mouthpiece of the T'ung-meng hui, and since his ultimate concern was the preservation of the national essence, from which other seemingly

---

2 Chang Ping-lin, *T'ai-yen hsien-sheng tzu-ting nien p'u* 太炎先生自訂年譜(Mr.[Chang] T'ai-yen's Chronological Autobiography), (Hereafter cited as *Nien-p'u*)(Taipei: Wen-hai ch'u-pan she, 1972), pp. 5~6.

3 Chang Ping-lin, "Po K'ang Yu-wei lun ke-ming shu"駁康有為論革命書(In Refutation of K'ang Yu-wei's Essay on Revolution), in *Chung-kuo chin-tai ssu-hsiang shih ts'an-k'ao tzu-liao chien-pien* 中國近代思想史參考資料簡編(Source Materials on the History of Modern Chinese Thought)(Hong Kong: San-lien shu-tien, 1957), pp. 598~611.

4 Chang Ping-lin was the chief editor of Min-pao, who edited Min-pao from no. 7 (Sept. 5, 1906) to no. 18 (Dec. 25, 1907) and from no. 23 (Aug. 10, 1908) to no. 24 (Oct. 10, 1908)

5 *Nien-p'u*, p. 11.

6 *CTYTPHW*, pp. 91~92.

7 Chang Ping-lin, "Tai-i jan-fou lun"代議然否論(On whether or Not to Have Representative Government), *Min-pao* 24 (Oct. 10, 1908), pp. 1~27.

參、中國思想：英文篇
Chang Ping-lin and His Concern for
the Preservation of the National Essence (Kuo-ts'ui 國粹), 1895~1911

conflicting ideas were derived, the inconsistencies in his thought were more apparent than real.

This essay is concerned with the life and thought of Chang Ping-lin from 1895 to 1911, and in particular with his concern to preserve the national essence of China and its association with other seemingly contradictory ideas in Chang's thought.

The related studies of this topic by Hsiao Kung-ch'uan and Michael Gasster unfortunately do not answer this question, although both of their works have pointed out the conflicts in Chang's writings.[8] We also do not receive a satisfactory explanation from two other Chinese scholars' works.[9]

My paper consists of four sections. The first section deals with Chang's concern to preserve China's national essence which is the core idea in Chang's thought. The second section analyzes Chang's career as a reformer from 1895 to 1899. Section three deals with the event that prompted Chang to change his stance from reform to revolution. The last section discusses the apparent conflicts which are marked in Chang's thought, from 1906 to 1911.

II. The Concern for the Preservation of the National Essence

Although Chang Ping-lin was a reformer from 1895 to 1899, who later supported the revolution wholeheartedly, the effort to preserve China's national essence was the most important mission in his life. By national essence, Chang meant those elements of China's historical and cultural attributes which were still appropriate to the modern Chinese nation.

Chang's education and home environment prepared him to be a transmitter of

---

8 They are: i) Hsiao Kung-ch'uan, "Chang Ping-lin", in *Chung-kuo cheng-chih ssu-hsiang shih* 中國政治思想史(A History of Chinese Political Thought)(Taipei: Chung-kuo wen-hua ta-hsueh ch'u-pan pu, 1980), pp. 867~898. ii) Michael Gasster, "Chang Ping-lin", in *Chinese Intellectuals and the Revolution of 1911: the Birth of Modern Chinese Radicalism* (Seattle: University of Washington, 1969), pp. 190~227.

9 They are:
i) Chang Yu-fa, "Chang Ping-lin", in Wang Shou- nan ed., *Chung-kuo li tai ssu-hsiang chia* 中國歷代思想家(Chinese Thinkers through the Ages), v. 10(Taipei: Shang- wu yin-shu kuan, 1978), pp. 5995~6059.
ii) Chu Hung-yuan, "Min-pao chung ti Chang T'ai-yen"民報中的章太炎(Chang T'ai-yen's Thought in Min-pao Period), *Ta-lu tsa-chih* 68/2. (Fed, 15, 1984), pp. 14~43.

traditional Chinese culture. During his childhood Chang was educated by his maternal grandfather, and then by his father, who instructed him in the Chinese classics and history.[10] At the age of twenty-three, Chang continued his studies in philology, history and classics at Ku-ching ching-she (Ku-ching Academy) in Hang-chou, where he was tutored by Yu Yueh(1821~1907)[11], a famous classical scholar. Before Chang was twenty-eight, his discipline in Chinese classical scholarship had become very profound. Although Chang was unwilling to enter civil service examinations under the Ch'ing[12], he was thoroughly committed to philology and classical studies throughout his life. Even during his careers as a reformer and a revolutionary, he was deeply interested in the study of classical learning, and published a number of his most important works on the Chinese classical studies.[13] After 1911, Chang published a monthly magazine entitled Hua-kuo[14], as well as a semi-monthly, Chih-yen[15], and founded a private school, Chang-shih kuo-hsueh chiang-hsi hui[16], through which he sought to keep Chinese culture alive.

As a classical scholar, Chang Ping-lin assumed the responsibility of maintaining Chinese culture voluntarily throughout his life. He formulated that his life-long ambition was "to revere Chinese history and preserve China's unique spoken and written languages".[17] He lamented that "the Chinese national essence will be extinct in my own hands"[18], when he was in prison in June, 1903. He also

---

10 *Nien-p'u*, p.2.

11 *Nien-p'u*, pp. 3~4.

12 *Nien-p'u*, pp. 2, 53.

13 They are:

    i) *Ch'un-ch'iu Tso-chuan tu* 春秋左傳讀(Notes on Tso's Commentary).

    ii) *Hsin fang-yen* 新方言(New Dialects).

    iii) *Chuang-tzu chieh-ku* 莊子解故(Interpretation of Chuang-tzu).

    iv) *Wen-shih* 文始(the Origins of Chinese Script).

    v) *Kuo-ku lun-heng* 國故論衡(Discussions of National Studies).

    vi) *Ch'i-wu-lun shih* 齊物論釋(Interpretation of the Equality of Things).

14 *Nien-p'u*, p. 50.

15 *Nien-p'u*, p. 50.

16 *Nien-p'u*, p. 50.

17 Chang Yu-fa, "Chang Ping-lin" p. 6048.

18 Chou Hung-jan ed., *Chang T'ai-yen hsuan-chi* 章太炎選集(The Selected Works of Chang Tai-yen)(Taipei: P'a-mi-erh shu-tien, 1979), p. 2.

參、中國思想：英文篇
Chang Ping-lin and His Concern for
the Preservation of the National Essence (Kuo-ts'ui 國粹), 1895~1911

asserted that after he died, Chinese culture would be extinguished.[19] He thought that the differences among nations were their histories, as well as spoken and written languages. Therefore, Chang had to maintain these two characteristics, especially when China was under the pressure from foreign powers.

Although Chang advocated the crucial need to preserve the national essence, he accepted Chinese culture in a critical way and was very definite about the elements of the culture which were to be maintained. His acceptance of Chinese culture became a matter of deliberate choice. National essence, Chang expressed, did not mean Confucian religion[20], as K'ang Yu-wei(1858~1927) claimed, but, in broad sense, Chinese history[21], which might be divided into three aspects.[22]

First, there were China's spoken and written languages. Through the spoken and written languages people could read ancient books and understand China's past. "If people have no idea of their past", Chang said, "what is the difference between them and the birds as well as the beasts?"[23] Second, there were China's laws and institutions. Chang maintained that although not all of the old systems might be esteemed, some features could be reformed, and others revived. Here, for example, he mentioned the Chun- t'ien (equal-field) system, the legal system, and the civil service examination system, which were unique in China and he felt, corresponded with socialism. In short, all of China's institutions tended toward socialism, and could apply equally to all. Finally, there were great men in China's history. At first, Chang mentioned Liu Yu and Yueh Fei, who were admirable, because they employed southern troops to defeat the barbarians. Their examples could heighten Chinese spirit. Chang also spoke highly of Chinese philosophy, and held that the most learned men were philosophers in the Chou and Ch'in dynasties. In sum, Chang said, "To promote the national essence means that people should cherish China's history".[24] Apparently Chang's conception of national essence was the essential or good elements in Chinese culture.

---

19 T'ang Kuo-li ed., *Chang T'ai-yen hsien-sheng chia-shu* 章太炎先生家書(Letters from Mr. Chang T'ai-yen to His Wife)(Taipei: Wen-hai ch'u-pan-she, 1966), p. 101.
20 *CTYTPHW*, p. 96.
21 *CTYTPHW*, p. 96.
22 *CTYTPHW*, p. 96.
23 Chou Hung-jan ed., *Chang T'ai-yen hsuan-chi*, p. 75.
24 *CTYTPHW*, p. 96.

Chang's concern to preserve the national essence was not only because he was a classical scholar, but also because it was essential for the survival of the nation. Under the pressure from Western powers, Chang was afraid that Chinese culture was threatened with extinction. In order to prevent foreign conquest, Chang believed that reform or revolution in China was necessary, and that the most important mission of the reformer or revolutionary was to keep China's unique culture alive. Therefore, Chang gave priority to the preservation of the national essence over the nation. The latter was important only because it was needed to save the former. And reform or revolution was in turn necessary to save the nation.

III. Chang Ping-lin As a Reformer: 1895~1899

Chang Ping-lin had been a reformer since 1895. After China's humiliating defeat in the Sino-Japanese War(1894~1895), Chang was convinced that it was necessary to implement reforms to save China. In 1895, Chang joined the Ch'iang-hsueh hui (Society for Study of National Strengthening)[25], a reform club, which was organized by K'ang Yu-wei. In 1896, Chang joined the staff of the Shih-wu pao (Current Affairs Journal), which was started by Liang Ch'i-ch'ao.[26] It was said that Chang was a firm supporter of the reform movement. Even after the failure of the reform, he remained a reformist. It was after the outbreak of the Boxer Uprising in 1900 that Chang abandoned his stance as a reformer.

Although Chang's anti-Manchu sentiments were inspired during his childhood, his support of reform was due to his main concern for preserving the Chinese national essence. With the foreign aggression, Chang hoped that the Manchu government could resist the foreign powers. A successful reform, he thought, would strengthen the government's ability to defend the nation. Therefore, he said, "After the downfall of the Ming dynasty(1368~1644), how can it be without the emperor in China for hundreds of years?"[27] However, it should be remembered that Chang's

---

25 Feng Tzu-yu, *Chung-hua min-kuo k'ai-kuo ch'ien ke-ming shih* 中華民國開國前革命史(A History of the Revolution before the Founding of the Republic of China)(Taipei: Shih-chieh shu-chu, 1954), v. 1, p. 112.

26 *Nien-p'u*, p.5.

27 T'ang Chih-chun ed., *Chang T'ai-yen cheng-lun hsuan-chi* 章太炎政論選集(The Selected Works of Chang T'ai-yen's Political Essays) (Hereafter cited as

參、中國思想：英文篇
Chang Ping-lin and His Concern for
the Preservation of the National Essence (Kuo-ts'ui 國粹), 1895~1911

support of reform was not to protect the Manchu regime, but to save the nation. And he saw national survival as the only way to keep the national essence alive.

Even after the failure of the reform in 1898, Chang still worked for the reformers, mainly because K'ang adopted Chinese culture to implement reform, and the basic aim of K'ang's reform was also to preserve China's tradition. Unlike K'ang Yu-wei, who was an advocate of the Chin-wen (New Text) school, and based his theories on the Kung-yang commentary, Chang Ping-lin was an adherent of the Ku-wen (Old Text) school of classical learning, and maintained the superiority of the Tso-chuan(Tso's commentary on the Spring and Autumn Annals) over the two other commentaries on the Ch'un-ch'iu, the Kung-yang chuan and the Ku-liang chuan. Although it was said that Chang already objected to K'ang's interpretation of Confucianism, this objection did not prevent Chang from joining the Ch'iang-hsueh-hui in 1895. Since Chang, at that time, was not a staunch advocate of the Old Text school, he also adopted some ideas from the works of the New Text school in his own writings[28], and even wrote an article to defend K'ang's view on interpreting the Classics.[29] Chang's opposition to K'ang's conceptions of Confucianism, at that time, was not so sharp, and this only showed that his primary understanding of the classics was different from K'ang's. It was after 1900 that Chang started to purify his conception of the elements of Chinese culture and to counter K'ang's view on the interpretation of Confucianism. Apparently it was K'ang's adoption of Chinese culture to implement reform, and the concern for the preservation of Chinese tradition, which he shared with K'ang, that permitted Chang to support K'ang's reform from 1895 to 1898.

IV. The Stance from Reform to Revolution: 1900~1906

The event that prompted Chang to change his position from reform to revolution was the outbreak of the Boxer Uprising in 1900. This event gave rise to a

---

CLHC)(Peiking: Chung-hua shu-chu 1977), v. 1, p. 87.

28 T'ang Chih-chun ed., *Chang T'ai-yen nien-p'u ch'ang-pian* 章太炎年譜長編 (A Chronological Biography of Chang T'ai-yen) (Hereafter cited as *NPCP*)(Peiking: Chung-hua shu-chu, 1979), v. 1. pp. 41~42.

29 T'ang Chih-chun ed., *Chang T'ai-yen nien-p'u ch'ang-pian* 章太炎年譜長編 (A Chronological Biography of Chang T'ai-yen), pp. 87~89.

national crisis: the allied forces of the eight powers occupied the Taku Forts on June 16, and the Manchu court declared war on foreign powers on June 21.[30] Because of the Boxer crisis, Chang Ping-lin attended a "national conference" (Kuo-hui), which was organized by T'ang Ts'ai-ch'ang[31], a disciple of K'ang Yu-wei. The purpose of the conference was to oppose the war policy of the Manchu government. Since, at the conference, T'ang and other leaders expressed their loyalty to the emperor Kuang-hsu, Chang protested bitterly and cut off his queue.[32] Since the queue was a symbol of Chinese submission to the Manchu conquest, the action showed his final break with the Manchu dynasty. He was convinced that China's survival could not depend on the Manchu regime, and therefore, it had to be overthrown. He said, "If we do not overthrow the Manchu government, we can not expect the people to love their own country and to resist foreign threats. Sooner or later, we will be gradually made slaves of the Europeans, and the Americans".[33] From then on, Chang apparently became an anti-Manchu revolutionary.

Since the Manchu government was unable to resist the foreign powers, Chang called for revolution to save the nation. However, revolution was perceived by Chang only as a means of serving an ultimate goal: the preservation of Chinese national essence. He said, "If Chinese people do not know the national essence, China will go the way of India, which has fallen under foreign rule".[34] In addition, Chang held that Chinese should find their revolutionary inspiration in Chinese culture, and employ the national essence to stimulate racial spirit and to promote people's patriotism.[35] Chang was also expressing his further and more fundamental belief that the preservation of Chinese national essence gave the nation its mission and meaning. He said:

---

30 Hsiao I-shan, *Ch'ing-tai t'ung shih* 清代通史 (A General History of Ch'ing Period)(Taipei: Shang-wu yin-shu-kuan, 1962), v. 4, pp. 196~198.

31 Feng Tzu-yu, *Ko-ming i-shih* 革命逸史(Untold Stories about the Revolution)(Peiking: Chung-hua shu-chu 1979), v. 2, p. 76.

32 *Nien-p'u*, p.7.

33 Shanghai Jen-min ch'u-pan-she ed., *Chang T'ai-yen ch'uan-chi* 章太炎全集(Complete Works of Chang T'ai-yen), (Hereafter cited as *CTYCC*)(Shanghai: Jen-min ch'u-pan-she, 1984), v. 3, p. 120.

34 *CLHC*, v. I, p. 307.

35 *CTYTPHW*; p. 91.

參、中國思想：英文篇
Chang Ping-lin and His Concern for
the Preservation of the National Essence (Kuo-ts'ui 國粹), 1895~1911

The reason that a nation is a nation lies in its essence.------The difference between the human and the birds as well as the beasts is only because the former can know their past. If the national essence is extinct, people will not know the past of their nation. In this case, what is the difference between them and the birds as well as the beasts.------If a nation is not conscious of its essence, it will be gradually conquered by other nations, and even perish.[36]

Apparently Chang's devotion to revolution was mainly as a means to protect China's culture and to guarantee the continuity of its literary and scholarly tradition.

V. The Conflicts in His Thought : 1906~1911

From 1906 to 1911, Chang's thought was very complicated and his ideas, put together, seemed to be in conflict with himself and his world. However, since his revolutionary and political ideas were derived from his concern for the preservation of the national essence, in fact, his thought was not inconsistent at all.

In spite of the fact that Chang was a leader of the revolutionary movement, he called for the preservation of Chinese culture. On 29 June 1906, upon his release from prison, Chang was welcomed by members of the T'ung-meng-hui, and made a speech to them.[37] However, in his speech, Chang did not discuss his conception of the national revolution and politics, but expounded on the importance of the national essence. Then, in his years as the chief editor of the Min-pao, aside from his duty as the editor, Chang was devoted to teaching and research on Chinese classical scholarship. Moreover, a number of his most important writings on the national studies were published at this time. Chang's emphasis on the national essence clearly distinguished him from all other members in the T'ung-meng-hui, and even seemed to conflict with his revolutionary stance. However, since in Chang's eyes, revolution was seen only as a means to keep the national essence alive, in fact, there was no conflict in his ideas at all.

Another seemingly conflicting idea was that Chang was a Confucian scholar,

---

36 Chou Hung-jan ed., *Chang T'ai-yen hsuan-chi,* pp. 75~76.

37 Shen Yen-kuo, *Chi Chang T'ai-yen hsien-sheng* 記章太炎先生(Remembering Mr. Chang T'ai-yen)(Taipei: Wen-hai ch'u-pan-she), pp. 29~30.

who rejected Confucian morality and even denounced some Confucian ideas.[38] However, in fact, there was no conflict in his thought. In Chang's view, Confucianism was linked with ideas of status and privilege. As he said, "The greatest defect of Confucianism is that it makes people pursue wealth and high position".[39] Thus, he continued to say that people who practiced Confucian morality tended to seek wealth and high positions. They can not endure all hardships but pursue their own selfish interests.[40] Nevertheless, Chang also regarded "Confucius as a good historian in ancient times"[41], and praised Confucius' great contributions to Chinese education and history.[42] Moreover, Confucianism also played an important role in China's national essence, which Chang promoted. For example, Confucius and Hsun Tzu were among the philosophers whom Chang admired, and actually Confucian scholars have also made contributions to the chun-t'ien system. Since Chang's acceptance of the Chinese tradition was highly selective, he kept the elements which were essential, and got rid of those were not. In Chang's eyes, not all of the constituent elements of Confucianism were essential, and the defect in Confucianism was the idea to pursue wealth and high positions. Because of his concern for preservation of the national essence, Chang praised the essentials in Confucianism and criticized those elements which were not essential in it.

Chang advocated that republicanism was the most advanced form of political organization[43], however, he condemned representative government.[44] This was because, in Chang's view, republicanism was consistent with equality. In Chang's eyes, republicanism was the anti-monarchical political institution, which excluded the feature of parliament. Although the form of government Chang preferred was republicanism, he did not accept it without reservation. As he said, "If it is necessary for a nation to have a government, then a republic is probably the least harmful form

---

38 *CLHC*, v. 1, pp. 289~291.
39 *CTYTPHW*, p. 92.
40 *CLHC*, v.1, pp. 289- 291.
41 *CTYCC*, v 3, p. 135.
42 *CLHC*, v.2, p.690.
43 *CTYTPHW*, p. 94.
44 Chang Ping-lin, "Tai-i jan-fou lun", pp. 456~470.

參、中國思想：英文篇
Chang Ping-lin and His Concern for
the Preservation of the National Essence (Kuo-ts'ui 國粹), 1895~1911

it can take. [45] Thus, in order to minimize its harmfulness, it needed some amendments: first, equal distribution of land to eliminate tenancy; second, government to establish industries to let the workers divide the profits equally; third, a ban on the inheritance of property to prevent wealth from being passed on to descendants; and fourth, to allow the people with the right to remove their representatives from office. [46] After these amendments, Chang saw republicanism as a political system with equality.

Although Chang accepted republicanism, he strongly opposed the idea of introducing representative government into China, for Chang thought, "It is a remnant of feudalism," [47] which was characterized by a class division between the nobles and the commoners. This division also existed in representative government [48], for Chang thought that its essential characteristic was "An upper house composed of nobles". [49] Chang asserted that a nation would adopt representative government, only if it was closer to its feudal stage, and still characterized by a division between nobility and commoners. [50] "China, however, had long outgrown her feudal stage". Chang said, "and in China all people are equal". [51] Since the representative government was inconsistent with equality, Chang urged that China should not adopt this system, which was inappropriate for her. [52] According to Chang's conception of the national essence, all of China's institutions were consistent with equality. Chang denounced representative government, because this institution was incompatible with equality, and was a remnant of feudalism, which was inconsistent with his conception of the national essence.

Despite his importance as one of the major Chinese thinkers, scholars and

---

45 *Chang-shih ts'ung-shu* 章氏叢書(The Collected Writings of Chang Ping-lin) (Hereafter cited as *CSTS*)(Taipei: Shih-chieh shu-chu, 1982), v. 2,p. 886, see also Gasster, *Chinese Intellectuals and the Revolution of 1911*, p. 214.
46 *CSTS*, v. 2, p. 886; Gasster, *Chinese Intellectuals and the Revolution of 1911*, p. 214.
47 Chang Ping-lin, "Tai-i jan-fou lun", p.456.
48 Chang Ping-lin, "Tai-i jan-fou lun", p.456.
49 Chang Ping-lin, "Tai-i jan-fou lun", p.456.
50 Chang Ping-lin, "Tai-i jan-fou lun", p.456.
51 Chang Ping-lin, "Tai-i jan-fou lun", p.456.
52 Chang Ping-lin, "Tai-i jan-fou lun", p.470.

political activists of this century, Chang has received little attention in the West. Even the scant scholarly treatment Chang has received in the West[53] fails to assess adequately his life and thought. His ideas, when taken together, are considered to be contradictory. Much of this appearance of inconsistency, however, is reduced, or even eliminated, if we keep in mind his efforts to preserve the national essence, which is the most consistent thread in his thinking, for all of his differing positions were assumed only as a means to serve an ultimate goal: the preservation of the national essence. This concern was always the unifier of apparent opposites.

The preservation of the national essence was the core idea and the most fundamental and constant characteristic of his thinking, and the foundation for his political action. A thorough study on Chang's life and thought is necessary to show this dimension of his thought. Unfortunately, both Chinese and Western scholars have overlooked this core idea, and thus have limited our understanding of Chang's thought. Therefore, there is a strong need for a reassessment of Chang Ping-lin. It is

---

53 There are only few articles in English: Charlotte Furth, "The Sage as Rebel: The Inner World of Chang Ping-lin", in Charlotte Furth ed., *The Limits of Change: Essays on Conservative Alternatives in Republican China*(Cambridge: Harvard University Press, 1976), pp. 113~150; Joshua A. Fogel, "Race and Class in Chinese Historiography: Divergent Interpretations of Zhang Bing-lin and Anti-Manchuism in the 1911 Revolution", *Modern China* 3/3 (July, 1977), pp. 346~375. Warren Sun, "Chang Ping-lin and His Political Thought", *Paper on Far Eastern History*(September, 1985), pp. 57~69; One chapter on Chang Ping-lin in both Michael Gasster's *Chinese Intellectuals and the Revolution of 1911: The Birth of Modern Chinese Radicalism*(Seattle: University of Washington Press, 1968), pp.190~227 , and Chang Hao's *Chinese Intellectuals in Crisis: Search for Order and Meaning*(1890~1911)(Berkeley: University of California Press, 1987), pp. 104~145; and a biography of Chang in Boorman, Howard L., and Howard, Richard eds., *Biographical Dictionary of Republican China*, 4 Vols.(New York: Columbia University Press, 1967), v.l, pp. 92~98. In 1989 Young-tsu Wong published a book on Chang: *Search for Modern Nationalism: Zhang Binglin and Revolutionary China, 1869~1936*(Oxford: Oxford University Press). In this book, he focused his study mainly on Chang's political ideas and activities and made great effort to evaluate Chang's contribution to revolution and politics. However, he failed to probe Chang's core idea, the preservation of the national essence and its significance to Chang's political ideas. Chinese scholars have also published on Chang, for example, see Li Zehou, "Zhang Taiyan As a Revolutionary and a Thinker", in *The 1911 Revolution: A Retrospective after 70 years*(Peking: New World Press, 1983), pp. 183~202; Mabel Lee, "Chang Ping-lin's Concept of Self and Society: Questions of Constancy and Continuity after the 1911 Revolution" in *Conference on the Early History of China, 1917~1927*(Taipei: Chung-yang yen-chiu-yuan chin-tai-shih yen-chiu-so, 1984), v.2, pp. 593~628.

參、中國思想：英文篇
Chang Ping-lin and His Concern for
the Preservation of the National Essence (Kuo-ts'ui 國粹), 1895~1911

also hoped that my study of Chang Ping-lin will begin this effort and provide a better understanding of his life and thought.

VI. Conclusion

Although Chang Ping-lin was noted for his role in the Chinese revolutionary movement, he was more famous in the field of Chinese classical learning. In Chang's career, reform and revolution were interludes while the preservation of Chinese national essence was a life-long calling. Therefore, the effort to maintain the national essence was the most consistent threads in Chang's life. With the national crisis, which was due to the pressure from foreign powers, Chang was afraid that Chinese culture was threatened with extinction. In order to save the national essence, Chang called for reform and then for revolution. However, reform or revolution was perceived by Chang only as a means to preserve the national essence.

Chang was a leader of T'ung-meng-hui, however, his emphasis on the preservation of the national essence distinguished him from all other members in the T'ung-meng-hui. And since his thought was very complicated, his ideas, put together, seemed to be contradictory. However, his ideas were derived from his overwhelming concern to preserve the national essence. In terms of this concern, his thought was not inconsistent at all.

While Chang was a proponent of Chinese culture, apart from his devotion to teaching and research, he participated in revolution and politics. He had to do so, because, as a classical scholar, he should be concerned about national affairs, especially when China was in crisis. Chang was a model of the traditional Chinese intellectual, who did not forget to do his duties for his country. Moreover, he was not only devoted to national studies, but also put his ideas in practice.

Chang Ping-lin and His Dilemma between Scholarship and Politics

I. Introduction

Although Chang Ping-lin(1869~1936) is well-known for his role in the revolutionary movement that culminated in the termination of imperial rule in 1911, he is more often remembered as a prominent clssical scholar.

While Chang Ping-lin was still a student at the Ku-ching Academy, he became involved in the reform movement which began after 1894. In 1895 Chang became an active reformist, and after 1900, a prominent revolutionary. Inasmuch as he was a serious student of the School of Han Learning, which stressed scholarship as purely textual studies divorced from politics, Chang found himself in a dilemma between scholarship and politics; which should be his priority, the promotion of national cultural heritage or national survival?[1] How did Chang resolve this dilemma?

Although Chang's anti-Manchu sentiments began during his childhood, he became a reformist before he became a revolutionary. Why did he favore reform when he was first involved in politics? Chang was also regarded as a racist, or an "ethnocentric nationalist"[2], for he was prominent as an anti-Manchu revolutionary

---

1 Chang Hao, *Chinese Intellectuals in Crisis: Search for Order and Meaning, 1890~1911*(Berkeley: University of California Press, 1987);Young-tsu Wong, *Search for Modern Nationalism: Zhang Binglin and Revolutionary China, 1869~1936*(Hong Kong: Oxford University Press, 1989).

2 Charlotte Furth, "The Sage as Rebel: The Inner World of Chang Ping-lin" in Charlotte

who had drawn a distinct line between the Manchus and the Han Chinese race. However, was it really the case?

This paper will examine these and related questions under two headings: first, Chang's dilemma between scholarship and politics and second, Chang as an anti-Manchu revolutionist.

II. Chang's Dilemma between Scholarship and Politics

After China was defeated in the Sino-Japanese War of 1894~1895, many Chinese intellectuals became convinced that it was imperative for China to undertake far-reaching reforms to survive as an independent nation. This defeat had greater impact on the Chinese than any of the other defeats China had previously suffered by foreign powers.[3] With this war, the efforts of self-strengthening reforms which has been under way for more than two decades failed as China's recently built modern navy was totally annihilated?[4] It seemed particularly shocking to most Chinese that China could be even defeated by such a small country which most Chinese had regarded as far inferior to China in both culture and power.[5] This defeat thus awakened most Chinese from the dream that by the adoption of Western technology in the method of the self-strengthening reform China could become a great power.[6] Therefore, many Chinese intellectuals began to realize that unless China implemented fundamental changes in the government, the survival of the nation would come into question. And K'ang Yu-wei's reformism became prominent in this intellectual ferment.

K'ang had petitioned the throne for the need of reform in 1888[7] to no avail . And only in 1895 after China's defeat did any large scale reform begin.[8] In this year, when

Furth ed., *The Limits of Change: Essays on Conservative Alternatives in Republican China* (Cambridge: Harvard University Press, 1976), pp. 117, 138, 149.

3 Chang Hao, "Intellectual Change and the Reform Movement, 1890~8" , in Denis Twitchett and John K. Fairbank eds., *The Cambridge History of China*(Cambridge: Cambridge University Press,1980), v. 11, p. 291.

4 C.Y. Hsu, "Late Ch'ing Foreign Relations, 1866~1905, in *The Cambridge History of China*, v. 11, pp. 106~107.

5 Chang Hao, "Intellectual Change and the Reform Movement, 1890~8", p. 291.

6 Leung Man-kam, "Chang Ping-lin: His Life and Career", *Lien-ho Shu-yüan hsüeh-pao* 8 (1976), p. 97.

7 Chang Hao, "Intellectual Change and the Reform Movement, 1890~8", p. 291.

8 Chang Hao, "Intellectual Change and the Reform Movement, 1890~8", p. 291.

K'ang was in Peking for the metropolitan civil service examination, he rallied hundreds of his fellow examination candidates to petition for resistance against the Japanese invasion and for initiating reform.[9] In August, 1895, K'ang established the Society for the Study of Self-strengthening (Ch'iang-hsüeh hui) in Peking, aiming at political reform.[10] Two months later, a Shanghai branch was also founded by K'ang.[11]

While Chang was still studying at the Ku-ching Academy, he learned of the humiliating defeat of China by Japan in 1894: it stimulated Chang's involvement in politics. He observed that the state of the nation was deplorable, and it was the age that even some wise men became recluses.[12] As he said, "When China was faced with partition [by foreign powers], I could not bear it."[13] Thus, like many intellectuals of the time, Chang was roused to action. In 1895, Chang sent a contribution and enlisted in K'ang's Ch'iang-hsüeh hui in Shanghai.[14] The next year Chang left Ku-ching Academy when he was invited to join the editorial staff of the reformist journal Shih-wu pao(Current Affairs Journal), edited by Liang Ch'i-ch'ao(1873~1929).[15]

Chang's departure from the academy was disapproved by his teacher, Yü Yüeh(1821~1907), who regarded it as a betrayal of the tradition of the School of Han Learning, which stressed the study for the sake of study with no political involvement. Chang's involvement in politics did place him in a dilemma between scholarship and politics.[16] However, Chang's conviction that the preservation of

---

9 Chang Hao, "Intellectual Change and the Reform Movement, 1890~8", pp. 291~292.

10 Chang Hao, "Intellectual Change and the Reform Movement, 1890~8", p. 293.

11 Chang Hao, "Intellectual Change and the Reform Movement, 1890~8", p. 294.

12 Chang Ping-lin, "Ming-tu" in Chiang I-hua and Chu Wei-cheng eds., *Chang T'ai-yen hsüan-chi* 章太炎選集(Selected Essays of Chang Tai-yen)(Shanghai: Jen-min ch'u-pan-she, 1981), p. 8; also see Lee, Mabel, "Chang Ping-lin's Concept of Self and Society: Questions of Constancy and Continuity after the 1911 Rovolution", in *Conference on the Early History of China, 1917~1927*(Taipei: the Institute of Modern History, Academia Sinica, 1984), v.2, p. 601.

13 Chang Ping-lin, "Ming-tu", p. 7.

14 Chang Ping-lin, *T'ai-yen hsien-sheng tzu-ting nien p'u* 太炎先生自訂年譜(Mr.[Chang] T'ai-yen's Chronological Autobiography), (Hereafter cited as *Nien-p'u*)(Taipei: Wen-hai ch'u-pan she, 1972), p. 5.

15 Chang Ping-lin, *T'ai-yen hsien-sheng tzu-ting nien p'u* 太炎先生自訂年譜(Mr.[Chang] T'ai-yen's Chronological Autobiography), p. 5.

16 Chang Hao, *Chinese Intellectuals in Crisis*, p. 105.

national culture could save the nation appeared to provide a resolution to this contradiction. Thus, while Chang was involved in politics, he never gave up the evidential scholarship of the school, for Chang believed that the survival of the nation depended on the survival of the national culture, and that the preservation of the national culture could strengthen the nation. Obviously, politics was perceived by Chang only as a means to protect China's culture. Even after Chang had become a revolutionary, he paid a visit to Yü Yüeh in 1901, who still scolded him very bitterly for his engagement in radical politics. Chang defended himself by appealing to the example of Ku Yen-wu(1613~1682), the founder of Han Learning, who combined scholarship with politics to justify his political involvement or anti-Manchuism.[17] Chang said, "The purpose of Ku's devotion to ching-hsüeh(classical studies) was to trace the origin of kuo-hsing(national character) and to draw a distinction between Han Chinese and barbarians [the Manchus]."[18] Thus, Chang's devotion to political radicalism was largely as a means to protect China's cultural heritage and to guarantee its continuity especially when China's culture was threatened with extinction by foreign powers.

While Chang had been exposed to anti-Manchu ideas in his early years, he did not become an instant revolutionary. In fact, he supported K'ang-Liang's reform from 1895. Chang was in favor of reform rather than revolution, because at that time K'ang-Liang's initiative was the most influential among those advocating change.[19] Besides, Chang at that time did not approve of Sun Yat-sen's(1866~1925) activities of revolution, for he doubted if Sun's revolution would benefit China. More important as far as Chang was concerned was that one of K'ang's aims of reform was to protect Chinese culture from the Western challenge; this shared goal permitted Chang to support K'ang in the mid-1890s. Although reform and revolution were regarded as the most practical means to deal with China's political crisis, until 1905~1909, most people were attracted to join the camp of reform, for they believed that reform would offer the greatest hopes to resolve China's problems.[20]

---

17 *Nien-p'u*, p. 8; see also Chang Hao, *Chinese Intellectuals in Crisis*, pp. 105~106.
18 *Nien-p'u*, p. 8.
19 Lee, p.602.
20 Lee, p. 598.

Although Sun Yat-sen had advocated revolution in 1894[21], it seemed that Chang was not attracted by Sun's political activities, for Chang did not think Sun's revolutionary activities would be promising, and he, before meeting Sun, even dismissed him as an "uncultured outlaw". [22] Sun Yat-sen had founded the revolutionary organization, the Hsing-Chung hui(Society to Revive China), in Honolulu in 1894, however, it had only a few members. [23] He also launched an uprising in Canton in 1895. The Chinese revolution was thus under way. However, the revolt was quickly suppressed by the Manchu government. [24] Even after his work on revolution for nine years, it had borne little fruit. By 1903, his revolutionary camp gained only little support and was short of funds, members and military equipment. [25] Thus, by 1903, no one would regard Sun as a promising revolutionary.

Besides, Sun was perceived by his contemporaries, especially the intellectuals, as a bandit (k'ou). For example, Wu Ching-heng (1864~1953) despised Sun as a "rustic ruffian", and even suspected that he was illiterate in Chinese.[26] This image was probably because Sun received Western education overseas in his early years. Chang also indicated that the students in Japan also thought that Sun was hard to get along with and they were rather indifferent toward him.[27] However, the suspicion was probably mutual, for Sun was also skeptical of trusting the intellectuals and students in the revolutionary movement.[28] This was evident that Sun did not attempt to recruit the intellectuals and students into Hsing-Chung hui, and he gained the

---

21 Michael Gasster, *Chinese Intellectuals and the Revolution of 1911:the Birth of Modern Chinese Radicalism*(Seattle:University of Washington, 1968), pp.28~29.

22 Chang Ping-lin, "Ch'in Li-shan chüan" 秦力山傳, in Shanghai Jen-min ch'u-pan-she ed., *Chang T'ai-yen ch'uan-chi* 章太炎全集(Complete Works of Chang T'ai-yen)(Hereafter cited as *CTYCC*)(Shanghai: Jen-min ch'u-pan-she, 1984), v. 5, p. 185; see also Hsüeh Chün-tu, *Huang Hsing and the Chinese Revolution* (Stanford: Stanford University Press, 1961), p. 33.

23 Gasster, p.28.

24 Gasster, p.29.

25 Gasster, p.30.

26 Schiffrin, Harold Z., *Sun Yat-sen and the Origins of the Chinese Revolution*(Berkeley: University of California Press, 1968), p. 300.

27 Hsüeh, p. 35.

28 Schiffrin, p. 300.

support mostly from overseas Chinese.[29]

While Chang was appreciative of Sun's anti-Manchu cause, he did not support revolution, not only because Chang suspected Sun's personality and leadership at that time, but because he doubted that revolution would save China. Chang began to take notice of Sun in 1896, when Sun was kidnapped in the Chinese embassy in London. Chang asked Liang Ch'i-ch'ao who Sun was? Liang told him that Sun was a die-hard anti-Manchu advocator. Chang was very much impressed.[30] While Chang was impressed with Sun who had "brilliant ideas" (chuo-shih) to advocate anti-Manchu revolution, he perceived Sun as a man who was unstable and not trustworthy, and thus, he could not become a Chang Chiao(?~184) or Wang Hsien-chih(?~878).[31] Chang also thought that revolution would bring chaos and lead to the division of China by the foreign powers, and only reform could save China. Therefore, while as early as 1894, Sun had already established the Hsing-Chung hui to engage in revolutionary activities, his influence among students and intellectuals was negligible. At that time, most Chinese intellectuals were ideologically dominated by K'ang-Liang's reformism. Thus, even Sun had formulated that the main goal of the Hsing-Chung hui was to overthrow the Manchus[32], Chang did not participate in Sun's revolutionary camp. In any case, Chang's anti-Manchu sentiments at that time could take no more radical form than refusal to enter the civil service examinations under the Ch'ing.[33]

---

29 Chang Yü-fa, *Ch'ing-chi te ke-ming t'uan-t'i* 清季的革命團體(Revolutionary Groups of the Late Ch'ing Period)(Taipei: Chung-yang yen-chiu-yüan chin-tai-shih yen-chiu-so, 1982), p. 202.

30 Chu Hsi-tsu, "Pen-shih Chang T'ai-yen k'ou-shou shao-nien shih-chi pi-chi"本師章太炎先生口授少年事跡筆記(Notes on My Teacher Mr.Chang Tai-yen's Reminiscences of His Early Years), *Chih-yen* 35 (1936), p. 1; see also Leung, p. 102.

31 T'ang Chih-chun ed., *Chang T'ai-yen nien-p'u ch'ang-pian* 章太炎年譜長編(A Chronological Biography of Chang T'ai-yen) (Hereafter cited as *NPCP*)(Peiking: Chung-hua shu-chu, 1979), v. 1, p. 83; see also Lee, p. 612. Chang Chiao was a leader of the Yellow Turban Uprising at the close of the Eastern Han dynasty. He started a rebellion in 184 A.D. Wang Hsien-chih was a leader of the peasant rebellion in the Late T'ang. He began his uprising in 875 A.D.

32 Gasster, p.30.

33 *NPCP*, v. 1, p. 7; see also Mary Backus Rankin, *Early Chinese Revolutionaries: Radical Intellectuals in Shanghai and Chekiang, 1902~1911*(Cambridge: Harvard University Press, 1971) p. 54.

Chang supported K'ang's reform, because he shared K'ang's concern to preserve China's tradition, for throughout his life the preservation of China's cultural heritage was Chang's ultimate concern or goal. And he perceived politics or reform was only as a means to fulfill this goal. At the very beginning, when K'ang proposed his reform, he saw China was threatened by Western aggression both politically and culturally. Apart from the national crisis, China also encountered a cultural crisis threatened by the Western culture, especially Christianity. In order to meet the Western challenge, it was therefore as important to preserve Chinese tradition or teachings (pao-chiao) as to preserve the nation (pao-kuo). These two goals thus formed the core of K'ang's reform program.[34] The objectives of K'ang's reform movement were formulated in the "Set of Regulations" (Chang-ch'eng) of the Pao-kuo hui (Society to Protect the Nation), which was formed in the spring of 1898. The aim of the society as stated in Article 2, was "to preserve intact the country's territory, its people, and its tradition" (pao-ch'uan kuo-t'u, kuo-min, kuo-chiao), or as defined in Article 9, "to study matters relative to the preservation of the country, the race and the tradition." (chiang-ch'iu pao-kuo, pao-chung, pao-chiao chih shih).[35]

While he was a supporter of the reform, Chang was said to have already objected to K'ang's interpretation of Confucianism due to their doctrinal differences.[36] Since K'ang was an advocate of the New Text School, and Chang was said to be an adherent of the Ancient Text School, scholars suggested that the conflict between these two scholars was a revival of the dispute between the New Text and Ancient Text Schools.[37] However, it was not necessarily the case. As we have stated above, Chang's intellectual tendency was characterized by the accommodation within the Han Learning of both the Ancient Text and the New Text persuasions. This undoubtedly was influenced by his teacher, Yü Yüeh, whose teaching included the scholarships of both of these schools. This was evident that Chang also adopted

---

34 Chang Hao, "Intellectual Change and the Reform Movement, 1890~8", p. 285.

35 Hsiao Kung-chuan, *A Modern China and a New World: K'ang Yu-wei, Reformer and Utopian, 1858~1927*(Seattle: University of Washington Press, 1975) p. 104.

36 *NPCP*, v. 1, p. 34.

37 For example, see Kuo Chan-p'o, *Chung-kuo chin-tai ssu-hsiang-shih* 中國近代思想史 (Modern Chinese Intellectual History)(Hong Kong: Lung-men shu-tien, 1965), p. 267.

ideas from the New Text school in his own writings, when he was studying in the Ku-ching Academy. Even after Chang became a supporter of reform, he still continued to employ New Text concepts to promote the cause of reform. Therefore, Chang's refutation of K'ang's views was not the revival of the debate between the Ancient Text and the New Text Schools as scholars suggested.

Nevertheless, Chang did oppose to K'ang's claim of the establishment of Confucianism as a state religion, for it made Chang feel uncomfortable. [38] For example, in 1896 when Chang joined the staff of Shih-wu pao, he asked Liang Ch'i-ch'ao what objectives K'ang was preaching. Liang answered that it was reform and the establishment of Confucianism as a state religion. Chang disapproved the latter by saying:

> Reform is the pressing and urgent matter to be dealt with today, however,
> to worship Confucius and to establish Confucianism as the state religion
> may risk the danger of stirring up religious agitation. [39]

Chang's anti-religious commitment could also be seen in his reply to Liang Ting-fen(dates unknown), a staff of Chang Chih-tung. When Chang was asked by Liang if K'ang intended to become emperor, Chang replied:

> I have only heard that K'ang attempts to become founder of a religion
> (chiao-chu), but I have never heard that he wants to make himself
> emperor. In fact, it is nothing strange that one has the desire to become
> emperor, however, it is improper if one attempts to become founder of a
> religion. [40]

Chang's opposition to K'ang's Confucian religion was because of his rational thinking as evidenced in his evaluation of Confucius. Chang regarded that the greatness of Confucius lay in his ability to free Chinese culture from superstitions,

---

38 *Nien-p'u*, p. 5.

39 Li Chien-nung, *Tsui-chin san-shih nien Chung-kuo cheng-chih shih* 最近三十年中國政治史(Chinese Political History in Recent Thirty Years)(Taipei: Hsueh-sheng shu-chü, 1976), p. 112; see also Leung, p. 100.

40 Feng Tzu-yu, *Chung-hua min-kuo k'ai-kuo ch'ien ke-ming shih* 中華民國開國前革命史(A History of the Revolution before the Founding of the Republic of China)(Taipei: Shih-chieh shu-chu, 1954), v. 1, p. 95.

gods and spirits. Therefore, Chang asserted that the establishment of Confucianism as a state religion, as K'ang claimed, was in effect to demote Confucius' teachings, for it introduced elements of mysticism into Confucianism that would make rational inquiry impossible.[41] Nevertheless, Chang's opposition to K'ang's Confucian religion did not prevent him from supporting reform. It was the concern to preserve China's tradition in general they had in common that was sufficient to override their differences and permitted Chang to support K'ang's reform in the 1890s. It was not until the 1900s that Chang started to purify his conceptions of the elements of Chinese culture and to establish his own concept of China's national essence, his different conception of tradition finally led him to counter K'ang's view on the interpretation of Confucianism, especially after their political differences were added.

In any case, Chang started his career as a reformist after 1895. After the collapse of the reform movement in 1898, Chang did allude to anti-Manchuism and even revolution. Nevertheless, He did not become openly a revolutionary until 1900, when Chang realized that the Manchu government was unable to resist the foreign powers in the Boxer Uprising.

In January, 1896, Chang left Ku-ching Academy for Shanghai to start his new position as the editorial staff of Shih-wu pao and to participate in political activities as a reformer. However, three months later Chang resigned because he had serious quarrels with many of K'ang's followers who supported K'ang's claim that Confucianism was a religion with which Chang felt uncomfortable.[42] However, Chang's resignation did not end his career as a reformer. Chang then returned to Hang-chou where he and Sung Shu organized Hsing-Che hui(The Association for Reviving Chekiang).[43] Chang wrote a preface for the association that praised five heros in Chekiang history who bravely fought against the barbarians.[44] In the

41 Wong, p. 9.
42 Chiang I-hua, *Chang T'ai-yen ssu-hsiang yen-chiu* 章太炎思想研究(A Study of Chang Ping-lin's Thought)(Shanghai: Jen-min ch'u-pan she, 1985), pp. 48~49.
43 Chiang I-hua, *Chang T'ai-yen ssu-hsiang yen-chiu* 章太炎思想研究(A Study of Chang Ping-lin's Thought), pp. 49~50.
44 Chiang I-hua, *Chang T'ai-yen ssu-hsiang yen-chiu* 章太炎思想研究(A Study of Chang Ping-lin's Thought), p. 51.

Chang-ch'eng, they also stressed the study of Chinese institutions and history.[45] In August, 1897, Chang and Sung also founded Ching-shih pao(The Statecraft Journal) with Chang as its editor-in-chief. The aim of the journal was to advocate reform by introducing new knowledge and theories from abroad.[46]

Chang also published a series of articles in the reformist journal, Shih-hsüeh pao(Journal of Practical Learning). These writings focused on a reappraisal of the Confucian tradition and the noncannonical philosophies of pre-Ch'in times, including Mohism, Taoism and Legalism. Chang maintained that Confucianism and noncannonical philosophies could complement each other and Confucianism thus should not monopolize Chinese cultural tradition [47], for he saw that while Confucianism has contributed significantly to Chinese cultural heritage, it could not be identified with Chinese culture, because there were still other schools of philosophies, such as Taoism and Mohism, in Chinese tradition. Thus, Chang wrote these essays to call for a critical and unbiased attitude towards Chinese culture. As for Confucianism, Chang was especially attracted by Hsün Tzu.[48] Chang's fervent interest in Hsün Tzu owed largely to his discipline in Han Learning, for the study of Hsün Tzu had been an undercurrent in the School of Han Learning since the mid-eighteenth century.[49] In an article entitled hou-sheng(The Later Sage) published in the Shih-hsüeh pao, Chang even promoted Hsün Tzu's standing second only to Confucius in the Confucian tradition. Chang said that Hsün Tzu was a figure who was eligible to be regarded as the later Sage following Confucius[50], for Chang asserted that like Confucius who was superior to such ancient sages as Yao, Shun and Duke of Chou because he was able to have a clear break from gods and spirits in ancient times, Hsün Tzu also revealed humanity and affairs (jen-shih) and freed

---

45 Chiang I-hua, *Chang T'ai-yen ssu-hsiang yen-chiu* 章太炎思想研究(A Study of Chang Ping-lin's Thought), p. 52.

46 Chiang I-hua, *Chang T'ai-yen ssu-hsiang yen-chiu* 章太炎思想研究(A Study of Chang Ping-lin's Thought), p. 53.

47 Chiang I-hua, *Chang T'ai-yen ssu-hsiang yen-chiu* 章太炎思想研究(A Study of Chang Ping-lin's Thought), pp. 56~57.

48 *Nien-p'u*, p. 6.

49 Chang Hao, *Chinese Intellectuals in Crisis*, p. 107.

50 *NPCP*, v. 1, p. 51.

from gods and spirits in his thinking.[51] According to Chang, before Han times Confucianism remained secular, it was only after Han dynasty that some elements of supernature permeated into Confucianism.[52] Following Hsün Tzu, Chang perceived Confucianism as a secular teaching which also revealed his rational thinking. Therefore, Chang's objective attitudes toward Chinese learning and his rational thinking provided him a basis to enable him not only to reappraise Chinese tradition but also to purify elements of Chinese cultural heritage and then to form his own conception of national essence afterwards.

In the spring of 1898, Chang left for Wu-ch'ang where he helped edit Cheng-hsüeh pao(the Journal of Orthodox Learning) proposed by Chang Chih-tung, who was regarded by his contemporaries as an open-minded and progressive scholar-official.[53] However, Chang was soon dismissed, for he had quite different ideas for reform from Chang Chih-tung's. While Chang Chih-tung showed his loyalty to the monarchy, Chang Ping-lin's support of reform was not to protect the Manchu regime, but to save the nation.[54] One account also showed that Chang's dismissal was because Chang Chih-tung discovered that Chang Ping-lin's intention was improper and that some of his expressions humiliated the emperor and offended superiors.[55]

On June 11, 1898, the Kuang-hsü Emperor issued an edict to announce reform. However, the reform movement failed when the empress dowager launched a successful coup d'etat on September 21st. With the failure of the reform movement, Chang was driven into exile due to his former connections with the Shih-wu pao.[56] Chang then fled to Taiwan in December, 1898, where he obtained a position as a writer (chuan-shu) at the Taiwan Daily News (Taiwan jih-jih hsin-pao).[57] After the

---

51 I NPCP, v. 1; see also T'ang Chih-chun ed., *Chang T'ai-yen cheng-lun hsuan-chi* 章太炎政論選集(The Selected Works of Chang T'ai-yen's Political Essays) (Hereafter cited as *CLHC*)(Peiking: Chung-hua shu-chu, 1977), v. 1, p. 120.

52 Wong, p. 17.

53 *NPCP*, v. 1, p. 63.

54 *NPCP*, v. 1, pp. 63~64.

55 Feng, v. 1, p. 113.

56 Boorman, Howard L., and Howard, Richard eds., *Biographical Dictionary of Republican China*(Hereafter cited as *BDRC*)(New York: Columbia University Press, 1967), v. 1, p. 93; see also Wong, p. 13.

57 Chiang, p. 80.

collapse of the reform movement in 1898, Chang, as an exile in Taiwan, did allude to anti-Manchuism. In an article, "Cheng-chiang lun"(On the rectification of territory), published in the Daily News, Chang said that the hatred of Han Chinese for the Manchus was not only because it was a different race but because of its brutal conquest of China. Since the Han Chinese hated the Manchus so bitterly, they could not live under the same sky.[58] Chang was also said to have written to K'ang and Liang, urging them not to be loyal to the Manchu dynasty. He said,

> Sun Wen [Sun Yat-sen] knows only a little about "foreign affairs" (yang-wu), however, he is still able to make distinction between the Han Chinese and the Manchus, and calls for revolution. Both of you are literati, but you fail to tell right from wrong, and are willing to serve the Manchu court. I am really regretful for that.[59]

While Chang was exposed to anti-Manchu ideas, he was also afraid that "if the Manchus were expelled at the time, the Western powers would take this occasion to seize China's territory."[60] Chang was thus in a dilemma as to whether to turn against the Manchus or not. To resolve this problem Chang made an expedient plan. He said that in order to meet the challenge of the West, the Kuang-hsü emperor could be accepted as the "guest ruler" (K'o-ti) or a feudal lord, and the descendant of Confucius should be honored as the ruler of China.[61] After he stayed in Taiwan for about six months Chang made his first visit to Japan on June 14, 1899, where he met Sun Yat-sen for the first time. They did not know each other very well at this time.[62] In any case, Chang remained a reformer in the 1890s. However, it should be remembered that Chang's support of reform was not to protect the Manchu regime, but to save the nation.

III. Chang as an anti-Manchu Revolutionist

When Chang was a supporter of reform, he asserted that a successful reform

---

58 Chiang, p. 86.
59 Feng, v. 1, p. 113.
60 *CTYCC*, v. 3, p. 67.
61 *CTYCC*, pp. 65~69.
62 *Nien-p'u*, p. 7.

would strengthen the ability of the Manchu government to resist foreign powers. His primary commitment to China meant that when the Manchu government failed to defend the nation against the foreign invasion in the Boxer Uprising in 1900, Chang would abandon the Manchus and become openly a revolutionary.[63] The choice of reform or revolution for Chang rested on assessments of means to save the nation; therefore, if reform could not save China, the only alterative could be revolution.

The event that prompted Chang to change his position was the Boxer Uprising in 1900. From the first allied actions of June 16 until the conclusion of the Boxer protocol, 1901, China was clearly the victim of a national crisis.[64] Because of the Boxer crisis, Chang attended a "National Conference" (Kuo-hui), which was organized by K'ang's follower T'ang Ts'ai-ch'ang(1867~1900), who was opposed to the war policy of the Manchu government.[65] The Conference was held in Shanghai on July 26, 1900, attended by approximately eighty people of reformist and revolutionary backgrounds; Jung Hung (Yung Wing)(1828~1912) was elected conference president, Yen Fu(1853~1921) vice president, and T'ang ts'ai-ch'ang secretary general.[66] The aims of the Conference were: first, to protect China's sovereignty, and to create a new independent nation, second, to claim that the Manchu government had no right to rule over China, and third, to reinstate the Kuang-hsü Emperor to power.[67] The last goal disturbed Chang; he denounced T'ang's political ambivalence towards the Manchu government, asserting that T'ang should not attempt to expel the Manchus on the one hand and to restore the Kuang-hsü Emperor on the other. Not only did he protest bitterly the ambiguity of the Conference, Chang also cut off his queue in front of those present at the conference.[68] Since the queue was a symbol of Chinese submission to the

---

63 Wong, p. 24.

64 Hsiao I-shan, *Ch'ing-tai t'ung-shih* 清代通史 (A General History of Ch'ing Period)(Taipei: Commercial Press, 1962), v. 4, pp. 196~198.

65 Feng Tzu-yu, *Ko-ming i-shih* 革命逸史(Untold Stories about the Revolution) (Peking: Chung-hua shu-chü, 1979), v. 2, p. 76; The Manchus declared war on the eight foreign nations involved in the catastrophe, June 21, 1900.

66 *NPCP*, v. 1, p. 109; see also Wong, p. 25.

67 *NPCP*, v. 1, p. 109.

68 *Nien-p'u*, p. 7.

conquering Manchu, the action showed his final break with the Manchu dynasty. He was convinced that the survival of China required the overthrow of the Manchu regime. He said, "If we do not overthrow the Manchu government, we can not expect the people to love their own country and to resist foreign threats. Sooner or later, we will be made slaves of the Europeans and the Americans."[69] From then on, Chang was committed to anti-Manchu revolution.

While Chang called for revolution to save China, his perception of "revolution" was only as a means to serve his ultimate goal: the preservation of China's unique national essence. He said, "If Chinese people do not know the national essence, China will go the way of India, which has fallen under foreign rule."[70] In addition, Chang held that Chinese people should find their revolutionary inspiration in Chinese culture, and employ the national essence to stimulate racial spirit and to promote people's patriotism.[71] Chang was also expressing his further and more fundamental belief that the preservation of the Chinese national essence gave the nation its mission and meaning. He said:

> The reason that a nation is a nation lies in its essence. …The difference between the humans and the birds as well as the beasts is only because the former can know their past. If the national essence is extinct, people will not know the past of their nation. In this case, what is the difference between them and the birds as well as the beasts. …If the people of a nation are not conscious of their own national essence, the nation will be gradually conquered by other nations, and even perish.[72]

Apparently, Chang's devotion to anti-Manchu revolution was mainly as a means to protect China's culture and to guarantee its continuity, for Chang said, "The study of national learning and the overthrow of Manchu rule are exactly the

---

69 *CTYCC*, v. 3, p. 120.
70 *CLHC*, v. 1, p. 302.
71 Chang Ping-lin, "Wo ti p'ing-sheng yu pan-shih fang-fa" 我的平生與辦事方法(My life and the Method for accomplishing Things), in *Chang T'ai-yen ti pai-hua wen* 章太炎的白話文(The Writing in Vernacular Chinese by Chang T'ai-yen)(Hereafter cited as *CTYTPHW*)(Taipei: I-wen yin -shu-kuan, 1972), p. 91.
72 *CTYCC*, v. 4, p. 366.

same thing."[73]

After Chang became a revolutionary, he began to revise his book, Ch'iu-shu(Book of Raillery), an effort which also indicated his conversion from reform to revolution. In the original edition, there were two essays with clear reformist implications, "K'o-ti"(the Guest Emperor) and "Fen-chen"(Decentralization). The former attempted to justify the Manchu emperor's rule over China and the latter placed a hope in the regional governors-general for reform.[74] The revised book incorporated two essays, "K'e-ti k'uang-miu"(Refuting the Guest Emperor), and "Fen-chen k'uang-miu"(Refuting the Decentralization), to counteract the erroneous views he had presented in the earlier articles. These two essays of refutation indicated Chang's strong anti-Manchu stance.[75]

Although Chang had become openly a revolutionary, he had no immediate direct connection with any other revolutionary, especially Sun Yat-sen. In August, 1901, Chang went to Soochow, where he obtained a teaching position at Soochow University (Tung-wu ta-hsüeh), a school managed by American missionaries.[76] While Chang was teaching there, he attacked the Manchu government openly, and spread anti-Manchu messages. As a result, the governor of Kiangsu, En Ming(1846~1907) pressed the school authorities and gave orders for the arrest of Chang.[77] In February, 1902, Chang escaped to Shanghai and then to Japan. There he renewed his acquaintance with and began his friendship with Sun. Chang was also in contact with many other revolutionists.[78] In order to advocate racial or anti-Manchu revolution and to stimulate a sense of China's history among Chinese students in Japan, Chang in April, 1902, proposed a rally to be held in Tokyo in commemoration of the 242nd anniversary of China's fall to the Manchus (Chung-Hsia wang-kuo erh-pai-ssu-shih-erh nien chi-nien hui).[79] The meeting was

---

73 *NPCP*, v. 2, p. 828.
74 See these two articles in *CTYCC*, v. 3, pp. 65~69 and pp. 72~74.
75 These two articles are placed as the forward of the revised edition of *Ch'iu-shu*, which was probably completed in 1902. These articles can be found in *CTYCC*, v. 3, pp. 116~120 and pp. 120~123.
76 *NPCP*, v. 1, pp. 121~122.
77 *Nien-p'u*, p. 8.
78 *Nien-p'u*, pp. 8~9.
79 *Nien-p'u*, p. 9.

approved by Sun, but prohibited by the Japanese authorities at the request of the Manchu government. However, the effort did arouse the anti-Manchuism of the Chinese students in Japan, and lead to the founding of many revolutionary organizations after 1902.[80]

In July, 1902, Chang returned from Japan to Shanghai, where he taught Chinese at the Patriotic Academy (Ai-Kuo hsüeh-she) from March, 1903.[81] The founding of the academy was sponsored by the Chinese Educational Society (Chung-kuo chiao-yü hui), established by Ts'ai Yüan-p'ei (1876~1940) and others in the spring of 1902 in Shanghai.[82] The members of the society went to Chang's Garden (Chang-yüan), to speak on revolution openly. Among them, Chang's speeches on anti-Manchu revolution were especially radical.[83]

In 1903, Chang wrote a preface to Tsou Jung's(1885~1905) "Ko-ming chün"(Revolutionary Army), in which he fiercely attacked the Manchu government's inability to deal with foreign powers and advocated a revolution to overthrow the Manchu regime.[84] Both Chang's preface and Tsou's pamphlet were published in Su-pao, a newspaper founded in 1896.[85] After Chang Shih-chao(1881~1973) was made editor-in-chief of the Su-pao, the newspaper became radical in tone, and became increasingly a revolutionary paper.[86] The Su-pao also carried Chang's booklet, "Po K'ang Yu-wei lun ko-ming shu"(A Letter Refuting K'ang Yu-wei's View on Revolution).

After the failure of the 1898 Reform Movement, K'ang had founded Pao-huang hui(Society to Protect the Emperor). It gained greater support from Chinese intellectuals and the overseas Chinese than Sun Yat-sen's Hsing-Chung hui.[87] In an effort to counter the rising revolutionary movement, K'ang had written an essay

---

80 *BDRC*, v. 1, p. 93. These revolutionary organizations included the *Ch'ing-nien hui* 青年會 in 1902, the *Chün kuo-min chiao-yü hui* 軍國民教育會 in 1902 and the *Kuang-fu hui* 光復會 in 1904.
81 *NPCP*, v. 1, p. 154.
82 *NPCP*, v. 1, p. 154.
83 *NPCP*, v. 1, p. 159.
84 *Nien-p'u*, p. 9; see also Leung, p. 104.
85 Chiang, p. 189.
86 *NPCP*, v. 1, p. 166.
87 Wong, p. 38.

against revolution in 1902. [88] K'ang claimed that revolution would require bloodshed and bring only chaos to the nation. Eventually it would lead to foreign intervention and make China the slave of other nations. On the contrary, China could be saved by reform without risking domestic violence and foreign invasion. And reform could be achieved without shedding blood and leaving China in disintegration, only after the Kuang-hsü Emperor regained his power.[89] As for anti-Manchuism, K'ang urged that there was no reason to overthrow the Manchu government, for the Manchus had already been sinicized. This was evident that after the Manchus took over China, they adopted the traditional Chinese culture and system.[90]

Since Kang's influence on intellectuals and overseas Chinese remained very strong, his view on revolution had created the impediment for the rising revolutionary radicalism. Chang, thus, had to refute K'ang's arguments against revolution. In his letter to K'ang, Chang agreed that revolution would shed blood, but he also maintained that reform would require bloodshed as well, as evident in the collapse of K'ang-Liang's 1898 Reform Movement. In fact, Chang held, revolution would be easier to accomplish than reform, for revolution required only leadership, while reform needed both leadership and the people's support. Chang rejected K'ang's argument that revolution would lead to partition of China by foreign powers by indicating that the Manchus were also foreign origin, and they had already ceded Chinese territories to other nations.[91] "Since all the Manchus are as stupid as deer and pigs," Chang said, "can we not launch a revolution?"[92] Chang then criticized K'ang's readiness to entrust the future of the nation to the timid Kuang-hsü Emperor, whom Chang ridiculed as "a little clown" (hsiao-ch'ou) who "can not distinguish beans from barley."[93] Chang continued to denounce K'ang's view that the Manchus had already been assimilated by the Chinese. Chang argued that instead

---

88 Wong, p. 38.
89 *CLHC*, v. 1, pp. 213~215.
90 *CLHC*, v. 1, pp. 220~221; pp. 195~196, and Gasster, p. 195.
91 *CLHC*, pp. 201~205; Gasster, p. 196.
92 *CLHC*, p. 200.
93 *CLHC*, p. 199.

of becoming sinized, the Manchus had already attempted to assimilate the Chinese as evidenced in the fact that they had forced Chinese people to adopt their own customs, such as the queue and the Manchu dress. If the Manchus had not been assimilated by the Chinese, they, as an incompetent minority race, were not justified to rule the majority Chinese.[94]

Chang's and Tsou's radical articles in the Su-pao greatly shocked the Manchu authorities. The open attack on the entire Manchu race and especially the denouncement of Kuang-hsü Emperor as a "little clown" brought forth the "Su-pao case".[95] The Manchu government gave orders to suppress the Su-pao and to arrest Chang and Tsou in particular. Although they were arrested, the authorities in the Shanghai International Settlement refused the Manchu government's request of extradition. The two were, however, tried by a mixed court of Chinese and foreigners in Shanghai, and Chang was imprisoned for three years and Tsou for two. Both were assigned to the prison in the International Settlement.[96] Tsou Jung died there in April, 1905, just shortly before the end of his term.[97]

While the Manchu government expected that the Su-pao case would curb anti-Manchu sentiments, the result was exactly the opposite.[98] Chang's courage and imprisonment not only made him more famous but also stimulated revolutionary fervor among many of his contemporaries.[99] The Manchu government's failure in attempting to extradite the prisoners was also an indication of its low credibility in dealing with the foreign powers and as a result it lost more prestige in the country.[100] More importantly, before the incident, K'ang's influence on Chinese people was so powerful that his reformism even overshadowed Sun's revolutionary force. However, after the Su-pao case, Sun's revolutionary cause attracted more Chinese

---

94 *CLHC*, pp. 194~200; see also Wong, p. 39.

95 Chu Hsi-tsu, p. 3; see also Wong, p. 41. On the *Su-pao* case, see details in Y.C. Wang, "The Su-Pao Case: A Study of Foreign Pressure, Intellectual Fermentation, and Dynastic Decline", *Monumenta Serica* 24(1965), pp. 84~129.

96 *NPCP*, v. 1, pp. 170~187; see also *BDRC*, v. 1, p. 94.

97 *Nien-p'u*, p. 10; *BDRC*, v. 1, p. 94.

98 Leung, p. 104.

99 Gasster, p. 197.

100 Rankin, p, p.94

people. Eventually, the revolutionaries became a formidable rival of K'ang and his followers. Revolution then became a political cause powerful enough to challenge K'ang's reformism.[101] In any event, the Su-pao case, not only undermined the Manchu regime, but also made revolution more popular at the time.[102]

Chang's three-year imprisonment was also very important for him both intellectually and politically. During his imprisonment, he started to study Buddhism seriously. For Chang, Buddhism thenceforth was included in Chang's concept of kuo-ts'ui, and was enlisted as a means to promote people's morality for the cause of the revolution. While Chang was imprisoned, he also was involved in the founding of the Restoration Society, which was formed in 1904 with Ts'ai Yüan-p'ei as its president. Chang claimed that he and Ts'ai initiated the idea to establish the Society.[103] When Chang was still in prison, he wrote to Ts'ai urging him and others to organize the society in order to promote anti-Manchu cause.[104] The title of the society, Kuang-fu, was originated from Chang.[105] Later, when T'ao Ch'eng-chang revived the society in 1910, Chang was made its president. Despite their common cause of anti-Manchuism, the Restoration Society then became a bitter rival of the T'ung-meng hui.[106]

After Chang's release from prison on June 29, 1906, he was invited to join the newly founded T'ung-meng-hui, the major political organization of the revolutionary camp, and to assume the editorship of the Min-pao, the official organ of the organization. The T'ung-meng hui had been founded on August 20, 1905, with Sun Yat-sen as its chairman (tsung-li). Its purpose was to drive out the Manchus, restore Chinese rule, establish a republic, and equalize land rights.[107] The formation

---

101 Wong, p. 45.
102 For the significance of the Su-pao case, especially the case of Chang Ping-lin, to the revolutionary movement, see Ibid., pp. 44~46.
103 NPCP, v. 1, p. 193; see also Wong, p. 46.
104 NPCP, p. 196; for Chang's involvement in the founding of the Restoration Society, see pp. 196~197.
105 The term "kuang-fu" appeared first in Chang's "Ko-ming-chün hsü"(Preface to the Revolutionary Army). In the preface, Chang said, "to expel the different race (i.e., the Manchus) is called kuang-fu (restoration)". See NPCP, v. 1, p. 197.
106 NPCP. v.1, pp. 318~320.
107 Michael Gasster, "The Republican Revolutionary Movement", in The Cambridge History of China, v. 11, p. 491.

of the T'ung-meng hui rested on the merger of the Hsing-Chung-hui, the Hua-hsing-hui(Society for the Revival of China), the Kuang-fu-hui and other splinter groups.[108] During 1905 and 1906 about one thousand people joined the organization, and a large majority came from the student class of 17 provinces.[109] The membership of the T'ung-meng hui was quite different from that of Sun Yat-sen's earlier Hsing-Chung-hui. The latter gained but little support, and even at its height its membership never exceeded 500 in number, most of which came from uneducated people in Kwangtung province.[110] The organization had even excluded students and intellectuals. In contrast, the membership of the T'ung-meng hui was multiprovincial and multiclass. It received new support from students, intellectuals and progressive army officers.[111] By the time of the Wu-ch'ang Uprising in October, 1911, about 10,000 members had joined the T'ung-meng hui and most of its officials were educated.[112]

Although the T'ung-meng hui was a larger and more unified organization than any other revolutionary groups, it was loosely organized. Since the T'ung-meng-hui was a conglomeration of different anti-Manchu groups and individuals, not all of its members were of one heart.[113] Most of the rank and file were more involved with their separate organizations instead of the T'ung-meng hui. They remained more loyal to the former and retained keen provincial sentiments.[114] Such provincialism characterized the late Ch'ing and early republican era.[115] While Sun was generally recognized as chairman by the members, his leadership was not unquestioned. This

108 Lee Ta-ling, *Foundations of the Chinese Revolution, 1905~1912: A Historical Record of the T'ung-meng Hui* (New York: St. John's University Press, 1970), p. 25. After the formation of the *T'ung-meng-hui*, however, the *Kung-fu-hui* still remained in existence.
109 Hsüeh, p. 44.
110 Mary Clabaugh Wright, "Introduction: The Rising Tide of Change", in *China in Revolution: The First Phase, 1900~1913*(New Haven: Yale University Press, 1973), p. 45.
111 Immanuel C.Y. Hsü, *The Rise of Modern China*(New York: Oxford University Press, 1975), p. 464.
112 Chang Yü-fa, pp. 343~349.
113 Lee Ta-ling, p. 39.
114 Gasster, *Chinese intellectuals and the Revolution of 1911*, pp. 55~56; see also Yoshirhiro Hatano, "The New Armies", in Mary C. Wright, ed., *China in Revolution: the First Phase, 1900~1913*, p. 366.
115 Hatano, p. 366.

was evident in the internal feud between him and the other leaders of the organization.[116] All these factors hindered the function of the T'ung-meng-hui. In addition, while the general headquarters remained in Tokyo, the center of the organization always shifted with Sun Yat-sen himself, wherever he was.[117] Thus, it was actually the personal leadership rather than organizational efforts that was largely responsible for the continuing function and growth of the T'ung-meng-hui.

Despite the fact that the T'ung-meng-hui was not perfectly effective, its formation did constitute a milestone for the revolutionary movement in China that culminated in the Wu-ch'ang Uprising in October, 1911. While there were many revolutionary groups at one time or another, the T'ung-meng-hui was a more unified organization than any others. The T'ung-meng-hui was the first organization that could unify the many different anti-Manchu groups and the large number of people with divergent origins and regional aspirations.[118] Although the T'ung-meng-hui was loosely organized, it did provide leadership and a central organization to foster the anti-Manchu cause.[119] Above all, with an important common purpose of carrying out a political revolution to overthrow the Manchu government, the T'ung-meng-hui did hold together for seven years, and made an important contribution to the Chinese revolutionary movement.[120] After the founding of the organization, revolutionary action was moving ahead quickly, and no less than eight revolts were carried out in South China between 1907 and 1911.[121] Thus, the T'ung-meng-hui was such an important organization that was largely responsible for leading Chinese revolutionary movement against the Manchu government from 1905 to 1911.

Before Chang assumed the editorship of the Min-pao, the Min-pao had already launched a series of bitter debates with the Hsin-min ts'ung-pao(New Citizen Journal), an organ of the reformers headed by Liang Ch'i-ch'ao. Although the Min-pao, especially under the editorship of Chang Ping-lin, did bring a large number of

---

116 For the personal conflicts within the rank and file of the *T'ung-meng-hui*, see Hsüeh, pp. 50~55.
117 Lee Ta-ling, pp. 39, 205.
118 Hsüeh, p. 45.
119 Lee Ta-ling, p. 39; see also Hsü, p. 465.
120 Gasster, *Chinese intellectuals and the Revolution of 1911*, p. 56.
121 Lee Ta-ling, p. iv.

students and intellectuals into the revolutionary movement[122], a majority of the students in Japan still favored Liang's reform cause of constitutional monarchy. Thus, in the debate, the Min-pao writers attempted not only to defend their revolutionary cause of republicanism against Liang's constitutional monarchy but also to gain more support from the overseas Chinese. While Chang had challenged K'ang's ideas before, after he took over the Min-pao editorship, his position changed for pragmatic reasons. As the debate with reformists grew, Chang even asserted his colleagues, Hu Han-min and Wang Ching-wei, attacked Liang Ch'i-ch'ao too harshly. This was not because Chang felt sympathy for Liang, despite Chang's earlier friendship, but because, as Chang said, the schism between the revolutionaries and the reformers would only benefit their common enemy, the Manchu government. Chang still hoped that Liang could cooperate with Sun to form a united anti-Manchu front, since Liang had once vacillated between revolution and reform.[123] Thus, when Liang proposed a truce with the Min-pao in January, 1907, Chang accepted Liang's request, but Sun rejected it.[124]

During the Min-pao period, from 1906 to 1908, apart from his expression of strong anti-Manchu views, Chang continued to advocate the preservation of China's national essence and Buddhism wholeheartedly, which distinguished him from most other members of the T'ung-meng-hui.

Although Chang was regarded as a member of the T'ung-meng-hui, aside from his anti-Manchu stance, he had little in common with other members of the T'ung-meng-hui.[125] Chang's concern for the preservation of the national essence was evident in the fact that he was also a frequent contributor to the "Journal of National Essence". Chang's focus was different. He believed that the most important mission of the revolution was the preservation of China's unique essence. His sense of history

---

122 *NPCP*, v. 1, p. 223; see also Wong, p. 50.
123 For Liang's vacillation between revolution and reform, see Chang Hao, *Liang Ch'i-ch'ao and Intellectual Transition in China, 1890~1907*(Berkeley: University of California Press, 1971), pp. 220~237; see also Chang P'eng-yüan, *Liang Ch'i-ch'ao yü Ch'ing-chi ko-ming* 梁啟超與清季革命 (Liang Ch'i-ch'ao and the Late Ch'ing Revolution)(Taipei: Academia Sinica, Institute of Modern History, 1964).
124 *NPCP*, v. 1, p. 233.
125 Mabel Lee, p. 613.

even influenced his methodology. Chang maintained that to accomplish the aim of overthrowing the Manchu government it was a necessity to draw from China's past to arouse people's patriotism and foster anti-Manchu sentiment. This approach was evident in his statement that "the overthrow of the Manchu government and the study of the national studies is the same thing."[126] Thus, Chang's revolutionary ideas were derived from "his concern to save the `Chinese essence'".[127] One of the reasons Chang advocated Buddhism was that "Buddhism attaches the greatest importance to equality, and endeavors to remove all obstacles to equality."[128] Since the Manchu government discriminated against Chinese people, it thus should be expelled[129], and Buddhism then could foster the anti-Manchu sentiment.

During the Min-pao period, Chang advocated anti-Manchuism wholeheartedly. Among the members of the T'ung-meng-hui, Chang was regarded as the most prominent anti-Manchu proponent. Since Chang had drawn a distinct line between the Manchus and the Han Chinese, and since he fiercely attacked the Manchu government and the Manchu race as a whole, modern scholars tended to regard Chang as a `racist', or an `ethnocentric nativist'.[130] However, this was not necessarily the case. Chang's anti-Manchu sentiment was inspired during his childhood. Chang became a revolutionary when this sentiment was reinforced by the events for the failure of K'ang's Reform Movement of 1898 and the Boxer Uprising. Chang called for the overthrow of the Manchus because the government was incapable of preventing foreign invasion. Obviously, Chang's opposition to the Manchus was not confined to simple racism but was inseparable from this anti-imperialism. As he said, "[If one considers revolution] in terms of racial enemies, then the Manchus are our chief enemies not the Europeans and the Americans. In regard to political and social challenges to Chinese, the Westerners are more harmful [to us Chinese] than are the Manchus".[131] Chang linked the overthrow of the

---

126 *NPCP*, v. 2, p. 828.

127 Joseph R. Levenson, *Confucian China and Its Modern Fate*(Berkeley: University of California Press, 1965) v. 1, p. 89.

128 *CTYTPHW*, p. 95.

129 *CTYTPHW*, p. 95.

130 For example, see Furth, pp. 117, 138, 149.

131 *CLHC*, v. 1, p. 432.

Manchus to resolution of imperialistic threats. Thus, Chang thought that unless the Manchu government was removed, China's struggle with the imperialist countries could not be launched.[132]

Although Chang called for overthrowing the Manchus, his anti-Manchuism was confined to the overthrow of the Manchu government only, rather than to expel it and its people. As Chang said, "To oppose the Manchus is to oppose its imperial household, its officials and its army."[133] He then continued, "To oppose the Manchus is not to oppose all governments and all the Manchu people, but to oppose the Manchu government."[134] He added, though, also non-Manchu people who worked for the Manchu government.

The Dynastic government then was his main target. Even after the success of the Wu-ch'ang Uprising, Chang did not discriminate against the Manchu people but treated them equally to Chinese people. In a letter he wrote to the Manchu students who studied in Japan, Chang said, "Your [the Manchu] government has been overthrown, while you are Manchus, [you are] also Chinese. Thus, you can get whatever jobs you want, [in] business or agriculture, and your voting rights will be equal to the Chinese."[135] This was the further evidence that Chang was not an ethnocentric nativist or racist.[136] His anti-Manchuism thus meant the overthrow of the Manchu government only. Since the Manchu government was incompetent to defend the nation from foreign aggression, Chang called for revolution to save China. His anti-Manchuism represented an ideological weapon for the republican revolution.

During the Min-pao period, the Japanese government, at the request of the Manchu government, asked Sun Yat-sen to leave the country in February, 1907. Sun was awarded some money. Before his departure, Sun left a small amount of money

---

132 Hu Sheng-wu and Chin Ch'ung-chi, "Hsin-hai ko-ming shih-ch'i Chang Ping-lin te cheng-chih ssu-hsiang"辛亥革命時期章炳麟的政治思想(The Political Thought of Chang Ping-lin at the Time of the 1911 Revolution), *Li-shih yen-chiu* 4 (1961), pp. 5~7.

133 *CTYCC*, v. 4, p. 269.

134 *CTYCC*, v. 4, p. 269.

135 *CLHC*, v. 1, p. 520.

136 Wong Young-tsu also argued that Chang was not a racist, see his *Search for Modern Nationalism*, pp. 62~64.

for the Min-pao, but took most of his money with him. Chang accused Sun of misappropriating party funds for his personal use.[137] After his conflict with Sun, Chang still edited the Min-pao, however, it was suspended, at the request of the Manchu government, by the Japanese authorities on October 19, 1908.[138] After the closure of the Min-pao, Chang's relationship with the T'ung-meng-hui became very tenuous. Even after he was made president of the revived Kuang-fu-hui in 1910, Chang remained a member of the T'ung-meng-hui until the 1911 revolution. After the success of the Wu-ch'ang Uprising on October 10, 1911, a new China was thus born.[139]

IV. Conclusion

Chang Ping-lin was one of the major thinkers, classical scholars and political activists in modern Chinses history. His life and thought illustrates the uneasy relationship between scholarship and politics among the intellectuals of his generation.

While Chang was still a serious student of the school of Han Learning, which emphasized scholarship for its own sake, and divorced from politics, at Ku-ching Academy, he became involved in politics.

His involvement in politices did place him in a dilemma between scholarship and politics. However, Chang's conviction that the preservation of national essence could save the nation appeared to provide a resolution to this dilemma. Obviously, politics was perceived by Chang only as a means to protect china's essence. Therefore, Chang gave priority to the preservation of the national essence over the nation. The latter was important only because it was needed to save the former. And reform or revolution was in turn necessary to save the nation.

As a prominent revolutionary, Chang openly and bitterly attacked Manchu government, and drew a distinct line between the Manchus and the Han Chinese race. As a result, Chang was regarded as an anti-Manchu racist and a Han chauvinist. This view, however, obscured the nature of Chang's thinking. Chang's anti-

---

137 Hsüeh, pp. 52~53.
138 *NPCP*, v. 1, p. 284.
139 *NPCP*, v. 1, p. 351.

Manchuism was derived from his anti-imperialism, and was confined to his opposition to the Manchu government only. Thus, after the overthrow of the Manchu government, Chang no longer advocated anti-Manchuism.

Chang's lifelong commitment to the preservation of the national essence manifested itself in his two careers: one as a political activist and the other as a classical scholar. Even after the founding of the republic, Chang remained active in the political arena. He continued to speak out against whatever he perceived to endanger China's sovereignty or its culture. Apart from his involvement in politics, Chang also devoted himself to teaching and the study of China's rich cultural heritage. This effort to preserve the national essence was the most consistent thread in his life.

附錄　美國漢學名著中文書摘

Homer Dubs, Hsüntze : The Moulder of Ancient Confucianism

一、作者姓名與著作名稱

作者：Homer H Dubs（德效騫）

書名：Hsüntze：The Moulder of Ancient Confucianism

出版項：London：Arthur Probsthain,1927

中文書名：荀子：古代儒學之塑造者

二、篇幅

共 308 頁（正文：293 頁，附錄：無，參考書目：3 頁，索引：10 頁）。

三、主題

本書係德效騫於 1927 年所出版之《荀子》一書之專著，亦是西方漢學界第一本荀子研究之專著。德氏並於次年又出了一本《荀子》之選譯，德氏可謂西方漢學界最早全面譯介《荀子》之學者，由此而開啟美國漢學界之荀子研究。德氏在本書中除了對荀子之學說作全面性之探討外，亦對荀子之生平和著作等相關問題作介紹。最重要的是，德氏提出「荀子乃古代儒學之塑造者」此一歷史定位。

四、關鍵辭

荀子、人性、倫理學、儒學、邏輯（名學）

五、主要論點

德氏在本書中之主要論點有：

（一）德氏指出「荀子乃古代儒學之塑造者」此一歷史定位。

（二）荀子的哲學是一種實踐哲學，依此，知識論和形上學皆被排擠到幕後，政治哲學成為哲學的最終目的。

（三）荀子之性惡說並非意謂人性是完全邪惡，而是意指人性是傾向於惡，且具有無限之能力朝向善之方向發展。

（四）荀子之倫理學是權威之倫理學，荀子亦是藉由性惡說賦予權威之原則一堅實之基礎。

（五）對荀子而言，禮是主要道德且是全部的道德。

（六）荀子以為，教育是環境塑造人性的結果，而不是在發展人的本性。

（七）德氏以為，邏輯意指名學而言。對荀子而言，邏輯是以倫理政治之要求為正名之目的。

六、目次

（一）背景

（二）荀子的生平與時代

（三）荀子的著作

（四）基本概念

（五）思辯哲學和迷信

（六）人性

（七）倫理學的基礎

（八）禮和仁

（九）其他的倫理學概念

（十）音樂

（十一）欲望和心；心理學

（十二）教育哲學

（十三）邏輯理論

（十四）不平等

（十五）政治哲學

（十六）理想主義和惡的問題

七、摘要

在本書中，德氏將荀子學說分別就人性、倫理學及邏輯理論等方面來加以論述，茲分述如下：

（一）基本概念

荀子之哲學是建立在兩個基本概念上，其一是人性概念；另一是一種特別的歷史詮釋。

荀子以為人性中的基本要素是形成社會組織的能力。德氏以為，人類生命中最顯著的特徵是誠如荀子所說的，為了生存而形成社會組織，從實際的人事觀點看來，群居性確是人類的一種特徵，亦是人禽之間的一種區別。

德氏指出，荀子的哲學明顯的是一種實踐哲學。依此，理論上的問題，諸如，知識論和形上學皆被排擠到幕後，政治哲學成為哲學的頂點和目的。而對政治哲學而言，所有其餘的皆是次要的。倫理問題成了適應別人的社會問題，並且在社會問題中，階級的權力和區分及正當行為的準則（禮）成為指導的原理。

德氏以為，荀子的倫理學是行動的、意志的、目的的及有好惡的人的倫理學，而非一種永恆的、非塵世的道德判斷的領域。

荀子哲學的另一基本要素是他的歷史詮釋。此一詮釋並非荀子所獨創，而是承自其先驅和經典而來。

荀子以為，在中國歷史上，每一朝代皆創始於一智德兼具之君主，而在一邪惡化身之暴君中逐漸墮落和衰敗，其後，暴君被推翻，但並非經由武力，而是由一有德者取而代之。此一理論對荀子而言，並非歷史的詮釋而是一歷史事實，是藉由歷史證據而建立的。此一理論為孔、孟、墨及所有儒者所接受。依荀子而言，善之終極征服並非是一信念而是一事實，此一歷史理論是荀子哲學的基礎之一。

（二）思辯哲學與迷信

荀子哲學的主要特色是它是實踐的而非理論的。荀子感興趣的是作為社會秩序中的人而非宇宙論思辯的人。此一特質表現在荀子拒絕所有在人類生活中並無實踐目的之思辯。而更明顯的是，荀子反對墨辯等之知識論的思辯。思辯是無益的，它放棄了人類最重要的特色——社會組織與社會生活，因此，荀子為了道德和政治哲學而反對思辯哲學。

荀子所反對的思辯包括任何鬼神或非人力量的信仰，此等力量是人類無法控制。而且荀子所追求的是人應該努力去發展存在於人性中的無限能力，而不是去依賴更高的力量，這是一種實證論（positivism）的立場，是在反對形上學的思辯。

中國古代宗教是一信仰諸多神靈的萬物有靈論，尤其是對祖先的崇拜和祭祀，以及對天的信仰。然而，這些信仰和實證論的立場並不一致，因此，荀子著手重新予以詮釋。

古代儒學之兩大形上學概念是「天」和「道」。老子將「天」等同於「道」，且使「天」成為非人格化之法則或「道」。荀子藉由接收老子作為普遍法則之道的概念和使儒家「天」之概念之意義成為法則，而完成將「天」去人格化之過程。

依荀子而言，天是不變的法則，其意義與自然的概念相同。當神靈的力量對人類社會的影響去除之後，人就會回歸自我；否則，人會依賴「天」而忽視其自身的責任。因此，荀子認為，沒有鬼神的信仰對人類是極為有利的。就像「天」被詮釋為非人格的法則，「道」也同樣被詮釋為人類的道德行為。因此，過去由天所擔負之責任，如今則落在人類身上。禍福來自人類自己的行為，政府的好壞是人類行為的結果，名譽和進步來自自身的努力而非神的禮物。

此一學說意味著德（善）是有回報而惡是會受罰的。對荀子而言，這種普遍法則的道德的特色是從歷史事實而來的一種合理的推論。法則是道德法則，依其自身之本質，它會賞善罰惡，此一學說將荀子從唯物論（materialism）之責難中解救出來。

（三）人性

德氏在〈人性〉一章中，首先提出，對荀子而言，欲望是人性之一種最根本的特徵。因此，很自然的，他應該會歸結出人性根本上是惡的。然而，德氏以為，荀子此一學說並非意謂著人性是完全邪惡，且是無望成善的，而是正好相反，因為，荀子意指人性是傾向於惡，因此，每一個人都必須格外努力去發展其本性以趨向於善。人性僅是傾向於惡，並且具有無限的能力朝著善的方向發展。

德氏指出，中國古代思想家大多有崇尚自然之思想，如老子、孔子、墨子、莊子和孟子等，然而，荀子極力反對此種崇尚自然之態度。荀子認為，儒學強調自我發展，每一個個人必須盡其所能去發展自我。德氏以為，荀子之所以主張性惡說的理由之一是此一學說可以迫使人們努力去成德。

荀子主張人之本性皆同，任何人皆可成就道德，然而，事實並非如此。荀子的回答是，雖然「性可化」，而就事實言之，則未必人人皆能受化而成善，此乃因有人避而不可化，如朱象獨不化。

德氏以為荀子的學說是非常具有現代性，它顯示出中國思想的根本的民主，亦即在人類之間並沒有根本的不平等，同時，中國思想也承認一種基於不同程度的道德發展而來的道德不平等。因此，荀子在他的人性學說中以一種令人注目的方式結合一種極理想化的人類平等的教義和一種實際的人生事實的認知。

（四）倫理學的基礎

荀子認為孔子的倫理學是一種教條式的倫理學。此後，教條主義和權威主義已是儒學的特色。對儒者而言，知識的問題首先是倫理知識的問題，真理不是思辯的而是實踐的。

荀子之所以反對孟子的性善說而主張性惡說，是為了確保權威之原則對其教義的重要。因此，在這方面，荀子較孟子更像儒家。荀子了解到權威是不需要解釋任何學說的來源。正確的學說是來自聖人，聖人在文明開始時建立此一民族的習俗和慣例。然而，聖人是如何獲得真理呢？為了回答此一問題，荀子發展出一種認識真理的經驗方法，其步驟有三，分別是：知道、可道和守道。

荀子指出，知道唯經由心，蓋心能統制身體和行動，而虛、壹、靜則是心行動的三種特性，且是正確行動的先決條件。荀子以為，知道的三個條件是：沒有成見（虛）、心之專一或專注於道（壹）和免除欲望（靜）。心必須免除成見和欲望且專注於真理之問題，如此，才能獲得真理。荀子認為，唯有聖人能克服這些限制且滿足知道的條件，因此，人們必須依賴權威。

對所有儒者而言，經典和聖人之權威已是一種主要學說。孟子主張道德來自先天之人心並由此提出性善說，此實背離儒家之基本重點。而荀子藉由主張性惡說並賦予權威之原則一堅實之基礎，就其強調權威而言，儒學是遵循荀子而非孟子。

荀子主張人性具有無限之能力，由於儒學強調教育和訓練的重要。因此，若人性是惡，則教育和訓練，甚至權威皆成為邏輯的必要。反之，若人性是善，則教育和權威等皆無其必要。

荀子倫理學之基礎主要是接受權威之倫理學，他必須為道德之權威完成哲學之基礎。荀子強調權威作為人生的指針似乎注定是多數的人和行動的事實。

（五）禮和仁

「道」不僅包括所有倫理學且包含整個儒家學說。此一事實指出，儒家哲學是非常徹底倫理的。在古代倫理學中有內在道德和外在道德的重大爭鬥，雖然並不明確，尤其是在正統或儒家思想潮流中，然而，此一事實的確構成諸多哲學討論的基礎。「仁」之概念成為內在道德之主角，而「禮」則是外在道德的主角。

荀子提到的禮的內容是喪、祭、朝、聘等禮，雖然，禮的內容是宗教儀式，但並不限於此。由於儀式是在任何場合中行止須合理，由此，禮成為具有「理」之意義。同樣地，禮亦伸展而意指外在道德。

由於宗教和宮廷儀式皆伴隨音樂，因此，樂和禮成為一對道德詞語，且「樂」成為擁有諸多「禮」字的道德涵義。因此，禮也發展成為中國人的主要道德概念之一，尤其是表現為外在和習慣性的道德。

對荀子而言，禮是主要道德且是全部的道德。禮即是道，且道、儒家之道和倫理學即是禮。此一與外在標準一致的行為概念是在倫理學中荀子學說的權威的必然的邏輯的結果。道德是迫使邪惡的人性走向正途的法則，而禮即是分辨善惡的外在標準。

在荀子的教義中，禮備受重視，而仁幾乎完全被排斥。仁只是作為尋求人民福祉的仁慈君主的屬性，它已成為僅僅是聖人的特質而已。

對荀子而言，禮不只是一系列的社會和宗教形式，它也是一種教育和社會的原則，它提供個人訓練自我的標準和一系列高度教育價值的實踐，尤其是訓練人們的欲望。它是社會組織的基石。社會必須立基於上下、老少、貧富和貴賤的分別，且為處理不同階級的適當儀式立法。

禮不只是一種純粹的道德原則。對儒者而言，在道德和形上學原則間並無終極分別。在《荀子》中，禮是宇宙論和倫理學的原則，荀子將禮等同於道。對荀子而言，禮包含全部的道德和所有形上學原則，至於其他倫理學和形上學的概念則只是禮的一方面的表現而已。

（六）其他的倫理學概念

仁和禮是不同的儒家學派衝突中的主角，而其他的德目則為所有人所接受。在其他德目中唯一受到荀子重視的是義。義常與禮結合，雖然有時會單獨使用。

「義」的意義是「正義」。荀子認為社會是建立在社會的不平等之上，如，統治者與被統治者，老少等。這些不平等必須加以調和。人們必須承認他們自己的低下和別人的優秀，並且依此對待他們——這種根據他們在生活中的地位所賦予的公正和應得權利，這種對待人們正如他們所應當接受的待遇就是「義」。

對荀子而言，義是社會的基石，且是在社會上承認不同的個人的相稱的權利。在荀子的教義中，義並未明確的與禮分開，禮也帶有義的特性。

此外，在荀子的學說中，忠、信、誠、孝、弟等德目也有簡略的提及。

（七）音樂

在中國古代的哲學中，音樂扮演一重要角色。在古代，音樂近於今日所謂藝術的概念。音樂是人類情感的表現，且對社會是絕對必要的，這是對墨子想要廢除音樂的一種回應。

為了反對墨子攻擊音樂是對社會無用的主張，荀子聲稱，音樂使聽者和諧，因為，他們擁有共同的經驗，因此，他們必定會和諧與虔誠，親切而順服。

針對墨子攻擊音樂無益於國，荀子宣稱，音樂影響人民極為深遠。它使人民和諧，因此，軍隊強大，人民安全，且由於人民安全，他們會對君主滿意，因此，君主的地位就會穩固。音樂也是一種有力的教育力量，它可使人心向善，且改變其習俗。人民若無音樂表達其情感，他們將只會有好惡的情感，但因情感無法適當表達，因此，社會將會失序。

荀子所謂的音樂是指好的音樂（雅樂），因為，在中國古代，音樂清楚地分為正統和非正統，且非正統音樂被認為不配音樂之名，此外，荀子的道是外在標準的概念，因此，荀子的整個理論可概括於一句話：「樂者所以道樂也，……所以道德也。」

（八）欲望和心；心理學

對荀子而言，欲望是人性的基本要素之一。欲望不但是意指有目的的行為方面，而且是指人類追求滿足。在欲望分析中，荀子被引入個人的心理學分析，這或許是荀子最富創意的作品之一。在荀子之前，從未有過諸多此一主題的討論，且幾乎未有任何人性的心理學分析。

荀子將靈魂二分為心或意志和欲望或情感。荀子認為欲望是人性的基本事實，是人類的天性且無法加以移除。人性是自然的產物，感情是人性的本質，欲望是感情的反應（所謂：「性者，天之就也；情者，性之質也；欲者，情之應也。」）。因此，根除欲望是不可能的，蓋欲望是人性基本而不變的性質。

荀子以為心能控制欲望而不需要移除或減少欲望，他賦予心統制整個人格的權力。雖然，荀子賦予心極大的權力，但心不可自作抉擇。確實，對一般人而言，心確會誤入歧途，而唯有君子或聖人才會具備虛、壹、靜的條件，且依內在的標準作判斷，至於其他人則必須遵循聖人所設計的標準即儒家之道。為了避免偏見和錯誤，心需要禮的指導，因此，荀子固守他行為的權威主義標準。

因此，心是欲望的控制者，心會被禮所控制，而後即使欲望很多時，心也能加以控制，但若心未受禮所控制，則即使欲望很少時，也會導致失序的行為，因此，行為的好壞是依於心而非依於欲望的多寡而定。

荀子以為，想要移除欲望是愚昧的，因為，它們從未實現過。荀子是一位實踐者，雖然，他的確有許多洞見，但是，他並沒有為知識而求知識的科學精神。他的心理學洞見只是他在解決一些較大的問題時的副產品，如，控制欲望等。荀子是一位真正的儒者，他的哲學是實踐的哲學。

（九）教育哲學

儒者首先是道德改革者。雖然，他們的主要重心是透過父權式的政府來解決問題，但是，他們也提供個人的發展和革新。此一或可稱之為救贖手段的過程是經由教育而來。對他們來說，教育是通往道德生活之路。

荀子主張性惡，因此，教育是絕對必要的。另一方面，這種惡的傾向並不會阻止善的發展，每人皆有提升至聖人的能力，因此，荀子強調在塑造性格中，環境所具有的力量。

教育是環境塑造人性的結果，而不是在發展人的本性。若沒有任何指導而去發展本性，則只會產生惡。因此，善的指導是必要的。在自我發展中，人是需要協助的，人所需之協助是透過「學」而來。「學」意謂著良好的規則和習慣的積累，因此，一個人的整個性情是可以改變，以致他可以成為聖人。

但是，「學」並不只是一種知識的過程，它也是一種道德的過程。它不僅是學習事物，而且在於使它們付諸實行。荀子認為，「學」的材料是經典。荀子或許是第一位塑造古典文獻正典的儒者。他所提倡的正典持續維持為官方之正典，此一事實只是荀子對中國思想影響的另一實例而已。荀子所陳述的正典是詩、書、禮、易、春秋（樂亡佚而以易代之）。在這些經典中，荀子認為禮是最重要的經典，此正如禮是最重要的倫理原則一樣。而比正典的形成更重要的是荀子是第一位將上述經典視為權威且採用作為教材的儒者。

　　荀子或許是以其教育哲學最為著稱。儒學尊重歷史和權威，而荀子即是儒學最合邏輯的典型。並且，荀子的教育學說是此一原則的邏輯和最生動的表現。

（十）邏輯理論

　　德氏在〈邏輯理論〉中，首先指出，在中文中，邏輯一詞，在字面上乃意指名學（the study of terms）而言，且邏輯問題之出現，首先是關於名之問題而非關於辭或判斷（judgment）之問題。德氏以為，荀子係中國古代哲學思潮中儒家之殿軍，作為孔子的真正傳人，荀子將「正名」視為他基本的邏輯原則。正如孔子一樣，荀子相信，公私生活中之所有罪惡和困境都是來自於名之不正，因而，沒有是非之真正標準。故唯有王者起而制名，名定而實辨，始能建立是非之正確標準。可見，對於荀子而言，邏輯是以倫理政治之要求為正名之目的。

　　德氏在本章中，主要是根據荀子〈正名〉篇之內容來加以疏解。其中包括「所為有名」，論制名之目的；「所緣以同異」，論同名異名之所由起；「制名之樞要」，論制名之原則，以及名之類別和名之用法等。在制名的原則方面，荀子特別強調名的社會性格。荀子認為名具有固定而確定的意義，但只是由約定俗成而來，但是約定俗成並無法賦予一種絕對而固定之標準，如荀子所想的，因為個人可以決定不去贊同約定俗成之原則。因此，荀子決定藉由王者或政府之力量來賦予名之絕對之性格。

　　又德氏亦提到荀子對於名之分類。德氏認為，墨辯將名分為達名、類名和私名三類；而荀子只分為達名和類名兩類（即大共名和大別名）。德氏以為，荀子可能並不認為私名是值得加以分類；或可能荀子認為所有的名都是類名，雖然，荀子並未明說。此外，德氏指出，對應於制名之三項原則，荀子亦提出各家用名之謬誤，即三惑。所謂三惑是指「用名以亂名」、「用實以亂名」和「用名以亂實」等。

（十一）不平等

　　所有古代儒家哲學是以促進統治的藝術為目的，儒家哲學幾乎可以政治學為其標記。政治學是中國哲學的核心。儒家政治理論的基本要素是人類的不平等，所有儒者皆堅持此種不平等的學說，但荀子是賦予它完全的理論基礎的第一人。

　　荀子認為，社會性是人類顯著的特性，此社會性意指階級的區分。荀子以為，透過造成社會差別的社會組織是在基本性質是欲望的人類之間獲得和睦與寧靜的必要手段。不平等是受到天生的人性強制之下可以保證有利的社會關係的一種必要手段。然而，不平等並不是天生的。儒學的基本教義之一是人的能力是平等的，因為，所有人都會達到最大的發展。

荀子以為，人們最初的能力在智愚方面是相同的，但他們發展的能力則不同，且他們是由智愚來區分的。此一不同是由於他們最初能力不同程度的發展而來。因此，它是一種道德的而不是一種貴族的、遺傳的不平等。它是天性的平等，而發展的不平等。

荀子藉由禮———一種權威主義的倫理制度，使個人奉行普遍的善。人們之所以接受是因為它是唯一可避免混亂的方法。於此，荀子將其政治哲學和倫理學緊密結合，且使其倫理學成為實現其政治哲學之目的的手段。

（十二）政治哲學

荀子之所以著重政治哲學是由於儒家哲學的一般傾向在於使政治學成為哲學思想的目標和實踐的正當性，而不是為了他自己的理論興趣。荀子在政治哲學方面的貢獻是理論的而不是實踐的。

荀子以為，一個成功的政府是因統治者的道德而定。決定統治者是否值得尊敬的是人民而不是他的權位，君主若暴虐無道則會被推翻。荀子接受並捍衛此一學說，但是，對荀子而言，天是不具人格的法則或自然，因此，超自然的制裁是完全不存在的，但是，道德的約束力卻因此而增強。此一學說從未導致任何朝代經常被推翻，但它已成為一種道德的歷史哲學的基礎，它是儒家真正偉大的學說之一。

（十三）理想主義和惡的問題

在儒家的教義中顯現出一種高度的理想主義，且似乎與一般人的日常經驗相牴觸。幾乎沒有任何超自然力量的信仰可提供儒家這種理想主義的基礎。關於超自然的存在，儒家傾向於不可知論，且其哲學整體而言，並未表現出一種強烈的宗教傾向。

儒家具有一種實現自己理想力量的信念，此一信念超越了通常人類生活所能提供的任何事物，這是一種他們的經驗所無法證實的對於善的力量的信念。這種道德的理想主義是一種在他們的生命和教義中的強而有力的力量，且歷代以來，持續成為中國偉大心靈的最偉大的寶藏。

此一理想主義在儒家的歷史哲學中表現得最清楚。其基本主題是善會得到回報，而惡會受罰。孔子主張一個真正有德之統治者藉由其自身獨有的善的力量可以改善他整個國家。孟子公開主張採用儒家的行動原則的統治者將可成為君王。荀子接受這種理想主義的理論，並進一步加以闡明。

儒家這種理想主義的理論引起諸多問題，如，從儒家內部所引發的問題是何以孔子本人未能成為君王。而人們也反對儒家這種理想主義，因為偉大的儒者從未提陞到高位，且偉大的儒者也不像人們所理解的那樣的賢明，並且當代的歷史和生活也不支持這種理想主義。

就個人的情形而言，最後，正義通常都會獲得回報。而在他們的道德理想主義中，儒家獲得一種對他們而言真正的宗教的堅定信仰。

（十四）結論

由荀子所賦予儒學發展的概觀中，可以看出，荀子是一位真正的儒者。在他所贊同的孔孟學說的精髓中，荀子是一位闡釋孔子學說之涵義並賦予孔子哲學以一理論基礎的天才。

荀子並非為人類思想發現新方向之先鋒，他只是盡其所能且奉獻其生命以發展和捍衛儒學。他的原創性在於賦傳統以新義，並為儒學提供一堅實之理論基礎。因此，荀子的確對儒家思想作出重要貢獻，並且在漢代，這些貢獻與儒家思想的大趨勢交織在一起，因此，即使荀子本人受到譴責，然而，其思想之精髓卻從未減損。

荀子將儒家學說構成一相當一致且圓滿的哲學。他的學說有系統且是有機的，此一特性在中國古代哲學中是尚未發現過的，然而，其學說絕非膚淺的，他深透入事物的核心和人性的知識，因此，其哲學是真正普遍的且是儒家的。荀子可確切被認為是一位具有非常奇特的心靈且是世界上偉大的哲學家之一。

H.G. Creel, Chinese Thought：From Confucius to Mao Tse-tung

一、作者姓名與著作名稱

作者：H.G.Creel（顧立雅）

書名：Chinese Thought：From Confucius to Mao Tse-tung

出版項：Chicago：University of Chicago Press,1953

中文書名：《中國思想：從孔子到毛澤東》

二、篇幅

共 240 頁（正文：211 頁，附錄：無，建議進階閱讀書目：3 頁，參考書目：6 頁，注釋：15 頁，索引：5 頁）。

三、主題

本書是一部中國思想史綜述，涵蓋之內容極為廣泛，從孔子之思想一直敘述到毛澤東為止。對於先秦儒、道、墨、法等主要學派之思想，漢代、佛學、宋明理學、清代及近代思想等皆有著墨，其中亦頗多精義。

四、關鍵辭

孔子、荀子、戴震、毛澤東、懷疑主義、折衷主義、極權主義、權威主義。

五、主要論點

（一）顧氏認同德效騫之稱荀子乃「古代儒學之塑造者」之歷史定位。此外，顧氏指出，荀子對儒學真正的傷害是他對人性的不信任，並將儒學發展成一種權威主義系統。

（二）道家是一種自然的神秘主義，而「自然」即是「道」。

（三）法家強調權威學說，且從《韓非子》一書中，可看出法家哲學最完整和成熟的圖像。

（四）折衷主義是漢代思想的特色所在。

（五）從第 8 到 16 世紀，在孔廟中供奉孔子及其弟子等之安排方式與佛寺類似，由此可看出佛教對中國影響之一般。

（六）明末清初之反理學思潮是大規模地反對佛教的影響，並試圖回歸孔孟學說之真義。

（七）中國共產黨的成功主要並非由於中國人民反抗貧窮和經濟剝削之革命浪潮所致，而是由於知識份子的領導和發起革命。

六、目次

（一）近代世界中的中國思想

（二）孔子之前

（三）孔子和爭取人類的幸福

（四）墨子和追求和平與秩序

（五）孟子和人性的注重

（六）道家神秘的懷疑主義

（七）荀子的權威主義

（八）法家的極權主義

（九）漢代的折衷主義者

（十）佛學和理學

（十一）理學的反動

（十二）西方的影響

（十三）回顧

七、摘要

（一）近代世界中的中國思想

一般而言，在十九世紀中葉，一個受過教育的中國人會認為，除了中國經典之外，並沒有什麼值得學習的。這例示了許多美國人認為，自我滿足和對外在世界缺乏好奇心是中國人的象徵。此一態度使中國人在與其他國家交涉時，極為不利，且是中國所以遭遇許多困境的原因。

而今日之情形則有些改觀。並非中國人忽視和不關心西方文化，而是西方人對中國幾乎無所知且並不努力去了解，而西方也正在付出且將持續付出無知的代價。

依此，中國和西方將無法和諧共存，直到彼此有一合理程度之相互了解。而我們要了解現代中國，則必須由孔子開始，而不是專注於馬克斯和毛澤東，因為，過去和現在是緊密地交織在一起。我們必須尊重中國的思想家，因為他們在造成今日的中國之過程中扮演主要的角色。

中國對文明的貢獻除了紙和火藥外，有關平等的理論和實踐在十七、八世紀的西方人類平等和政治民主的概念發展中扮演重要的角色。如，美國的文官考試制度是來自英國的影響，而英國的文官考試制度則和中國的科舉制度頗為類似，此外，西方人強調征服自然，雖然帶來物質上的滿足，但也忽略人際關係，其結果是人們在精神上較為不安。而中國人則是尋求與自然和諧相處，且極為注重人際關係，結果是似乎缺乏物質的進步，但在面對困境時，較能隨遇而安，且較少為心理失調所苦。當然，中國有很多地方可向西方學習，反之亦然，而有些是現成的存在於他們偉大思想家的著作中。

（二）孔子之前

西元前 1122 年，周克商，周朝藉由歷史只是自我重複的說辭來為其征服商朝的正當性作辯護。周人說，幾世紀以前，商湯承接天命，以同樣的方式取代其前朝夏，此一說法提供周之克殷一種先例，並使它成為一種循環的偶發事件。

周公似乎是天命說的主要倡導者。根據天命說，若統治者不能善待人民，將會被天所罷黜，其結果是在理論上建立了統治者是為人民而存在的原則。統治者是由於人民的信任，民心的歸向才能擁有政權的。

此外，在中國思想中亦已存在其他的重要觀念，如，對家庭的重視。西方人有時會認為，孝道是孔子所發明或至少是他所首先加以強調的。但是，在周初實已有此一說法：孝道不僅是一種道德的並且甚至是一種法定的責任。

周克殷之後所面對的統治工作絕非易事。面對新征服的廣大土地，周天子所能做的就是將其領土分封給他的親戚等貴族來協助管轄。起初，這種封建制度運作得很好，但隨著周天子的權力變弱，而某些貴族的勢力變強，他們不僅疏忽他們的職責，甚至運用其私有軍隊去嘲弄或企圖篡奪統治者的權力。

孔子即生活於此種政局不安定的背景中，他是一位具有高度智慧和崇高
理想的人。他雖周遊列國欲伸展其政治抱負，但未受任何國君重用，最後，他
奉獻其心力於教育。孔子去世後，他對中國政治在理論和實踐方面皆具有重大
的影響和貢獻。

（三）孔子和爭取人類的幸福

孔子是藉由個人和知性天賦與成就的力量深深地影響人類歷史的少數人
之一。孔子於西元前 551 年生於魯國（今山東省）。孔子自言：「吾少也賤，故
多能鄙事。」因此，孔子必須自力更生，且其學問多是自修而來。這些經驗無
疑地使孔子能貼近地關心百姓之疾苦，並認識一些貴族。

孔子並非一和平主義者。他相信，有德者為了避免他們自身和世界受到黷
武者的奴役，有時必須使用武力。但是，他認為，任何人不僅在理想上並且在
實際上必須順服正義的力量。依此，他相信軍隊不可能有效地作戰，除非士兵
知道他們為何而戰，且能使他們信服是基於正義而戰。

孔子的觀念和當時的貴族完全相異。他不僅知道且試著加以實踐。如，
「君子」一詞，當時是指出身貴族者，但孔子完全改變此一用法。他主張人
人皆可成為「君子」，如果他們行為是高尚、不自私、公正和善良。另一方面，
他主張「君子」的認定不是依據出身而僅是居於行為和品德。

孔子認為，人人皆渴望幸福。他相信，所有人都應該擁有他們所想要的東
西。然而，孔子發現，他周遭的人都不快樂。人民生活窮困，有時飢餓，被戰
爭或貴族壓迫。甚至貴族也總是無法從他們不合法和不安的生活方式中獲得
快樂。既然如此，那麼，這兒有一明顯的目標：使人人幸福。因此，我們發現
孔子將良好的政府界定為使其人民幸福。由於幸福是美好的，且人通常是社會
的動物，因此，它只是通往孔子互惠主義之原則的一小步。孔子界定互惠主義
為：「己所不欲；勿施於人。」其積極義為：「己欲立而立人；己欲達而達人。」
依此，欲使人達成幸福的目的，孔子強調普遍教育的必要。

孔子於西元前 479 年去世，然而其思想對中國人，甚至西方人皆有莫大的
影響。

（四）墨子和追求和平與秩序

雖然，墨子的生卒年並不確定，但他的出生似乎並不早於西元前 480 年，
而去世的時間亦不會晚於 390 年。有學者認為他生於魯國，但也有人認為他是
宋國人，據說他曾在宋國為官。

墨子出身卑微，據說他曾學於孔子之後學，然而，他認為儒學未能解決人民之困境，因此，他與儒家分道揚鑣，並創立自己的學派。

墨子與儒家的學說不同。墨子曾攻擊儒家所提出的貧富、壽夭皆依於天（命），且不可改變的學說。然而，墨子最激烈的批評是反對儒家主張厚葬、久喪。墨子認為，實行厚葬、久喪將使國家貧困、干擾經濟生產和政府的正常運作，且會使人口減少，因此，他們是應該被譴責的。

墨子也反對戰爭。首先，他試圖說服統治者，戰爭是無利可圖的。其次，更有說服力的是，他主張戰爭對勝、敗雙方皆並非是建設的而是破壞的過程。因為，被征服的土地通常都已經荒蕪了。最後，墨子有一更積極的構想。墨子提出「兼愛」作為根本解決戰爭和許多其他罪惡的方法。墨子相信，每一個人都應該愛世上的任何人，且沒有任何差別。墨子認為，「兼愛」之「愛」並非感情的，而是純粹理智之事。為了使人接受其「兼愛」之主張，墨子提出其功利主義之學說，因為，兼愛是良善的且對人是有利的。由此，墨子也反對音樂（非樂），因為，音樂是無益於民生的。

此外，墨子提出「尚同」之主張。「尚同」，他似乎意指意志和利益的認同。墨子指出，臣子必須尚同於天子，而天子必須尚同於天志，如此，「尚同」之原則才能確實地運作。

墨家早期與儒家並稱顯學，然而，不久即沒落，並從歷史舞台上消失，直到近代才又開始復興。

（五）孟子和人性的注重

孔子去世之後，到了西元前四世紀，孟子曾抱怨：楊朱、墨翟之言盈天下，天下不歸楊、則歸墨。孟子是一位很有趣的人，並且具有一種很複雜的性格。孟子相信在他的時代，他是儒家傳統的繼承者。孟子認為，他的觀念和行為與孔子是完全一致的。但在這一點上，他是錯的，孟子和孔子是完全不同，並且，時代也已改變。孔子曾多次坦承自己的過錯，但孟子卻從未公開承認其錯誤。顧立雅指出，I. A. Richards 認為。孟子通常對贏得論證比試著發現真理更有興趣。這並非意指孟子並不關心真哩，而是他相信，他已獲得真理，並且只需要去說服其對手此一事實而已。

孟子政治綱領的基本主張是德行會帶來成功，因此，他告訴梁惠王，即使是一小國亦足以作為稱王天下之始點。若梁惠王施仁政於民，則誰與王敵，此即仁者無敵之謂。孟子指出，統治可依循之準則是光有德行是不夠的，為政者必須效法古代的聖王，若君臣並無缺失，他們只需效法堯舜的行為，在徵收賦稅方面亦是如此。孟子相信，古代聖王的教誨是構成人類思想和行為的完美典範。依此，聖王如何獲得教誨？是來自超自然之啟示或聖人是超人？當然不是，孟子說：堯舜與人同耳。

孟子相信，人生而有相同之人性，且人性是善。此一學說已是儒家內部極具爭議之主題，此一爭議似乎是從錯誤方向的進路而來。通常注意力是放在「人性」一詞上，然而，檢證「善」一詞可能更為有利。對孟子正如同對孔子是一樣的「善」，即是與人性完全一致的。如，使人胃痛的食物即非「善」（good）的食物，對牛而言，草是「善」的食物，但對人則不是，因為，它不適合人的「性」（nature）。因此，當孟子說人之性善，他在某種程度上是同語反覆（tautologically）的說法。因為，他意指「善」是與人性是完全調和的。因此，對孟子而言，倫理學與心理學之間的關係是非常密切的。孟子確有一種心與欲間之心理學的二元論，若心能控制欲望，則不致流於惡。孟子雖認為欲望應被控制，但不應予以壓制或去除。

（六）道家神秘的懷疑主義

一般而言，道家最早的著作和代表作是《老子》和《莊子》。傳統上認為，《老子》一書是由老子所作，並且，老子與孔子是同時代的人。然而，許多學者主張，老子的時代應晚於孔子，並且，即使如此，《老子》一書亦非由老子本人或其他任何人所獨力完成。

《老子》又名《道德經》，全書約五千言，是一部有趣而重要的書籍。然而，《老子》一書並非成於一人之手，而是由多人所寫而後編輯成書的。至於其成書年代，顧氏認為，不會早於西元前四世紀。

至於莊子，他生於今日的河南省，曾在此擔任過小吏，一般認為，莊子在西元前 300 年之後不久去世。而《莊子》一書，學者多認為並非成於莊子一人之手，且其目前之版本應成於西元前二世紀。

誠如馬伯樂（Maspero）所言，道家是一種神秘主義哲學，是一種自然的神秘主義。在我們的城市當中，道家理所當然的似乎是無稽的，但是，它似乎具有一種強過於最複雜之邏輯的效力。基督教或伊斯蘭教之神秘主義者在追求與上帝的靈交與和諧，而道家則試圖成為具有自然的神秘主義者，而他們將「自然」稱之曰「道」。

在孔子之前，「道」一詞通常意指道路或行為之方式。孔子把它當作一哲學概念來使用，是代表道德、社會和政治行為的適當方式。然而，對孔子而言，「道」並非一形上學概念。對道家而言，「道」則是一形上學概念。他們使用「道」一詞代表萬物之全體，相當於有些西方哲學家所謂的「絕對」。「道」是產生萬物之基本要素，是質樸、無形、無欲、不爭和無上滿足的。

至於「德」，依儒家之意是指道德而言，但卻為道家所譴責。對於「德」，道家是指自然的、天性的、原始的性質，而與受社會認可和教育所責成之性質相反對。

道家之理想是質樸，其目的是回歸於「道」。人若要回歸於道則應與宇宙之根本法則相和諧而不是與之對抗。道家又主張萬物皆是相對的，這種相對主義可應用於道德問題和我們的存在。由於萬物皆不確定，因此，人若努力想獲得成功則是荒謬的。人不應該想要去擁有外在事物，而應試圖去獲得自知和滿足。那麼，我們要如何做呢？道家告訴我們要「無為」。「無為」是道家著名的訓諭。「無為」並非什麼都不做，而是不去做不自然或非自發性的事，重要的是不要以任何方式去做過度的努力。

（七）荀子的權威主義

顧氏在本文中將荀子之生平、著作和學說作一般之論述。顧氏指出，荀子對儒學的影響很大，而德效騫也極為正確地稱他為「古代儒學之塑造者」。然而，在過去數千年中，荀子在儒家學者中並未受到高度寵愛。在中國之外，那些熟悉孟子大名之人甚至並不確定荀子是何方神聖。

有謂荀子之所以缺乏崇高的聲譽乃是由於他反對孟子之性善說，而受到朱熹的譴責。顧氏以為這只是原因之一，但是，真正遮蔽荀子之聲譽的乃是由於他本身思想中之一種特殊限制。顧氏指出，毫無疑問的，荀子是世界上最出色的哲學家之一。然而，由於荀子對人性缺乏信心，不僅使其名譽受損，且強迫其後之儒學披上一件學術正統之外衣（按，意指權威主義）。

顧氏指出作為一位哲學家，荀子令人感到興趣的是，當他討論語言理論時。荀子所處理之問題，甚至仍困擾著今日之哲學家。荀子提出之問題有：何謂名或語詞？何謂概念？概念如何產生？何以人們在使用概念時是如此的不同？

在中國古代有所謂的辯者（dialectician）提出詭辯，如「白馬非馬」等來贏得人心。作為當時儒家之主要代表，荀子必須與這些論辯對抗。荀子並不滿足於只是處理這些問題，而是，試圖研究語言的本質，並且建立語言之正確使用的規則。

荀子首先提出的問題是「所為有名」，荀子的回答：名是為了滿足談論事物和事件之方便的需求而來，同時，名亦是人們所發明來提供這種需求。荀子指出制名之目的在於辨同異和明貴賤。

其次，荀子提出「名之同異的基礎」此一問題。顧氏指出荀子認為名之同異的基礎在於感官。根據感官，感官認為事物屬於同一類的，就是同類。顧氏指出荀子並不相信名與實之關係是固定不變的。荀子說：

> 名無固宜，約之以命，約定俗成謂之宜。……名有固善，徑易而不拂，謂之善名。

荀子使用各種不同的關於語言的原則來分析先秦諸子之令人困惑之命題。此外，他更確立語言之正確使用來表達觀念。可惜，後人並未重視荀子之學說。

顧氏以為，荀子一書應是荀子本人所作，但部分篇章明顯的是出自其學生之手。最後六篇與《荀子》一書之其他篇章頗為不同，可能是出自漢代儒者所附加。而在本文中之其他地方亦有似乎是插入的簡短的添加文字。

顧氏指出，荀子最著名的學說是性惡論，此一學說係荀子持之以反對孟子之性善說。依荀子之意，人之性惡，且人人皆然。故荀子說：「凡人之性者，堯舜之與桀跖，其性一也；君子之與小人，其性一也。」又說，君子與小人不論是材性知能、好榮惡辱或好利惡害等皆同，且塗之人透過實踐善則可成聖，只是人若無師法之開導則無法實踐善，故荀子說：「今是人之口腹，安知禮義？安知辭讓？安知廉恥隅積？亦哺哺而噍，鄉鄉而飽矣。人無師無法，則其心正其口腹也。」依此，荀子以為人若無師之教化則無法成善，然而，此中有一難題，即第一位教師如何能施行教化？蓋依荀子之意，教化及其原則皆聖人所創制，但荀子又否認聖人和任何人在本性上有所不同。荀子承認此一難題，並試著加以處理。

荀子在〈性惡〉篇中，藉由問答之方式來說明此一難題。有人問說：「人之性惡，則禮義惡生？」荀子回答說：「凡禮義者，是生於聖人之偽，非故生於人之性也。……聖人積思慮、習偽故，以生禮義而起法度，則禮義法度者，是生於聖人之偽，非故生於人之性也。」

依此，顧氏以為，荀子承認聖人之成善係經由其自我之努力且無師法之助。然而，他同時亦否認在他的時代一般人可以成聖，即使他們天生的能力與聖人相同。於此，顧氏以為，吾人已經接近荀子思想之基本弱點。他的對手偵知其弱點，並加以挑戰。荀子試著加以回答如下：有問曰：「聖可以積而致，然而皆不可積，何也？」荀子回答說：「可以而不可使也。故小人可以為君子，而不肯為君子；君子可以為小人，而不肯為小人。小人君子者，未嘗不可以相為也，然而不相為者，可以而不可使也。故塗之人可以為禹，則然；塗之人能為禹，則未必然也。雖不能為禹，無害可以為禹。」

顧氏以為此段論述，並無法令人完全信服。當然，人們訓練自我的能力有所不同，因此，不論我們是否相信荀子之論點，我們必須承認那些荀子所提到的與聖人相似的人並不多。然而，就是這種不同，似乎掩飾了荀子的主張──人在能力和道德方面是一樣的。荀子所相信的，似乎是曾經有人自己發現善和真，但是這種人在荀子的時代是不存在的。

顧氏指出，不僅是眾人且是所有人都無法為自己去思考一些基本問題，荀子此一信念之結果，不僅抑制道德和知性之進步，且甚而使得道德和知性之健全發展不可能。對於人或心靈而言，永遠遵循別人所安排的軌跡並非正常之作用。

顧氏以為，荀子對儒學真正的傷害是他對人性的不信任。他不相信人能為自己思考，他想要將道德安置在一受到保證的基礎上，且強迫每一世代的人盲目地遵循經師所詮釋之經典。荀子說：「不是師法，而好自用，譬之是猶以盲辨色，以聾辨聲也，舍亂妄無為也。因此，正如同德效騫所說：「荀子將儒學發展成一種權威主義系統，在這系統中，所有真理皆來自於聖人之名言，由於荀子對人的不信任，對儒學而言，荀子失去了許多。」

（八）法家的極權主義

從孔子到道家，中國古代哲學有一共通點，即它們關心中國古代人民不幸的處境，被貧窮所折磨和受戰爭的壓迫和荼毒。它們都批評統治者；試圖防止人民受壓迫並試圖結束戰爭。反觀法家則非如此，法家哲學在很大程度上是一種反革命的哲學，它們試圖捍衛統治者的權威，並反對下列主張：政治是為人民存在，而不是為統治者而存在；任何政府若無法滿足人民的需求，將會受到譴責。

荀子建立一種儒家和法家間的橋樑。雖然，荀子反對法家的觀念，但是，他的性惡學說和權威主義卻傾向於法家的方向。荀子最著名的兩個學生──李斯和韓非，都是法家，而韓非是所有法家中最偉大的一位。

顧氏認為，法家不能說是一個學派，因為，該學派中空無一物。法家強調權威學說，但是它並沒有創派者，即使韓非是法家中最偉大的，但是他的老師並非法家而是儒家的荀子。只有不同的人和書以不同的方式和程度擁護我們稱之為法家的思想。並且，有些法家的著作是編輯而成，其中包含一些根本無法說明法家哲學的部份。

或許最早被稱為法家的人是管仲，一位西元前七世紀的宰相。他並非總是被歸類為法家。他強調「術」對政府的重要。申不害死於西元前 337 年，在韓國當官 15 年，他也強調「術」對政府的重要。慎到與孟子同時，約在西元前300 年前，他強調「勢」，即權力和地位的重要。

從學術的觀點而言，最重要的法家是韓非子。他死於西元前 233 年。從《韓非子》一書中，可看出法家哲學最完整和成熟的圖像。法家的歷史觀與儒家不同。儒家強調託古改制，而韓非則認為，即使在古代，不同的時代有不同的方法，尤其是時代產生巨變時。因此，治國之道宜隨時代之推移而有不同之應變對策，才能因時制宜。

在人性論方面，韓非和其他法家一樣，他接受人是自私自利且不會試圖以任何方式減輕的觀點，即使是在家庭中。韓非相信，自私自利即是法則。既然人性是自私自利的，因此，唯有以嚴刑峻罰來抑制這種趨勢，君主才能保有其地位甚或其性命。

韓非認為，君主必須採用法家理論所列出的「法」、「術」、「勢」三者，才能治好國家。「勢」是權力和地位；「術」是方法；「法」是法條。韓非認為，即使是聖王也要擁有「勢」，才能使人民服從，因此，德、智是無法與「勢」相提並論的。

（九）漢代的折衷主義者

在西方，通常不會想到政府和哲學是密切相關的，然而，在中國，它們通常是非常緊密相連的。政府和哲學之間的關係在西曆紀元前最後幾世紀裡變得特別明顯。西元前 213 年，在秦朝統治下，幾乎所有哲學文獻和儒家經典都被禁止，而法家則是當令。幾年後，隨著漢朝的建立，情況則改觀。到了武帝在位期間（r.140～87B.C.），法家之著作從官方地位被剔除，而為了研究儒家經典，太學也建立了。因此，不到一世紀之內，整個情勢丕變，由秦時法家是官方學說轉變成漢武帝時儒家成為當令的學說。

儒家正統的性質和它在過去二千年間在中國所佔有的地位是深深地受到

儒學在漢代所謂的勝利（triumph）的影響。有些學者認為，儒學在漢代所以獲得重視是因為時代的政治和經濟環境的不可避免的結果。其他學者則以為，這是因為某統治者和顧問的偏好所致。更有許多學者主張，漢武帝之所以採用儒學作為統治的官方哲學是因為儒家強調臣子對君主的奉承，並提升皇帝和統治階層的權力和威望。無論如何，以上學者的說法都太簡單。顧氏指出，要了解此一問題，宜考慮下列三個要素：統治者、學者和廣大的百姓。

一般認為，漢武帝採用董仲舒之建議，罷黜百家，獨尊儒術。但事實上，並非如此。1. 漢武帝 15 歲繼承王位時，曾是一位儒者，但他成年之後，卻一直是個法家，並為了政治因素，假裝自己是一位儒者。2. 武帝所採用之政策是法家和反儒家之學說。3. 即使表面上儒學受到重視，但在武帝在位期間，儒學已是被曲解的儒學。

漢武帝在其任內，不僅未將秦朝之苛法完全廢止，且更擴充成一嚴密而詳細之法典，且無情地嚴屬施行。漢武帝不僅行為像個法家且有學者指出，他自覺地以秦始皇為師。由於許多文獻在秦朝遭受毀壞，因此，學者對復原古籍，尤其是經典，大感興趣，再加上皇帝的鼓勵，在這期間，開啟了解經的偉大時代。漢代學者以其時代之思想來註解古代文獻，由於他們的努力，直到 20 世紀，這些典籍還能被研究和翻譯。

易經是古代占卜之書，但在漢代卻被認為是儒家之經典。他們認為，易經之「十翼」是孔子所作，並公開說明一種藉由神秘的術數來了解甚或控制事件的方法。顧氏以為，「十翼」可能是由深受道家影響之儒者所作。

在西元前 4 世紀興起另外一種觀念，即萬物皆被歸類為陰、陽原理，任何事物皆從陰、陽這兩種原理導出。然而，這並非西方之二元論，相反的，陰、陽二者之互補，維持宇宙之和諧，且可能彼此互相轉化，因此，冬天的陰可轉變成夏天的陽。

此外，一種幾乎是同時出現的重要概念是「五行」，它們是木、火、土、金、水。五行與方位相關，在哲學上，五行之次序極為重要。五行相生相克。木生火；火生土；土生金；金生水；水生木。而五形相克之次序則是：水克火；火克金；金克木；木克土；土克水，因此，周期再次完成。

藉由古代的技術，如，易經、術數、陰陽和五行等之占卜技術，漢代發展出一種廣泛而嚴密的系統來分析和控制現象。然而，這種理論並未經由實驗加以證明，因此，它幾乎是教條和假科學的。此外，在武帝時期，淮南子及其門下食客合編《淮南子》一書，此書本質上是道家思想，但是呈現出強烈之折衷主義之傾向，此亦漢代思想之特色所在。

（十）佛學和理學

大約西曆紀年始，佛教由印度傳入中國。其意義遠大於只是一種宗教之降臨。對某些中國人來說，它意指一種新的生活方式。對所有中國人而言，不管他們接受與否，它意謂著，從此將會以新的方式去看這個世界，並對宇宙之了解也會與之前有很大的不同。整個中國人的思考方式，某種程度上，如此漸進地且普遍地改變，以致幾乎無人意識到發生何事。中國人的心靈被佛教所支配大約一千年左右。

顧氏以為，我們不知道佛教是如何和何時傳到中國，但我們確知，傳統上所接受的解釋是不正確的。據指出，道家的老莊思想和有些印度著作之觀念有其相似性。印度思想很早進入中國的確足以影響這些道家的作品，但有關詳細的證據則有待未來的研究。然而，我們有證據顯示，佛教大約在西曆紀年開始時為中國人所知。雖然如此，幾世紀以來，佛教似乎對中國學術圈幾乎都沒有影響。

在中國文獻中，直到三世紀時，幾乎沒有提到，而入侵中國的西、北部族反而是提供這種新信仰的沃土，有些統治者成為虔誠之皈依者。據說，到了 381 年，中國西北部族有十分之九成為佛教徒。著名的印度僧人鳩摩羅什（344～412）在西元 400 年後不久任職西安並開設譯場，在他的監督下，翻譯了 94 部佛典。

佛寺和出家眾成倍數成長，信徒也捐出廣大土地建寺，如此減少生產田地和賦稅，造成政府財政短缺，不僅百姓和皇帝成為佛教徒，甚至一些士人也轉向佛教。最令人之吃驚的是，雖然有些學者持續批評佛教是一外來迷信，但從第 8 到 16 世紀，孔廟供奉孔子及其弟子等，其安排方式竟與佛寺類似，由此可見，佛教對中國影響之一般。

宋朝（960～1279）興起所謂「理學」（Neo-Confucianism），其始點可追溯至唐朝。理學試圖呈現它能提供任何佛教所想望的所有東西。它著手下列工作：1. 與佛教宇宙論相匹敵 2. 形上地解釋新世界和儒家倫理學 3. 證明政治和社會活動的正當性及證明在日常的正常生活的追求中，人有得到幸福的權力。

在宋代理學中，重要之學派有二，其領導者分別是朱熹（1130～1200）和陸象山（1139～1193）。朱熹年輕時，曾研讀道、佛，但不久他成為一堅定之儒者。他為許多重要的經典作注，為官方認可且成為科舉考試之標準本。

　　朱熹可說是集北宋理學之大成，其哲學之中心概念「理」。所有存在之事物皆由「理」和「氣」所構成。「氣」類似實體（substance）或物質（matter）之概念，萬物皆由「氣」和「理」所組成，但「理」具有優先性，是先於任何個體而存在。朱熹指出，「理」無生滅，是太極（the Supreme Ultimate）之一部分。

　　朱熹主張，人之「性」即「理」，凡人之「理」皆同，但「氣」則不同。「氣」若不純，則人愚昧而墮落，因此，人必須去除晦暗之「氣」的障礙，以恢復人之本性。朱熹非常重視「格物」作為獲得道德理解之手段。在政治方面，朱熹認為，「理」是建立政治行為之理想型態。若觀察之政府與此理想政府符合則是良好政府；反之，則否。

　　朱熹最大的對手是陸象山。朱熹哲學強調格物窮理；而陸象山則是冥想和直覺。雖然，陸氏所強調的與禪學相似，但它在儒學中已有一段長久的歷史。或許朱、陸二人最基本之不同在於其形上學。朱熹相信，萬物皆由「理」和「氣」所組成，而陸象山則相信，所有存在之事物皆只是「理」。因此，陸氏是一元論者。的確，一元論思想似乎比朱氏二元論與中國早期思想較為相像。

　　陸氏主張收回放心之實際方法。他認為，透過靜坐與冥想可以致知，並且可得到頓悟，使人之心與萬物合一。陸氏似乎受到禪學的影響，他相當忽略經典之權威，而事實上，他的著作也不多。在他死後，與朱熹相比，此無疑對他的學說不利，蓋朱熹係一多產作家。雖然，朱熹哲學受到官方之支持，但在明代，王陽明（1472～1529）卻是發展陸象山而非朱熹之哲學。

　　王陽明似曾研究過道家和佛學，但最後卻成為一堅定之儒家。王氏早年曾奉行朱熹之格物說，但七天後卻病倒。事實上，王氏是附和陸氏之學說，認為，人不宜研究事物而僅研究其「理」，而「理」則在人之心中。王氏最具特色之學說是「知行合一」。王氏認為，沒有人是真知而不能行，知而不行事實上是不知。聖人教人要知行並重，主要是希望人們回歸其真實之本性。沒有人能確切地說他了解孝弟，除非他確實加以實踐。

　　很明顯的，王陽明哲學受到禪學的影響。他默認道家和佛家之學說，但王氏將道、佛擺在儒學之下，並宣稱，佛教不去試圖解決世界之問題，卻予以逃避。

（十一）理學的反動

直到今天，佛教在中國仍有其重要性，尤其在一般民眾之間。作為一種學術力量，佛教在推翻滿清之革命中扮演某種角色。但是，近數百年來，佛教之影響力已大不如前。在近 4 世紀中，中國思想發展中興起兩股扮演重要角色的力量，其一是西方的衝擊。起初並不重要，而至今已成長至有人預測，在將來，西方的觀念幾乎將會完全取代中國之傳統思想。另一則是反理學。它是以十分不同的方向進行，是大規模地反對佛教的影響，並試圖回歸孔孟學說的真義。

清初興起反理學的漢學學派之開山者是顧炎武（1613～1682）。作為學者，顧氏經由廣泛旅遊蒐集和校勘資訊，且博覽群籍，這對當時狹隘的經學而言，是一重要矯正法。或許顧氏最大的貢獻是在音韻學研究方面，他運用音韻學作為文獻學和歷史研究之工具。作為哲學家，顧氏強力抨擊陸、王之理學，他認為陸王是受惠於佛學。他指出，與他同時代的多數人沉浸於理學，幾乎不會採取任何有效行動去反對敗壞明代政府和壓迫人民之罪惡。他們無力反抗滿清之侵略，並早早地向滿清投懷送抱。

在當代學者中，顧氏對黃宗羲（1610～1695）表示推崇，蓋黃氏勇於表達自由思想。黃氏在〈原君〉一文中指出，在古代，君主願意將其利益擺一邊而為人民謀福利，這些是古代的聖王。然而，後代之君主則非如此。在古代，人民愛戴其君主，視之如君、父，且事實上，亦如此，而今日則民視君如寇讎，如獨夫，而事實上亦如是。

至於強調實用作為哲學之基礎的是顏元（1635～1704）。顏元批評朱熹主張萬物皆由理、氣所構成之學說，顏元指出，人性是一而非二。顏元亦鄙視書呆子，宣稱讀書是無用的，除非將其所學付諸實踐。古代聖王和周公、孔子皆教人行動之必要。顏元之藥方是以實際行動去醫治世間之疾病。

一般相信，顏元之思想影響了清代最重要之哲學家戴震（1724～1777）。戴震較顏元更徹底地反駁朱熹之二元論。戴震無法了解「理」是由天所賦予，他認為，萬物是由氣所組成。而人禽之辨在於人能擴充其德性並發展其知識到極致。戴震之主要著作是《孟子字義疏證》，其目的在於努力獲得孔孟之真正學說。

清初有一導向早期注疏及古代文本之精密研究的運動，它可以提供較古老權威的基礎，且因此較理學家的著作更具權威性。顧炎武對音韻學研究的貢獻極大，他成功地建立古音學系統，這是清代學者用來批評古代文獻，揭示偽書，甚至重建亡佚文本的工具之一。

最早的經典注疏是漢代的經典。由於漢代注疏者在時間上與經典書寫的時間最接近，因此，他們應最了解這些經典。因此，漢代之注疏被認為最是可靠，依此，清代學術之此一分支被稱為漢學學派。漢學派學者批評理學家之形上學思辯，因此，他們強調歸納法研究。考證在中國絕非新方法，但清代學者將之提升到一新的高點。

清代學者使用考證學將其研究推擴到政治、社會和經濟領域，並研究歷史和經典。漢學派學者主要關切的是使用這些不同的方法去批判理學家的著作及其研究所依據的資料。

戴震繼承漢學派的技巧，誠如房兆楹所指出，戴震相信，這些研究本身並非即是目的，而是用來發展一種新的哲學。依此，戴震幾乎是獨一無二的。甚至在他的時代，戴震的觀念並未被完全了解，且他在中國思想史中之重要性亦是最近才受到承認。〔註1〕

（十二）西方的影響

中國在十九世紀中葉和二十世紀中葉之間發生之變動較之前兩千年更為劇烈。這種轉變在不同程度上，已經影響了政治制度、社會結構和經濟生活。不可免的，中國人的思考同時也已經改變了。這些改變及其產生之原因實在多而雜，實無法完全加以分析，但有一基本事實卻可提供整個情況之解答。

中國長久以來即自認是世界上最有文化且最重要之民族，他們相信其他民族皆是野蠻人，且應確認中國皇帝的王權。中國人幾乎與外在世界隔絕，除了承認其文化優越性之鄰國外。因此，當英國派遣使者與中國朝廷交涉時，大部分中國人相信，他是來朝貢並對中國皇帝宣誓忠心的。然而，突然之間，一切都改變了。

西方國家為了擴張和尋求貿易，在十六世紀時開始向中國叩關。但他們遭遇了反抗，直到 1842 年，中國被英國打敗。從此以後，中國無法通過西方勢力的考驗，並被迫逐步向西方屈服，就愈發明顯了。中國領土被瓜分或被佔為租界。這種權力的損失雖然難堪，但中國人失去威信，卻使有思想的中國人更

〔註1〕譯者案：直到二十世紀，戴震在中國思想史上之地位首先被章太炎（1869～1936）所認同，並使之為大眾所知曉。有關章太炎之英文論著，見 Jer-shiarn Lee, *Chang Ping-lin (1869～1936): A Political Radical and Cultural Conservative*（台北：文史哲出版社，1993 年）。

加困惑。

因此，中國人以三種方式試圖迎接西方的挑戰。1. 中國傳統的生活和思想方式較其他任何國家優越，中國人已發現他們的困境並非由於他們太保守而是因為他們並未遵從傳統的理想而行動。假如他們如此做，中國將會強盛，而它的困境也會消失。2. 他們相信，中國文化提供了中國發展最健全的基礎，他們希望加以修正來滿足現代世界的情況，且希望接收西方的技術。3. 中國整個傳統政治、社會和經濟組織是不適合今日世界，且整個生活和思想態度必須予以改革。

愈來愈多的中國人了解到，要繼續享受中國傳統的文化方式，並同時驅逐外國勢力，且贏得中國獨立是不可能的。無可避免的，中國在某種程度上必須「西化」。很自然地，中國人所仰賴的西化方式是西方的「民主」。「科學」和「民主」被相信是必會導向新時代的康莊大道。英國被推崇的是它的政治制度及經濟與軍事力量。1905 年孫逸仙組織一個革命團體，其宗旨是「自由、平等、博愛」，1912 年中華民國成立。

一般而言，大部分改革者沉醉於科學和民主，而幾乎很少提到中國傳統文化。雖然，胡適和少數其他知識份子承認古典儒學的民主精神，但是他們幾乎並不打算使用它作為近代民主哲學的基礎。從 1917 年起，中國知識份子受到「新潮」和「中國文藝復興」運動的影響，其中，發起此一運動最著名的學者是胡適。他是實用主義的倡導者杜威的學生。

胡適首先提倡白話文運動，目的在於以白話文取代傳統文言文作為寫作和表達文學、思想等的工具。此運動並非只是文學的，它成為許多為新觀念奮鬥者的中心。

民主是一種成長，它不可能一夕成功，要發展成一完全民主的國家，中國需要時間，但時不我予。民國成立後，中國經歷內戰、日本侵略等，在此情況下，任何國家要發展完全民主都是困難的。

中國傳統包含至少三千年的逐步演化，是世界上最古老的傳統之一。此一傳統似已來到盡頭，當中國共產黨在 1949 年取得政權後。一般認為，中國共產黨的成功主要是由於中國人民反抗貧窮和經濟剝削的革命浪潮所致。實者，中國共產黨革命的領導和發起並非來自農民而是來自知識份子。在過去，西方國家不斷使用武力來壓迫中國，而毛澤東則說，未來中國共產黨將會使用武力來面對所有拒絕改造成中國共產黨的人。

（十三）回顧

中國哲學對現代世界是有用的。中國人發現西方文化的特色是侵略和競爭的精神。這些精神若過度發展，將引起個人和國家不必要的傷害。這種侵略和競爭的傾向表現出我們擴張主義的精神，其結果是造成衝突。

「知足」這個字詞在現代西方很少聽到，但在中國，大部分中國哲學家都鼓吹「知足」的美德，且大部分中國人在顯著的程度上會加以實踐。雖然，中國人不像西方人會沉浸於彼此之間的競爭，但這並不意謂著他們是生活在停滯的狀態。

或許有人會說，這是理想化了中國人的生活方式，但「知足」也曾經被批評是使中國人在現代世界中無法進步和競爭的罪惡。果真如此，則並非由於「知足」本身不好，而是因為它被引入極端且未受中國傳統哲學核心的中庸和均衡所監督。

中庸、均衡是中國人的標記。它是從何而來？它不僅是一種思想方式且是一種生活方式，且此一生活方式部份是來自「禮」的實踐。